D1331123

GUNNING
FOR GOD

JOHN C. LENNOX

GUNNING FOR GOD

WHY THE NEW ATHEISTS ARE MISSING THE TARGET

Copyright © 2011 John C. Lennox
This edition copyright © 2011 Lion Hudson

The author asserts the moral right
to be identified as the author of this work

A Lion Book
an imprint of
Lion Hudson plc
Wilkinson House, Jordan Hill Road,
Oxford OX2 8DR, England
www.lionhudson.com
ISBN 978 0 7459 5322 9 (print)
ISBN 978 0 7459 5840 8 (epub)
ISBN 978 0 7459 5839 2 (Kindle)
ISBN 978 0 7459 5841 5 (pdf)

Distributed by:
UK: Marston Book Services, PO Box 269, Abingdon, Oxon, OX14 4YN
USA: Trafalgar Square Publishing, 814 N. Franklin Street, Chicago, IL 60610
USA Christian Market: Kregel Publications, PO Box 2607, Grand Rapids, Michigan 49501

First edition 2011
10 9 8 7 6 5 4 3 2
First electronic format 2011

All rights reserved

Acknowledgments

All Scripture quotations are from The Holy bible, English Standard Version® (ESV®)
copyright © 2001 by Crossway, a publishing ministry of Good News Publishers. All right
reserved.

pp.122, 156 Scripture taken from the New King James Version. Copyright © 1982 by
Thomas Nelson, Inc. Used by permission. All right reserved.

p.123 Extract from The Authorized (King James) Version. Rights in the Authorized
Version are vested in the Crown. Reproduced by permission of the Crown's patentee,
Cambridge University Press.

pp. 23–24 *In God we Doubt: Confessions of a Failed Atheist* by John Humpreys © John
Humphrys 2007, reproduced by permission of Hodder and Stoughton Limited.

pp.137–38 David Bentley Hart "Believe It or Not" *First Things* (www.firstthings.com),
May 2010, reprinted by permission.

pp. 161–362 This extract is from According to Luke by David Gooding, published by
Inter-Varsity Press 1987, Used by permission.

A catalogue record for this book is available
from the British Library

Typeset in 10.5/13 Palatino

CONTENTS

To my friends and colleagues
David Gooding, Michael Middleton, and
Arthur Williamson, with deep appreciation

INTRODUCTION

"Even if they can't be herded, cats in sufficient numbers can make a lot of noise and they cannot be ignored."
Richard Dawkins

"There's probably no God, now stop worrying and enjoy your life."
British Humanist bus advertising campaign

Atheism is on the march in the Western world. Noisily. A concerted attempt is still being made to marshal the atheist faithful, to encourage them not to be ashamed of their atheism but to stand up and fight as a united army. The enemy is God. They are gunning for God. The biggest gun, otherwise known as the former Oxford Professor of the Public Understanding of Science, has been Richard Dawkins. In 2005 he was voted by the magazine *Prospect UK* as one of the three leading public intellectuals in the world. His book *The God Delusion*,[1] published in 2006, has dominated best-seller lists and sold over 2 million copies in English alone.

However, there now an even bigger gun, certainly so far as scientific credentials are concerned – the Cambridge theoretical physicist Stephen Hawking. For years Hawking appeared to have left the question of God open. At the end of his best-selling *A Brief History of Time* he wrote: "If we discover a complete theory… it would be the ultimate triumph of human reason – for then we would know the mind of God."[2] However, in his latest book, *The Grand Design*,[3] co-authored with Leonard Mlodinow, he claims there is now no room for God. Richard Dawkins is delighted, of course, and speaking of God he says: "Darwin kicked him out of biology, but physics remained more uncertain. Hawking is now administering the coup de grâce." Trailing behind Dawkins come a phalanx of lesser calibre but equally trigger-happy fusiliers. First, the highly articulate British-born, US-based Christopher Hitchens, a writer and professor of liberal studies in New York, who has written *God is not Great*.[4] Next is a scientist, Daniel Dennett, who produced *Breaking the Spell: Religion as a Natural Phenomenon*.[5] He describes himself as a "godless philosopher".[6] Finally, the more junior Sam Harris, a graduate in neuroscience, who has written *The End of Faith*;[7] *Letter to a Christian Nation*,[8] and, more recently, *The Moral Landscape*.[9]

The anti-God adrenalin is not only running in the English-speaking world. In France the most prominent activist is, unsurprisingly, not a scientist but a philosopher. He is the prolific author Michel Onfray, who has written *In Defence of Atheism*.[10] Dressed from head to foot in black, he regularly addresses overflowing crowds of eager listeners. In Italy the mathematician Piergiorgio Odifreddi has stirred up controversy with his essay *Why we cannot be Christians (much less Catholics)*.[11] The Vatican is not amused by his parody of the Latin blessing, in which he replaces the Trinity by Pythagoras, Archimedes, and Newton.

Dawkins hopes that he can orchestrate an atheist revival – although the task, he feels, is as tricky as the proverbial herding of cats: "Even if they can't be herded, cats in sufficient numbers can make a lot of noise and they cannot be ignored."[12] Well, he, as Cat herder-in-Chief, and his colleagues are certainly showing how to make plenty of noise. Whether that noise can be resolved into intelligible language is another matter entirely.

One attempt they have made to get their message across is by advertising it on the sides of buses. For a time bendy buses became the medium that carried the atheist message. They charged around the UK's major cities bringing the remarkably underwhelming missive: "There's probably no God, now stop worrying and enjoy your life." Apart from the advertisement for a well-known beer, there are probably very few advertisements containing the word "probably". After all, can one imagine being caught by advertisements like: "This medicine has probably no serious side effects…; this bank will probably not collapse…; this plane will probably get you to your destination"? Yet Richard Dawkins was prepared to dip into his own pocket to help finance the campaign.

Not to be outdone, German atheists, failing to get permission from local authorities to mount a similar campaign on public buses, rented one of their own to carry the message. In grand teutonic style it carefully announced: "There is (with probability bounding on certainty) no God. A fulfilled life needs no faith." As the bus toured Germany it was shadowed by another, similar, vehicle, hired this time by Christians. It, more modestly, simply asked a question: "And what if He does exist?" The media were delighted at the sight of both buses parked together in city after city. The net effect? God was firmly on the agenda.

Now I imagine that the word "probably" may well have been included for legal reasons, to avoid prosecution under trade-description legislation. The atheists realize, of course, that they could not amass enough evidence to convince a court that the probability of God's existence was zero; and if it is not zero, then God's existence is possible. Come to think of it, the *a priori* probability of Richard Dawkins' existence is very low. His existence, like that of the rest of us, is improbable. In spite of that, lo and behold, Richard Dawkins, you and I, are all actual. The message on the bus is beside the point. The real question is not, "How probable is God?" but rather, "Is there evidence that God is actual?"

If we have not yet boarded the atheist bus, we might well want to ask what kind of a God is it whose existence is deemed improbable? The slogan proudly informs us that it is a God whose existence is associated (at least in atheist minds) with worry and lack of enjoyment – no doubt with the implication that atheism is the fount of joy that will dismiss this gloomy God and alleviate all of life's concerns.

Mathematician David Berlinski comes in with a reality check:

The thesis that *if* there is no God, then disbelievers may contemplate many new enjoyments prompts an obvious question. Have atheists, at least, stopped worrying and begun to enjoy their lives? To be sure, it has not been widely observed that prominent atheists have in recent years blistered their conscience with anxiety. Short of retiring into a coma, it is hard to imagine how Richard Dawkins, Sam Harris, Daniel Dennett or Christopher Hitchens could have stopped worrying more than they had already stopped worrying and so hard to credit atheism for their ebullience.

Berlinski continues:

Those considering atheism as a *new* doctrinal commitment, however, will not find plausible the alleviation of anxiety it is said to afford. If the great concern occasioned by atheism is God's indignation, then given the very tentative way in which his *in*existence has been affirmed, it might seem that atheists have drawn their worries prematurely to an end. Whatever its other benefits, atheism is not generally counted a position calculated to assuage the worst fears of mankind; and as the work of prominent atheists indicates, those who *have* stopped worrying have done so only because they have stopped thinking.[13]

One of those prominent atheists, Jean-Paul Sartre, said: "Atheism is a long, hard, cruel business." Might it not, therefore, rather be that worry is part and parcel of the *rejection* of God rather than a consequence of belief in him? And might it not be wise then to ask exactly where the atheist bus is headed before jumping on board? Slogans on the side of a bus can distract one from noticing the bus's destination.

But the atheists' poster campaign did not end here. In 2009 Richard Dawkins and the British Humanist Association commissioned posters depicting two very happy looking children with the legend: "Please don't label me. Let me grow up and choose for myself." However, in an exquisitely ironical contradiction of their first poster campaign's claim, that atheism was the prerequisite for joy, it turned out that the grinning children, selected by the atheists to embody their vision of childlike happiness, were children from a devout Christian family. As the father of the children commented, it was quite a compliment that the atheists judged these particular children to be happy and free, without knowing about their family background.[14]

I shall comment later on why I am in fact sympathetic to the atheists' desire not to have children labelled and to allow them to choose for themselves. The question of parents teaching children what they believe is, of course, a very different matter.

At the moment, Richard Dawkins would appear to be the principal driver of the atheist bus. Like him, I am a scientist (a mathematician in fact); like him, I believe in truth; and also like him, I am a professor at Oxford University. But, unlike him, I am a theist – a Christian, to be precise. I do not associate the existence of God as such with worry, but rather with joy. Indeed, if I were impelled to come up with a bus slogan, it might go something like this: "There is good evidence for the existence of God. Therefore trust him and experience real joy." Of course, I am aware that God might be a potential source of worry for atheists. After all, as Lucretius noted centuries ago, if God exists, atheists will meet him one day. More of that in due course.

Richard Dawkins and I have engaged in two major public debates, the first in Birmingham, Alabama in 2007, where we discussed some of the major theses of his best-selling book *The God Delusion*.[15] The second debate was on the question "Has Science Buried God?", which is the subtitle of my own book, *God's Undertaker*.[16] This latter debate[17] was held in 2008 in the Oxford Natural History Museum, the place where in 1860 Thomas Henry Huxley had his famous interchange with Bishop Samuel Wilberforce over Darwin's *The Origin of Species*. The setting was both unusual and dramatic. Dawkins and I were perched on stools, with the vast head and jaws of the museum's showpiece, the Tyrannosaurus Rex skeleton, towering threateningly above us. T-Rex is certainly extinct. On that Dawkins and I agree. Dawkins also thinks God is extinct, or, more exactly, that he never existed. I disagree.

I also have had two public debates with Christopher Hitchens, who describes himself as a contrarian. Our first encounter was before a large audience in the Usher Hall at the Edinburgh Festival in 2008, where the motion under consideration was "The New Europe should prefer the New Atheism."[18] At the end of the debate a number of members of the audience, who had initially indicated their indecision on the issue, surprised many by moving to reject the motion. Consequently it was pronounced lost by the moderator, James Naughtie of the BBC, when Hitchens graciously conceded. One member of the audience who did not contribute to that shift of opinion was Richard Dawkins. He did not seem to be at all pleased with the outcome.

I met Hitchens again in March 2009 for an equally lively re-match. This was an even larger event, organized by the Socratic Club at Samford University in Birmingham, Alabama. The issue before the house was "Is God Great?" – the topic of Hitchens' best-seller.[19] Not surprisingly, perhaps, no vote was taken on that occasion.

I have also debated the physicist Victor Stenger (among others) in Australia at an IQ^2 Debate [20] organized by *The Sydney Morning Herald* in August 2008, on the topic "The world would be better off without religion." As part of Sydney Science Week 2008 I encountered Michael

Shermer, the editor of *Sceptic Magazine*, to debate the question "Does
God exist?" In July 2009 I had a lengthy moderated discussion for
Australian Television with Peter Atkins, Emeritus Professor of
Chemistry at Oxford.[21] In addition, in April 2011 I engaged in a very
warm-hearted public discussion with Daniel Lowenstein, Professor
of Law at UCLA on the topic "Is Christianity true?"[22]

That brings me to my motivation for this book. In each of my
debates and discussions I have tried to present in the public space
a credible, rational alternative to the fare which the New Atheists
offer, rather than simply attempting to use rhetoric or emotional
appeal to "win" the argument on the day. Whether I have succeeded
or not is up to the respective audiences to judge. However, these
public events do not, of course, permit full development of
arguments. I thought it worthwhile, therefore, to draw from such
experience and give in book form a more thorough presentation of
the central issues.

I have already written at length on the science aspect in my book
God's Undertaker; and have addressed the more recent entry into the
debate by Stephen Hawking and Leonard Mlodinow in a further book
God and Stephen Hawking: Whose Design is it Anyway?[23] Because of
their topicality I shall include some of the flavour of these arguments
here. The main debate, however, is not limited to science. Indeed, the
arguments that often grip the attention of the general public have to
do with morality and the alleged dangers of religion. These issues
will be our main concern here.

Other authors have paved the way. Alister and Joanna McGrath
have impressively deconstructed many of the major arguments in *The
Dawkins Delusion?*;[24] as has Keith Ward in *Why There Almost Certainly
Is a God*.[25] At a more accessible level, David Robertson's *The Dawkins
Letters* is an excellent guide.[26] More recently David Bentley Hart, in
Atheist Delusions: The Christian Revolution and Its Fashionable Enemies,[27]
very effectively exposes the superficiality of the New Atheist approach
to history. One might ask, so why add yet another book?

The New Atheists want to "raise the consciousness" of atheists and
encourage them to stand up and be counted for their faith. Hence
they are constantly adding to the ranks of their spokespeople. They
are out to get converts.[28] The importance of the issues and the extent
of public interest warrant analysis of the New Atheism arguments
from as many different angles as possible, so that everybody's
"consciousness is raised" – including that of Christians.

My aim is to provide one of these angles, in the hope that it will be of help. This book is not simply a product of passive analysis, important though that is. It is a product of public engagement with the New Atheists and their ideas. I have stepped into the public arena in order to add my voice to those who are convinced that the New Atheism is not the automatic default position for all thinking people who hold science in high regard. Like me, there are many scientists and others who think that the New Atheism is a belief system which, ironically, provides a classic example of the blind faith it so vocally despises in others. I should like to make my own small contribution towards raising public awareness of this fact.

I have, however, a further reason for writing. The debate has necessarily given prominence to atheist arguments and reactions to them, which means that the positive presentation of the alternative tends to come short. Perhaps it is for this reason that the New Atheists incessantly chant Bertrand Russell's famous mantra about there not being enough evidence. In light of this, I propose in this book not only to deal reactively with atheist objections to Christianity, but also positively to present detailed evidence for the truth of Christianity.

I would like to express my thanks to the many people who over the years have stimulated my thinking on these issues, including those representatives of the atheist worldview that I have encountered in both public debate and private conversation. I am also grateful to my research assistant Simon Wenham and to Barbara Hamilton for her invaluable help with the production of the typescript.

THE CHARGE OF THE BRIGHT BRIGADE

The New Atheists regard themselves as distinguished and worthy offspring of the Enlightenment, and, in an attempt to jettison the negative image they feel atheism has had hitherto, they have accordingly styled themselves as "the Brights". Christopher Hitchens deserves credit for objecting to such a "conceited cringe-making proposal".[29] Just imagine what the reaction would have been had the Christians equally foolishly and condescendingly called themselves "the Clevers".

No doubt those of us who disagree with the Brights will by default be dubbed "the Dims" or "Dulls", or perhaps even "Darks". Dennett, however, says that this is not necessarily the case, and that those who believe in the supernatural should call themselves the "Supers".[30] "Super-Bright", therefore, would be an oxymoron.

Hitchens' objection to this rather tasteless bit of hubris has been ignored; and the Brights have now staked their claim to a piece of cyberspace by setting up a dedicated multilingual website under that name. We find there the following explanation of the term: "A bright is a person who has a naturalistic worldview. A bright's worldview is free of supernatural and mystical elements. The ethics and actions of a bright are based on a naturalistic worldview."

As children of the Enlightenment, the Brights see themselves as luminaries of a new era of rational understanding, dispelling the darkness of religious superstition and error. Michel Onfray displays a rather limited memory in explaining their objectives thus: "We need a return to the spirit of Light, of Enlightenment, that gave its name to the eighteenth century"; as if there was no high calibre intellectual discussion before the eighteenth century, and, as Alasdair MacIntyre points out,[31] as if the Enlightenment project was not a failure in its ability to supply a foundation for morality. As if the Enlightenment took us on an upward path from barbarism to peace, instead of ushering in one violent revolution after another until we reached the depths of human wickedness in the bloodiest century to date – the twentieth.[32] In its headlong charge, the Bright Brigade does not appear to wish to pause and consider such things. We must, however – and we shall.

WHAT IS NEW ABOUT THE NEW ATHEISTS?

The New Atheists have been around for some time now; so, in that trivial sense, they are no longer new. What is more, at the intellectual level, their arguments never were really new. However, the new thing about them is their tone and their emphasis. The New Atheists are much louder and shriller than their predecessors. They are also more aggressive. This change in tone centres on the fact that they are no longer content simply to deny God's existence. For instance, Christopher Hitchens says: "I'm not even an atheist so much as I am an antitheist; I not only maintain that all religions are versions of the same untruth, but I hold that the influence of churches, and the effect of religious belief is positively harmful."[33] The agenda of the New

Atheists has widened, therefore, to include attack on the existence of belief itself. This particular feature is described by them as their way of expressing their "loss of respect" for religion. As Richard Dawkins puts it, "I am utterly fed up with the respect we have been brainwashed into bestowing upon religion." Christopher Hitchens sums up the position in his all-encompassing, and characteristically wild, statement: "Religion poisons everything."[34] Bradley Hagerty on National Public Radio reports Hitchens as saying (to roars of approval from a capacity audience at the University of Toronto): "I think religion should be treated with ridicule, hatred, and contempt, and I claim that right."[35] Sam Harris's intention is "to destroy the intellectual and moral pretensions of Christianity in its most committed forms".[36]

WHY THE AGGRESSION?

Something appears to have snapped. And it has: the Twin Towers on 9/11. According to the leading German weekly news magazine *Der Spiegel*, it was that horrific event in 2001 that gave birth to the New Atheism. A cover article entitled "God is to blame for everything"[37] says: "Without the attacks on New York and Washington, there would be no New Atheism." In a later interview with the same magazine, Dawkins says that 9/11 "radicalised" him,[38] thus confirming his earlier statement:

> **My last vestige of "hands-off religion" respect disappeared in the smoke and choking dust of September 11, 2001, followed by the "National Day of Prayer", when prelates and pastors did their tremulous Martin Luther King impersonation and urged people of mutually incompatible faiths to hold hands, united in homage to the very force that caused the problem in the first place.[39]**

The logic is simple. "Imagine with John Lennon," says Dawkins, "a world without religion. Imagine no suicide bombers, no 9/11, no 7/7, no Crusades, no witch-hunts, no Gunpowder plot, no Indian partition, no Israeli/Palestinian wars, no Serb/Croat/Muslim massacres, no persecution of Jews as 'Christ-killers', no Northern Ireland 'troubles', no 'honour killings', no shiny-suited bouffant-haired televangelists fleecing gullible people of their money ('God wants you to give till it hurts'). Imagine no Taliban to blow up ancient statues, no public beheadings of blasphemers, no flogging of female skin for the crime of showing an inch of it."[40]

This message resonates powerfully in a world rendered fearful by fanatical acts of terror perpetrated by extremists. Which of us, apart from the violent themselves, would not like a world purged of such horrors? Most of us have no hesitation in agreeing with the New Atheists that there are problems, major problems, with aspects of religion. How could we "respect" religious extremists that encourage young men and women to become living bombs in order to gain instant access to paradise? The New Atheists are quite right in drawing attention to this kind of thing, especially in societies that are in danger of having public discourse paralysed by political correctness.

In page after page the New Atheists spell out in lurid detail the tragic history of horror and evil associated with religion – from the atrocious acts of fundamentalist Islamic suicide bombers, killing and maiming their innocent victims, to the unspeakable abuse of children by priests, robbing them of their childhood innocence and often inflicting on them brutal and permanent psychological trauma; from the fearful brainwashing of the cults, to the ethnic cleansing of the Balkans, and the kneecappings and shootings inflicted on each other by extremist Protestants and Roman Catholics in Northern Ireland. Indeed, a cursory glance around the world at the moment shows that not only are there wars between different religious groups, but vicious fighting between various factions of the same religious group. It is a sickening litany. Religion would certainly appear to be a major problem.

Well then, if religion is the problem, then the solution is obvious, say the New Atheists: get rid of religion. Civilized society, they say, can no longer afford the luxury of smiling indulgently at religion that has become far too dangerous and extreme for such complacency. It must therefore be eliminated; and Nobel Laureate Steven Weinberg, for one, has no hesitation in saying so: "The world needs to wake up from the long nightmare of religion… Anything we scientists can do to weaken the hold of religion should be done, and may in fact be our greatest contribution to civilization."

That is the New Atheists' stated goal in a nutshell; and the observant reader will not miss the totalitarian sounding word "anything" in Weinberg's statement.[41] Dawkins states the goal this way: "If this book works as I intend, religious readers who open it will be atheists when they put it down,"[42] even though in his next sentence he recognizes that this might just be presumptuous optimism. He wants not only to rally the faithful (atheists) and to encourage them to "come out" for their faith (for such it is, despite their protests to the contrary as we shall see); but also to proselytize – to "raise the consciousness" of others, by describing the attractions of the New Atheism – thus increasing the footprint of atheism on the demographic landscape.

THE RELIGIOUS LANDSCAPE

To gain some idea of what that landscape looks like, we refer to a YouGov poll in the UK, commissioned by the BBC broadcaster John Humphrys in 2007. According to it, 16 per cent of the 2,200 polled called themselves atheists; 28 per cent believed in God; 26 per cent believed in "something" but were not sure what; 9 per cent regarded themselves as agnostics, among them Humphrys himself; 5 per cent said they would like to believe and envied those who did, but couldn't; 3 per cent didn't know; 10 per cent hadn't given it much thought; and 3% gave the response "other".[43] It is interesting to set these figures in the wider context of an earlier (2004) international survey of ten countries, again commissioned by the BBC, entitled "What the world thinks of God".[44]

Overall, about 8 per cent of those polled considered themselves to be atheists; so the UK came out at about twice that average with the highest percentage of atheists – 16 per cent. In the USA about 10 per cent said they did not believe in God; although a 2005 Gallup poll put the figure much lower, at 5 per cent. An internet trawl through a selection of recent polls seems to indicate that more people are comfortable with making the negative statement, that they do not believe in God, than the positive statement, that they are atheists – however illogical that may seem. For instance, the *American Religious Identification Survey (ARIS)* conducted in 2001 gives the figure for atheists in the USA as 0.4 per cent, although 14 per cent identify themselves as non-religious.[45]

However interesting these figures may be as indicators of the uphill nature of the New Atheists' struggle to gain a hearing, the central issue, whether their atheism is true or not, is not going to be settled by mere recourse to statistical analysis. To ascertain truth, we need more robust evidence than that.

THE NEW ATHEISM AND TRUTH

One refreshing feature of the New Atheism is that it is not noticeably influenced by postmodernist relativism, at least in the realm of truth. Richard Dawkins amusingly writes: "Show me a cultural relativist at 30,000 feet and I'll show you a hypocrite."[46] Addressing his Christian readers, Sam Harris says, "I would like to acknowledge that there are many points on which you and I agree. We agree, for instance, that if one of us is right, the other is wrong." The New Atheists believe therefore that truth exists that is accessible to the human mind. They accept the law of the excluded middle – either this universe is all that there is, or it isn't; either there is a God, or there isn't; either the resurrection of Jesus happened, or it didn't. In that sense they are thoroughly modernist in persuasion. This means, in particular, that we can be clear from the start what it is we are talking about; we have at least some basis for rational debate.

IN PLACE OF GOD

In 2006 a conference took place at the Salk Institute, La Jolla, California, on the theme "Beyond Belief: Science, Religion, Reason, and Survival". Its remit was to address three questions: Should science do away with religion? What would science put in religion's place? Can we be good without God? Leading New Atheists like Richard Dawkins and Steven Weinberg were among the speakers. *The New Scientist* judged this conference to be of such importance that, in its fiftieth anniversary special edition, it included a report of it in an article entitled, "In place of God".[47]

This title reveals that the objective of the New Atheists is not simply to complete the process of secularization by banishing God from the universe; but it is to put something in place of God. And it is not simply that society should replace God with something else; it is that science should do so. Apparently no area of human thought or activity other than science is qualified to contribute anything useful. Science is king. Of course, science is a set of disciplines practised by human beings; so the ultimate objective would appear to be to make these scientists the ultimate arbiter of what is not only to be believed by all other human beings, but what is to be worshipped by them –

remember it is God they wish to replace. Do we detect more shades of totalitarianism?

The first two questions on the La Jolla conference agenda show that propagating atheism is part of a wider goal, the enthronement of science as supreme. This aim has powerful echoes of the similar crusade of T. H. Huxley in the years following the publication of Darwin's *The Origin of Species*. Huxley saw Darwin's theory as his main weapon to loosen the grip of Christianity and achieve the secularization of society through the domination of science. In 1874 this theme was evident at a famous meeting of the British Association in Belfast, at which Huxley, J. D. Hooker (botanist), and John Tyndall (President of the British Association for Science – who worked on atmospheric gases), were main speakers. Tyndall said: "All religious theories must submit to the control of science and relinquish all thought of controlling it."[48]

THE MORAL DIMENSION

Inevitably, therefore, the New Atheists have to tackle the issue of morality and ethics. That is why the third question (Can we be good without God?) appears on the conference agenda, even though it might seem incongruous at first sight. The conference organizers clearly felt they had to address the incontrovertible fact that for centuries the source of morality, at least in the West, has been the Judaeo-Christian tradition. The New Atheists wish to abolish religion, so they have to solve the problem of giving an alternative source for morality, not least because their main attack on religion is that it is not only intellectually but morally wrong.

We can therefore express the major elements in the New Atheists' agenda as follows:

1. Religion is a dangerous delusion: it leads to violence and war.

2. We must therefore get rid of religion: science will achieve that.

3. We do not need God to be good: atheism can provide a perfectly adequate base for ethics.

SOME DEFINITIONS

We need first to say something about the meaning of the terms "atheism" and "religion". According to the Oxford English Dictionary (OED), atheism (a-theism) is "disbelief in or denial of the existence of a God". The OED cites Shaftesbury (1709): "To believe nothing of a designing Principle or Mind, nor any Cause, Measure or Rule of things but Chance... is to be a perfect atheist." Dawkins (citing Steven Weinberg) defines his concept of God: "If the word 'God' is not to become completely useless, it should be used in the way people have generally understood it: to denote a supernatural creator that is 'appropriate for us to worship'."[49] Dawkins' stated antipathy, therefore, is only to what he calls "supernatural gods". They are the delusional gods and are to be distinguished from the God of some (enlightened – according to Dawkins) scientists and philosophers, where the term "God" has become a synonym for the laws of nature, or for some kind of cosmic natural intelligence that, although superior to human intelligence, ultimately evolved from the primitive stuff of the universe like any other lesser intelligence. Thus, the principle target of the New Atheists is the supernatural God of the Bible, who is the Maker and Upholder of the universe.

I use the term "target" in order to draw attention to the fact that the New Atheists are not simply atheists. They are perhaps better described as anti-theists, by contrast with the type of atheist who, though she does not believe in God herself, is quite happy for others to believe in God provided they do not disturb her.

One corollary of their anti-theism is that by "religion" the New Atheists have particularly in mind the great monotheistic religions of Judaism, Christianity, and Islam, with the main emphasis being on Christianity. Pantheistic religions like Hinduism, and religions that could reasonably be alternatively classified as philosophies, like Confucianism and certain forms of Buddhism, play little or no role in New Atheist literature.

I grew up in Northern Ireland and can understand those who think that the only solution to the world's problems is to get rid of religion. But, precisely because I was brought up in Northern Ireland and nevertheless remain a convinced Christian, I may just have a contribution to make in correcting what I feel is a disquietingly dangerous imbalance in the logic of the New Atheists' approach, both in terms of the diagnosis they make and the solution they propose.

I am not alone in that disquiet. Many atheists share it. Barbara Hagerty, in her NPR report[50] mentioned previously, points out that the reaction to increased atheist aggressiveness has not met with universal approval among atheists. She cites atheist Paul Kurtz on the New Atheists: "I consider them atheist fundamentalists. They're anti-religious and they're mean-spirited, unfortunately. Now, they're very good atheists and very dedicated people who do not believe in God. But you have this aggressive and militant phase of atheism, and that does more damage than good." The interesting thing here is that Paul Kurtz was the founder of the Center for Inquiry, whose mission is to "foster a secular society based on science, reason, freedom of inquiry, and humanist values", and which is the organizer of a "Blasphemy Contest" that invites contestants to submit short statements critical of religious beliefs. Hagerty reported that Kurtz claims to have been ousted from his position at the Center for Inquiry by a "palace coup".

Atheists are clearly divided about the aggressive approach of the New Atheists, and some find it positively embarrassing. Their embarrassment echoes that of philosopher Michael Ruse when he penned the following endorsement for the McGraths' book, *The Dawkins Delusion?*:[51] "*The God Delusion* makes me embarrassed to be an atheist and the McGraths show why." For this reason it is important to realize from the outset that the New Atheists are far from being representative of all atheists. Indeed, many of my atheist friends and acquaintances are, not surprisingly, at pains to distance themselves from the aggressiveness of the New Atheists.

The agnostic fraternity is also disturbed by the New Atheist onslaught. In his book *In God We Doubt*,[52] the well-known BBC Radio Presenter John Humphrys presents the main ideas of the New Atheists, and his responses to them, in his inimical, pithy way. It goes like this:[53]

1. **Believers are mostly naive or stupid. Or, at least, they're not as clever as atheists.**

   Response: This is so clearly untrue it's barely worth bothering with. Richard Dawkins, in his bestselling The God Delusion, *was reduced to producing a "study" by Mensa that purported to show an inverse relationship between intelligence and belief. He also claimed that only a very few members of the Royal Society believe in a personal god. So what? Some believers are undoubtedly stupid (witness the creationists) but I've met one or two atheists I wouldn't trust to change a light-bulb.*

2. The few clever ones are pathetic because they need a crutch to get them through life.

   Response: Don't we all? Some use booze rather than the Bible. It doesn't prove anything about either.

3. They are also pathetic because they can't accept the finality of death.

   Response: Maybe, but it doesn't mean they're wrong. Count the number of atheists in the foxholes or the cancer wards.

4. They have been brainwashed into believing. There is no such thing as a "Christian child", for instance – just a child whose parents have had her baptised.

   Response: True, and many children reject it when they get older. But many others stay with it.

5. They have been bullied into believing.

   Response: This is also true in many cases but you can't actually bully someone into believing – just into pretending to believe.

6. If we don't wipe out religious belief by next Thursday week, civilisation as we know it is doomed.

   Response: Of course the mad mullahs are dangerous and extreme Islamism is a threat to be taken seriously. But we've survived monotheist religion for 4,000 years or so, and I can think of one or two other things that are a greater threat to civilisation.

7. Trust me: I'm an atheist.

   Response: Why?

   Humphrys adds wryly: "I make no apology if I have oversimplified their views with that little list: it's what they do to believers all the time." Quite so!

More needs to be said, of course. But this kind of reaction on the part of John Humphrys, who is a highly intelligent person with no religious affiliation (he classifies himself as a doubter), serves to show why many people are left uneasy by the New Atheists' message. They find it unbalanced and often extreme in many places; at best unsubstantiated and at worst plainly wrong. Dawkins is constantly encouraging us to be critical; but we shall see that he himself is highly selective in what he chooses to criticize, and indeed in what he understands by criticism.

THE IRONY OF THE ATTEMPT TO ELIMINATE RELIGION

One of the ironies emerging about the New Atheists has to do with the fact that they assign an important role to evolutionary theory[54] in their attempt to annihilate religious belief. However, evolution does not appear to be playing ball! *The Sunday Times*[55] ran an article by the science editor John Leake, entitled, "Atheists are a dying breed as nature 'favours faithful'". He reports on an eighty-two country study entitled *The Reproductive Advantage of Religiosity*, led by Michael Blume of Jena, which found that those whose inhabitants worship at least once a week have 2.5 children each, and those who never worship have 1.7 – which is less than the number needed to replace themselves. Leake contrasts Dawkins' argument that religions are like mental viruses that infect people and impose great costs in terms of money and health risks, with Blume's work, which suggests the opposite: evolution favours believers so strongly that over time a tendency to be religious has become embedded in our genes.

One might have thought that, if the New Atheists are right about evolution, they, of all people, would be the most enthusiastic about spreading their genes. Clearly not.

Perhaps, then, all we have to do is wait?

However, perhaps not; for even though the New Atheists seem to have lost interest in spreading their genes they have not yet abandoned the propagation of their "memes".

CHAPTER 1

ARE GOD AND FAITH ENEMIES OF REASON AND SCIENCE?

"Monotheism loathes intelligence."

"God puts to death everything that stands up to him, beginning with reason, intelligence and the critical mind."
Both Michel Onfray

"Faith is an evil precisely because it requires no justification and brooks no argument."
Richard Dawkins

"These things are written that you might believe."
St John

Michel Onfray thinks that God is not dead. But theists should not cheer prematurely, for his explanation is:

> A fiction does not die, an illusion never passes away, a fairy tale does not refute itself… You cannot kill a breeze, a wind, a fragrance; you cannot kill a dream or an ambition. God, manufactured by mortals in their own quintessential image, exists only to make daily life bearable despite the path that every one of us treads towards extinction… We cannot assassinate or kill an illusion. In fact illusion is more likely to kill us – for God puts to death everything that stands up to him, beginning with reason, intelligence and the critical mind. All the rest follows in a chain reaction.[1]

For Onfray, then, it is this fictional god that is an enemy of reason. Well, fictional gods may well be enemies of reason: the God of the Bible certainly is not. The very first of the biblical Ten Commandments contains the instruction to "love the Lord your God with all your *mind*". This should be enough to tell us that God is not to be regarded as an enemy of reason. After all, as Creator he is responsible for the very existence of the human mind; the biblical view is that human beings are the pinnacle of creation. They alone are created as rational beings in the image of God, capable of a relationship with God and given by him the capacity to understand the universe in which they live.

Consistent with this, far from being anti-scientific, the Bible positively encourages science. It could be said that it gave science its initial mandate. One of the activities fundamental to all branches of science (indeed to all intellectual disciplines) is the naming, and therefore classifying, of things and phenomena. Every intellectual discipline has its special dictionary of words. According to Genesis, in the biological field it was God who initiated this process by telling humans to name the animals.[2] Taxonomy thus got underway. With time this broadened into a vision of nature as a rational unity that was (at least in part) amenable to human comprehension, because it was designed by the mind of God in whose image the human mind was made.

In fact, as Alfred North Whitehead and others have pointed out, there is strong evidence that the biblical worldview was intimately involved in the meteoric rise of science in the sixteenth and seventeenth centuries. C. S. Lewis summarizes as follows: "Men became scientific because they expected law in nature and they expected law in nature because they believed in a lawgiver." More recently Oxford's Professor of Science and Religion, Peter Harrison, has argued an impressive case for a sharpening of Whitehead's thesis. He shows that it was not only theism in general, but also the particular principles of biblical interpretation used by the Reformers that made a significant contribution to the rise of science.[3]

The Bible teaches that creation is contingent; that is, God as Creator is free to make the world as and how he likes. Thus, in order to find out what the universe is like and how it works, we have to go and look. We cannot, as Aristotle thought, determine the nature of the universe by starting with abstract philosophical principles. He held that there were certain *a priori* principles[4] to which the universe had to conform – a view that dominated thinking for centuries. One of these principles was that perfect motion must be circular. Since Aristotle thought that everything beyond the moon was perfect, it followed that the planets must move in circles. It was only when Kepler, a Christian, decided to break free of this Aristotelian metaphysical constraint, and allow the astronomical data on the movement of Mars (already collected by Tycho Brahe) to speak, that he discovered that the planets actually moved in equally "perfect" ellipses.

We admire Kepler for his willingness to follow where the evidence led, rather than allowing himself to be intellectually fettered by a metaphysical restraint – even though that restraint represented the established wisdom of centuries. Yet a storm of protest greeted world-renowned philosopher Anthony Flew when he announced his conversion to deism, on the basis of the evidence of the complexity of life. It would seem that stepping outside the naturalistic paradigm is fraught with as much difficulty as stepping outside the Aristotelian one. The largely irrational protest against Flew, by people whose intellectual pretensions should have moderated their reaction, is unequivocal evidence that an *a priori* naturalism can effectively stop intelligent minds entertaining the notion that some features of the universe point towards a designing intelligence, even though such an explanation may be the most logical and obvious way of interpreting the evidence.

Again it was a theist, not an atheist, who had the idea that led to the current widely accepted Big Bang model of the origin of the universe. Georges Lemaitre (1894–1966), a Belgian priest and astronomer, challenged the theory of an eternal universe that had held sway for centuries, and which even Einstein held at the time (Aristotle's influence, once more). Lemaitre made a brilliant application of Einstein's theory of relativity to cosmology, and in 1927 worked out a precursor of Hubble's Law regarding the fact that the universe is expanding. In 1931 he went on to propose his hypothesis of the "primeval atom", by which he meant that the universe began in a "day that did not have a yesterday". Like Alexander Friedman, Lemaitre had discovered that the universe must be expanding; but Lemaitre went further than Friedman in arguing that a creation-like event must have occurred. Interestingly, Einstein was suspicious of this, because for him it was too reminiscent of the Christian doctrine of creation. So was Sir Arthur Eddington (1882–1944), who had taught Lemaitre at Cambridge and regarded his 1927 work as a "brilliant solution" to an outstanding problem in cosmology. Nonetheless the idea of a creation was too much for Eddington: "Philosophically, the notion of a beginning of the present order of Nature is repugnant... I should like to find a genuine loophole."[5]

Much later – in the 1960s – another well-known scientist, Sir John Maddox, then Editor of *Nature*, responded equally negatively to the discovery of further evidence supporting the Big Bang theory. For him, the idea of a beginning was "thoroughly unacceptable", since it implied an "ultimate origin of our world", and gave those who believed in the biblical doctrine of creation "ample justification" for their beliefs.[6] It is rather ironical that in the sixteenth century some people resisted advance in science because it seemed to threaten belief in God; whereas in the twentieth century scientific models of a beginning were resisted because they might increase the plausibility of belief in God.

An anti-scientific stance is completely antipathetic to the biblical worldview, and I am as opposed to it as the New Atheists are. That is not to say that no religious people hold anti-scientific attitudes. It is the sad fact that they do. From the Christian perspective such views are inexcusable, and it is lamentable that they are still to be found. On the other hand, it is also regrettable that the New Atheists are not always as scientific as they profess to be, particularly when it comes to following evidence where it leads – especially when that evidence threatens their materialistic or naturalistic presuppositions. The New Atheists can then be just as anti-scientific as anyone else.[7]

We note in passing that it is often claimed that scientists who believe in a Creator are being unscientific, because their model of the universe is incapable of generating testable predictions. But Maddox's statement above shows that this is not the case. Maddox was hostile to the notion of a beginning precisely because the Genesis creation-model clearly entailed such a beginning, and he did not welcome scientific confirmation of that model. However, his protests had to give way when confronted with the evidence. The discovery of the galactic red-shift and the cosmic echo of creation, the microwave background, confirmed the obvious prediction that the biblical account implied – there was a beginning to space-time.

Maddox's reaction is to be contrasted with that of Richard Dawkins. When I made this point to him in our Alabama debate he was not impressed. His response was that, since either there was a beginning or there was not, the Bible had a 50-50 chance of getting it right. However, quite apart from the gratuitous assumption that the biblical account is simply a matter of guesswork, the probability of a correct guess is not quite the issue. The Big Bang theory met fierce resistance because there was a palpable desire among scientists that the Bible should not get it right. It took massive and convincing scientific evidence to establish the standard model. The irony is that the very same Big Bang model of the universe, which confirms the biblical teaching that there was a beginning, is now being used to banish God by one of the brilliant theoretical physicists involved in developing the theory – Stephen Hawking.

STEPHEN HAWKING AND GOD

In his latest book *The Grand Design*, co-authored with Leonard Mlodinow, Hawking mounts an audacious challenge to the traditional religious belief in the divine creation of the universe. According to him, the laws of physics (not the will of God) provide the real explanation as to how life on earth came into being. He argues that the Big Bang was the inevitable consequence of these laws: "Because there is a law such as gravity, the universe can and will create itself from nothing."[8]

Hawking is guilty of a number of serious misunderstandings and logical fallacies. Firstly, his view of God is defective. From what he says, he clearly thinks of God as a "God of the Gaps", to be put forward as an explanation if we don't yet have a scientific one. Hence his conclusion that physics has no room for God as it has removed the last place where he might be found – the moment of creation.

But this is certainly not what any of the great monotheistic religions believe. For them, God is author of the whole show. God both created the universe and constantly sustains it in existence. Without him, there would be nothing there for physicists to study. In particular, therefore, God is the creator both of the bits of the universe we don't understand, and the bits we do. And of course, it is the bits we do understand that give the most evidence of God's existence and activity. Just as I can admire the genius behind a work of engineering or art, the more I understand it; so my worship of the Creator increases, the more I understand what he has done.

Hawking's inadequate view of God could well be linked with his attitude to philosophy in general. He writes: "Philosophy is dead."[9] But this itself is a philosophical statement. It is manifestly not a statement of science. Therefore, because it says that philosophy is dead, it contradicts itself. It is a classic example of logical incoherence. Not only that: Hawking's book, insofar as it is interpreting and applying science to ultimate questions like the existence of God, is a book about metaphysics – philosophy par excellence.

Imagining that philosophy is dead is hardly the wisest thing to do, especially when you yourself are about to engage in it. Take, for instance, Hawking's key assertion quoted above: "Because there is a law such as gravity the universe can and will create itself from nothing." Clearly, he assumes that gravity (or perhaps only the law of gravity?) exists. That is not nothing. So the universe is not created from nothing. Worse still, the statement "the Universe can and will create itself from nothing" is self-contradictory. If I say "X creates Y", this presupposes the existence of X in the first place in order to bring Y into existence. If I say "X creates X", I presuppose the existence of X in order to account for the existence of X. To presuppose the existence of the universe, to account for its existence, is logically incoherent. What this shows is that nonsense remains nonsense even when talked by world-famous scientists. It also shows that a little bit of philosophy might have helped.

Because Hawking has an inadequate concept both of God and of philosophy, he blunders into a further series of errors by asking us to choose between God and the laws of physics. Here he confuses two very different things: physical law and personal agency. The choice he asks us to make is between false alternatives. This is a classic example of category error. His call for us to choose between physics and God is as manifestly absurd as demanding that we choose either the laws of physics or aeronautical engineer Sir Frank Whittle, in order to explain the jet engine.

That mistake was not made by a previous holder of Hawking's chair at Cambridge, Sir Isaac Newton, when he discovered his law of gravitation. He did not say: "Now that I have the law of gravity I don't need God." What he did was to write *Principia Mathematica*, the most famous book in the history of science, expressing the hope that it would "persuade the thinking man" to believe in God.

The point here is that the laws of physics can explain how the jet engine works, but not how it came to exist in the first place. It is self-evident that a jet engine could not have been created by the laws of physics on their own. That task needed the intelligence and creative engineering work of Whittle. Come to think of it, even the laws of physics plus Frank Whittle could not on their own produce a jet engine. There also needs to be some material around the place that is subject to those laws, and that can be worked on by Whittle. Matter may be humble stuff, but laws don't produce it.

Not only did scientists not put the universe there; neither did science or the laws of mathematical physics. Yet Hawking seems to think they did. In *A Brief History of Time* he hinted at this kind of explanation in suggesting that a theory might bring the universe into existence:

> **The usual approach of science of constructing a mathematical model cannot answer the questions of why there should be a universe for the model to describe. Why does the universe go to all the bother of existing? Is the unified theory so compelling that it brings about its own existence? Or does it need a creator, and, if so, does he have any other effect on the universe?**[10]

However, the idea of a *theory* or *physical laws* bringing the universe into existence does not make sense. Or am I missing something? Scientists expect to develop theories involving mathematical laws that describe natural phenomena, and have done so with spectacular success. However, the laws that we find cannot themselves even cause anything, let alone create it.

Physical laws on their own cannot *create* anything; they are merely a (mathematical) description of what normally happens under certain given conditions. Newton's law of gravitation does not create gravity; it does not even explain gravity, as Newton himself realized. In fact, the laws of physics are not only incapable of creating anything; they cannot even cause anything to happen. For instance, Newton's celebrated laws of motion never caused a snooker ball to race across the green baize table: that can only be done by people using a snooker cue and the actions of their own muscles. The laws enable us to analyse the motion and to map the trajectory of the ball's movement in the future (provided nothing external interferes[11]), but they are powerless to move the ball, let alone bring it into existence.

Yet well-known physicist Paul Davies appears to agree with Hawking: "There's no need to invoke anything supernatural in the origins of the universe or of life. I have never liked the idea of divine tinkering: for me it is much more inspiring to believe that a set of mathematical laws can be so clever as to bring all these things into being."[12]

However, in the ordinary world in which most of us live, the simple law of arithmetic $1+1 = 2$ never by itself brought anything into being. It certainly has never put any money into my bank account. If I put £1,000 into the bank and then later another £1,000, the laws of arithmetic will rationally explain how it is that I now have £2,000 in the bank. But if I never myself put any money into the bank, and simply leave it to the laws of arithmetic to bring money into being in my bank account, I shall remain permanently bankrupt.

C. S. Lewis saw this long ago. Of the laws of nature he says:

They produce no events: they state the pattern to which every event – if only it can be induced to happen – must conform, just as the rules of arithmetic state the pattern to which all transactions with money must conform – if only you can get hold of any money. Thus, in one sense, the laws of Nature cover the whole field of space and time; in another, what they leave out is precisely the whole real universe – the incessant torrent of actual events which makes up true history. That must come from somewhere else. To think the laws can produce it is like thinking that you can create real money by simply doing sums. For every law says in the last resort: "If you have A, then you will get B. But first catch your A: the laws won't do it for you."[13]

The world of strict naturalism, in which clever mathematical laws all by themselves bring the universe and life into existence, is pure (science) fiction. Theories and laws do not bring matter/energy into existence. The view that nevertheless they somehow have that capacity seems a rather desperate refuge (and it is hard to see what else it could be but a refuge), from the alternative possibility implied in Hawking's question cited above: "or does it need a creator?"

If Hawking were not so dismissive of philosophy, then he might have come across Wittgenstein's statement that the "deception of modernism" is the idea that the laws of nature *explain* the world to us when all they do is to *describe* structural regularities. Richard Feynman, a Nobel Laureate in physics, takes the matter further: "The fact that there are rules at all to be checked is a kind of miracle; that it is possible to find a rule, like the inverse square law of gravitation, is some sort of miracle. It is not understood at all, but it leads to the possibility of prediction – that means it tells you what you would expect to happen in an experiment you have not yet done."[14] The very fact that those laws can be mathematically formulated was for

Einstein a constant source of amazement that pointed beyond the physical universe to that "spirit vastly superior to that of man".

Hawking has signally failed to answer the central question: why is there something rather than nothing? He says that the existence of gravity means the creation of the universe was inevitable. But how did gravity come to exist in the first place? What was the creative force behind its birth? Who put it there, with all its properties and potential for mathematical description? Similarly, when, in support of his theory of spontaneous creation, Hawking argues that it was only necessary for "the blue touch paper" to be lit to "set the universe going", I am tempted to ask: where did this blue touch paper come from? It is clearly not part of the universe, if it set the universe going. So who lit it, if not God?

Allan Sandage, widely regarded as the father of modern astronomy (discoverer of quasars and winner of the Crafoord Prize, astronomy's equivalent of the Nobel), is in no doubt about his answer: "I find it quite improbable that such order came out of chaos. There has to be some organizing principle. God to me is a mystery but is the explanation for the miracle of existence – why there is something rather than nothing."[15]

In trying to avoid the clear evidence for the existence of a divine intelligence behind nature, atheist-scientists are forced to ascribe creative powers to less and less credible candidates, such as mass/ energy and the laws of nature. In fact, Hawking has not only not got rid of God; he has not even got rid of the God of the Gaps in which no sensible person believes. For the very theories he advances to banish the God of the Gaps are themselves highly speculative and untestable.

Like every other physicist Hawking is confronted with powerful evidence of design, as he explains in his book:

Our universe and its laws appear to have a design that both is tailor-made to support us and, if we are to exist, leaves little room for alteration. That is not easily explained and raises the natural question of why it is that way... The discovery relatively recently of the extreme fine-tuning of so many of the laws of nature could lead at least some of us back to the old idea that this grand design is the work of some grand designer... That is not the answer of modern science... our universe seems to be one of many, each with different laws.[16]

Thus we arrive at the multiverse. Roughly speaking, the idea here is that there are so many universes (some suggest infinitely many) that anything that can happen will happen in some universe. It is not surprising then, so the argument goes, that there is at least one universe like ours.[17]

We note in passing that Hawking has once again fallen into the trap of offering false alternatives: God, or the multiverse. From a theoretical point of view, as philosophers (that despised race) have pointed out, God could create as many universes as he pleases. Of itself, the multiverse concept does not rule God out.

But back to Hawking's multiverse. Here he moves out beyond science into the very realm of philosophy whose death he has announced at the beginning of his book. Furthermore, Hawking claims to be the voice of modern science. This gives a false impression where the multiverse is concerned, since there are weighty voices within science that do not support Hawking's view.

For instance, Professor John Polkinghorne, an eminent theoretical physicist himself, rejects the multiverse concept:

> Let us recognise these speculations for what they are. They are not physics, but in the strictest sense, metaphysics. There is no purely scientific reason to believe in an ensemble of universes. By construction these other worlds are unknowable by us. A possible explanation of equal intellectual respectability – and to my mind greater economy and elegance – would be that this one world is the way it is, because it is the creation of the will of a Creator who purposes that it should be so.[18]

I am tempted to add that belief in God seems an infinitely more rational option, if the alternative is to believe that every other universe that possibly can exist does exist, including one in which Richard Dawkins is the Archbishop of Canterbury, Christopher Hitchens the Pope, and Billy Graham has just been voted atheist of the year!

Hawking's ultimate theory, to explain why the laws of physics are as they are, is called M-theory: a theory of supersymmetric gravity that involves very sophisticated concepts, such as vibrating strings in eleven dimensions. Hawking confidently calls it "the unified theory that Einstein was expecting to find". However, Paul Davies (cited above), who is not a theist, says of M-theory: "It is not testable, not even in any foreseeable future."[19] Oxford physicist Frank Close goes further: "M-theory is not even defined... we are even told 'No one seems to know what the M stands for.' Perhaps it is 'myth'." Close concludes: "I don't see that M-theory adds one iota to the God debate, either pro or con."[20] Jon Butterworth, who works at the Large Hadron Collider in Switzerland, states that "M-theory is highly speculative and certainly not in the zone of science that we have got any evidence for." Butterworth argues, however, that although M-theory could not be tested, it did not require faith in the religious sense, but was more of a scientific hunch.[21]

Half a minute! Don't scientific hunches require faith to pursue the research that may establish them? Doesn't Hawking have faith in M-theory – even if it is faith without much evidence to back it up?

Clearly, we need to do some hard thinking about faith. But before we do, we might just sum up the discussion about Hawking as follows:

We are presented with the following argument in the form of a syllogism:

If M-theory is true, then there is no God;

M-theory is true;

Therefore there is no God.

We have seen that the first premise is false, whether or not the second is true. The second premise has not been established; some think it not even well defined, let alone testable. The conclusion is therefore invalid. The Grand Design still points unwaveringly to the Grand Designer.[22]

Now to the all-important question of faith.

WHAT IS FAITH?

There is widespread confusion about the nature of faith – especially among atheists. This confusion arises from the fact that the term "faith" has developed a range of meanings and is often used without making clear which meaning is intended. Let's start with the dictionary. According to the OED, the word "faith" derives from the Latin *fides* (from which we get "fidelity"), so its basic meaning is "trust", "reliance". "The Latin *fides* like its Greek etymological cognate *pistes*, which it renders in the New Testament, had the following principal senses: 1. belief, trust; 2. that which produces belief, evidence, token, pledge, engagement; 3. trust in its objective aspect, troth, observance of trust, fidelity."

So, according to the OED, the main meanings given to the word "faith" are: belief, trust, confidence, reliance, and belief proceeding from reliance on testimony or authority. Thus, the statements "I believe in science"; "I trust in science", and "I have faith in science" all mean essentially the same – and we should note that such faith/belief/trust is regarded by most people as warranted.

This all seems plain sailing until we begin to read the New Atheists. On the one hand, they say that they *believe* that God does not exist. On the other, they say that they have no *faith*. Richard Dawkins claims that: "Atheists do not have faith; and reason alone could not propel one to total conviction that anything does not exist."[23] He thinks that: "a case can be made that *faith* is one of the world's great evils, comparable to the smallpox virus but harder to eradicate. Faith, being belief that isn't based on evidence, is the principal vice of any religion."[24] "Scientific belief" according to him "is based upon publicly checkable evidence. Religious faith not only lacks evidence; its independence from evidence is its joy, shouted from the rooftops."[25] Michel Onfray accuses religious believers of "unbelievable credulity because they do not want to see the evidence".[26]

These statements bring us to the heart of the matter. Dawkins here contrasts "scientific *belief*" with "religious *faith*". This shows that he thinks that "faith" is not the same as "belief" but means a special kind of belief: belief where there is no evidence. This idiosyncratic view seems to be shared by many atheists, Julian Baggini among them. He asks the question: is atheism a faith position? His answer is no:

The atheist position is based on evidence and arguments to best explanation. The atheist believes in what she has good reason to believe in and doesn't believe in supernatural entities that there are few reasons to believe in, none of them strong. If this is a faith position then the amount of faith required is very small. Contrast this with believers in the supernatural and we can see what a true faith position is. Belief in the supernatural is belief in what there is a lack of strong evidence to believe in.

Baggini deduces from this: "The status of atheist and religious belief are thus quite different. Only religious belief requires faith because only[27] religious belief postulates the existence of entities which we have no good evidence to believe exist."[28] For Baggini, therefore, a "faith-position" is, by definition, belief without evidence. In other words, for the New Atheists, "belief" would seem to be the neutral term (it may or may not be warranted by evidence), whereas they use "faith" as a special term for belief without warrant.

Furthermore, Baggini confuses two very different things: 1) the terms "faith", "belief", or "trust" and 2) the grounds for such "faith", "belief", or "trust". The point is that, contrary to what Baggini thinks, according to the OED, the normal use of the word "faith" does not contain within it implications for the strength or weakness of the evidence that might justify that faith. From that perspective, it would be much more accurate to say that atheism, agnosticism, and theism are all "faith positions", and we can ask of each of them: What evidence supports them and what speaks against them? What warrant do they have? The confusion arises from an idiosyncratic, implicit, re-definition of "faith" as a peculiarly religious term (which it isn't) and that it only means a special kind of believing, that is, believing without evidence (which it doesn't).

If, for instance, instead of the OED, we consult the popular Merriam Webster's Online Dictionary we find the following entry under "faith":

> **1. a: allegiance to duty or a person: loyalty; b (1): fidelity to one's promises (2): sincerity of intentions. 2. a (1): belief and trust in and loyalty to God (2): belief in the traditional doctrines of a religion; b (1): *firm belief in something for which there is no proof* [italics mine] (2): complete trust.**

According to Webster's, then, firm belief in something for which there is no proof is an allowable use of the word "faith". Perhaps the most famous example of such use is Mark Twain who said that faith is "believing what you know ain't true". The New Atheists all follow him. A leading atheist website (that quotes Mark Twain) says it all: "Simply put, faith means belief or trust. Faith is a particular kind of belief. It is strong, it is often unwavering and it does not require proof or evidence. Most would agree that belief is faith when it is quite strong and does not involve evidence or practical reasoning."[29]

However, faith conceived as belief that lacks warrant is very different from faith conceived as belief that has warrant. To avoid confusion, therefore, it will be helpful to use the much more common and unambiguous term "blind faith" when referring to belief without warrant. Use of the adjective "blind" to describe "faith" indicates that faith is not necessarily, or always, or indeed normally, blind. Nevertheless, Baggini seems to think that it is: "When such grounds for belief are available we have no need for faith. It is not faith that justifies my belief that drinking fresh, clean water is good for me, but evidence. It is not faith that tells me it is not a good idea to jump out of the windows of tall buildings, but experience."[30] In the first sentence here "faith" is contrasted with "grounds for belief"; in the second it is contrasted with "evidence"; and in the third with "experience". This is pure Mark Twain, and for someone who takes the OED seriously, it sounds absurd since, in ordinary language, saying that "it is not faith that justifies my belief" is like saying that belief doesn't justify belief or, equivalently, that faith doesn't justify faith. This simply makes no sense.

In normal language, what Baggini presumably means is that he puts his faith in drinking fresh, clean water on the basis of such and such evidence, and that he trusts (or puts faith in) his experience to tell him that it is not a good idea to jump from tall buildings. Far from him not exercising faith at all, he is exercising it on both occasions.

It follows from this that the *validity*, or *warrant*, of faith or belief depends on the strength of the evidence on which the belief is based. Indeed, for most people that is the common sense view. Asked to believe something, they will want to know what the supporting evidence is, especially if the matter is of some importance to them. A bank manager will not have faith in (trust, believe) a potential borrower who asks for a substantial loan unless the bank manager can see sufficient evidence on which to base that trust.

Think of the financial crisis of 2009. Before it happened many had faith in the banking system, because they believed in the integrity of most bank officials. Then it was discovered that ethically responsible risk management was not a strongpoint for some senior bankers who, out of sheer greed, gambled our money away on risky ventures. Any basis for trust in them was eroded to such an extent, therefore, that the economy was paralysed, and the banks had to be bailed out. Public faith in the bankers was shown to be blind. Indeed, even the bankers' faith in their own ability also turned out to be blind. As a result the banks were faced with the very difficult task of recovering the faith, the confidence, of the public. The system could not get moving again until a basis for trust (faith) was restored.

What is this telling us? We all know how to distinguish between blind faith and evidence-based faith. We are well aware that faith is only justified if there is evidence to back it up. When buying a car, we don't just throw our hard-earned money at any vehicle. We check out the reliability ratings of the manufacturer; we check with friends who own similar cars. In other words, we look for reasons – we look for evidence – to justify our decision to have faith in buying a particular vehicle.

We also know that blind faith can be dangerous – even in the everyday matter of buying a car, to say nothing of the kind of blind fanaticism that fuels terrorism. Most of us would surely agree with Richard Dawkins when he says: "If children were taught to question and think through their beliefs, instead of being taught the superior virtues of faith without question, it is a good bet that there would be no suicide bombers."[31]

FAITH IN PEOPLE

In our everyday usage of the words "faith" and "belief", we tend to distinguish between "belief that something", and "belief in someone". Here once more, it is surely obvious that trust in other human beings is based on evidence, unless we happen to be gullible. I made this point in my first debate with Richard Dawkins in response to his assertion that faith is blind. I asked him about his faith in his wife. His instinctive, positive reaction confirmed to me that he understands very well that faith is normally evidence-based. In fact, Dawkins explains this in some detail in a letter written to his daughter:

> People sometimes say that you must believe in feelings deep inside, otherwise you'd never be confident of things like "My wife loves me." But this is a bad argument. There can be plenty of evidence that somebody loves you. All through the day when you are with somebody who loves you, you see and hear lots of little tidbits of evidence, and they all add up. It isn't a purely inside feeling, like the feeling that priests call revelation.[32] There are outside things to back up the inside

feeling: looks in the eye, tender notes in the voice, little favours and kindnesses; this is all real evidence.

Sometimes people have a strong inside feeling that somebody loves them when it is not based upon any evidence, and then they are likely to be completely wrong. There are people with a strong inside feeling that a famous film star loves them, when really the film star hasn't even met them. People like that are ill in their minds. Inside feelings must be backed up by evidence otherwise you just can't trust them.[33]

Exactly! Evidence-based faith is not an unfamiliar idea – even to the New Atheists.

In all of these examples we should note that faith is not something that makes up for lack of evidence, so that strength of faith is inversely proportional to strength of evidence. Nor is faith that which "supports beliefs that lack the ordinary support of evidence or argument."[34] It is the other way round, as we all surely know very well. The more evidence I see for trusting a document or a person, the stronger will be my trust in it or her.

In light of all of this it is quite astonishing just how deep the Mark Twain definition of faith has been adopted by the New Atheists as the *only* definition of faith, so that they imagine that evidence somehow displaces faith rather than justifies it. A further classic example of this is given by Christopher Hitchens: "If one must have faith to believe in something, then the likelihood of that something having truth or value is considerably diminished." Exit science then! Exit also Christopher Hitchens, as I pointed out to him in our Alabama debate, "Is God Great?" After all, on the presumption that Christopher Hitchens has sufficient faith to believe in his own existence, his argument would tell me that the likelihood that he actually exists is considerably diminished. Such "logic" is not exactly impressive, is it? Worse still, what Hitchens says about faith refutes itself, since it is itself an expression of faith. He believes it, and he expects you to believe it; so if it is true the likelihood of its having truth is diminished! It contradicts itself. It is incoherent.

Indeed, Hitchens appears to have confused himself almost completely in this issue. Consider his wondrously foolish statement: "Our belief is not a belief. Our principles are not a faith."[35]

A further root of this endemic confusion about faith is traceable to the Enlightenment philosopher Immanuel Kant. He introduced a false disjunction between faith and knowledge that has caused endless trouble ever since. Kant wrote: "I have... found it necessary to deny *knowledge,* in order to make room for *faith.*"[36] Many have taken Kant to mean that if there were convincing evidence for the existence of God, then there would be no room left for faith.

This bizarre notion is very common, and yet it is plainly false. For instance, the late Warden of Green College Oxford, the eminent epidemiologist Sir Richard Doll, demonstrated beyond reasonable doubt that smoking causes lung cancer. We can therefore say that we *know* that smoking causes lung cancer. Does this knowledge leave no room for faith? Of course it leaves room for faith. Some people have faith in Doll's work and stop smoking, thus dramatically decreasing the potential risk to their health. Other people do not have faith in the scientific results; even though they know it, and are reminded of it every time they purchase a packet of cigarettes. Their lack of faith is perverse, of course, and frequently fatal – yet they go on smoking. To say that knowledge somehow displaces faith reveals very muddled thinking. After all, knowledge of facts and people increases our faith in them and not the opposite.

IS FAITH IN GOD BLIND OR EVIDENCE-BASED?

As we have seen, blind faith exists, and can be dangerous. Therefore, our next question must be: Is the Christian faith[37] like that?[38] Is it Mark Twain faith? Yes, says Baggini, and, what is more, the Bible itself says that faith means believing something for which there is no evidence. In support, Baggini quotes the story of "doubting" Thomas's encounter with Jesus in Jerusalem after the resurrection. In his Gospel, John tells how Thomas was not with the other disciples when they saw Jesus, and refused to accept their story unless he was given visual and tangible evidence: "Unless I see in his hands the mark of the nails, and place my finger into the mark of the nails, and place my hand into his side, I will never believe."[39]

The account continues as follows:

> **Eight days later, his disciples were inside again, and Thomas was with them. Although the doors were locked, Jesus came and stood among them and said, "Peace be with you." Then he said to Thomas, "Put your finger here, and see my hands; and put out your hand, and place it in my**

side. Do not disbelieve, but believe." Thomas answered him, "My Lord
and my God!" Jesus said to him, "Have you believed because you have
seen me? Blessed are those who have not seen and yet have believed."[40]

Baggini gives his interpretation: "Thus Christianity endorsed the
principle that it is good to believe what you have no evidence to
believe, a rather convenient maxim for a belief system for which
there is no evidence."[41]

This is a completely unwarranted, and indeed, rather foolish,
deduction, as a moment's thought will show. Thomas believed, says
the text, because he *saw*. Does that mean that the millions of people
(including myself) who have not seen Jesus with their own eyes,
yet believe in him, do so without evidence? Of course not! Seeing is
only one kind of evidence. There are many other kinds of evidence,
and we shall consider it in detail later. For the moment, let us simply
note that Baggini's interpretation is on the level of suggesting that,
because you have not *seen* gravity or atoms or X-rays, your belief in
their existence cannot be evidence-based; or because you have not
seen Napoleon, your belief that he fought the battle of Waterloo is
blind. And Baggini is a philosopher![42]

Before putting pen to paper he would have been well advised to
read the statement in the Gospel of John immediately following the
Thomas incident that explains just how John himself understood the
concept of faith. "Now Jesus did many other signs in the presence of
the disciples, which are not written in this book; but these are written
so that you may believe that Jesus is the Christ, the Son of God, and
that by believing you may have life in his name."[43] John is stating here
the purpose for which he wrote his book. It records a collection of signs
– special things that Jesus did, that pointed towards a reality beyond
themselves, and thus bore witness to his identity as God incarnate. For
instance, Jesus multiplied loaves of bread to feed a large crowd and
then used what he had done to point to himself as the "bread of life"
at a deeper level. John records how people believed in Jesus because
of the evidence he provided through the performance of such signs.[44]
And John regarded that evidence to be sufficient also for those, like
ourselves, who did not directly observe the events in question. The
belief (= faith) required by Christ is anything but blind, according to
John. The blindness is on the part of the people who cannot see this.

Terry Eagleton, a distinguished British literary critic, is
characteristically trenchant:

Dawkins considers that all faith is blind faith, and that Christian and Muslim children are brought up to believe unquestioningly. Not even the dim-witted clerics who knocked me about at grammar school thought that. For mainstream Christianity, reason, argument and honest doubt have always played an integral role in belief.[45]

FAITH AND FREUD: IS FAITH A DELUSION?

Faith, seen through the distorting lens of the New Atheism, is a psychological aberration only to be found in deluded religious minds, or "faith-heads", as Dawkins mockingly dubs them. In his considered opinion, faith is not only a delusion, but a morally reprehensible one: "Faith is an evil precisely because it requires no justification and brooks no argument."[46] It is also insane, in his view. Dawkins quotes Robert Pirsig, author of *Zen and the Art of Motorcycle Maintenance*: "When one person suffers from a delusion, it is called insanity. When many people suffer from a delusion, it is called Religion."[47]

The idea that faith in God is a delusion did not, of course, have to wait for Richard Dawkins. Before sailing under guard for Rome to be heard by Caesar, the Christian apostle Paul made his final defence of the gospel in Caesarea, when he was summoned to appear before the Roman governor Porcius Festus and King Herod Agrippa. Festus famously interrupted Paul's defence speech saying: "Paul, you are out of your mind; your great learning is driving you out of your mind."[48] If Paul was accused of delusion in those early days, then it is perhaps not surprising that we are seeing another wave of it today.

According to the OED, the word "delude" (Latin *de-ludere* – to play false, mock, deceive) originally meant simply "to deceive the mind or judgement to cause that which is false to be accepted as true"; but nowadays it almost invariably implies the suspicion of psychiatric illness. A delusion is "a fixed false belief", "a persistent false belief held in the face of strong contradictory evidence, especially as a symptom of psychiatric disorder".

It is to be noted that Dawkins classifies faith under the first part of this statement; and it is clear that, in this sense, some of what goes under the name of faith is clearly delusional – faith in the flying spaghetti monster; or even faith in leprechauns, if you happen to be Irish. Indeed, the New Atheists love to classify faith in God along with faith in Santa Claus and the Tooth Fairy. But that is rather silly. Alister McGrath recalls:

> **As a child I believed (for a very short while) in Santa Claus. However I soon sussed the real situation out, although I must confess I kept my doubts about Santa's existence to myself for some time because I also noticed that there was material advantage in so doing. I have never heard of an adult coming to believe in Santa Claus or the Tooth Fairy. I have known many adult people come to believe in God. So clearly there is a great difference. But it is still worth asking the question: why is faith in the Tooth Fairy a delusion? The answer is obvious – the Tooth Fairy does not exist.[49]**

This brings us to a key issue that is very easily overlooked. It is this. Faith in God certainly is a delusion, if God does not exist. But what if God does exist? Then atheism is the delusion. So the real question to ask is: does God exist?

This point is so important that I wish to put it another way, and simultaneously confront another objection. Many atheists (inspired by Sigmund Freud, who himself thought that faith in God is an illusion)[50] claim that they have a very simple and convincing explanation of why people believe in God. It arises from incapacity to cope with the real world and its uncertainties. Michel Onfray tells us that "religion is imagined because people do not wish to face reality".[51] They would "rather have the faith to soothe than reason at the price of a perpetually infantile mentality".[52]

For the New Atheists, then, God is a wish fulfilment, a fictional father figure projected on the sky of our imagination and created by our desire for comfort and security. On this view, heaven is an invention to cope with human fear of extinction at death, and religion is simply a psychological escape mechanism so that we don't have to face life as it really is.

In his best-selling book *God: A Brief History of the Greatest One*,[53] the German psychiatrist Manfred Lütz points out that this Freudian explanation for belief in God works very well – *provided only that God does not exist*. However, he continues, by the very same token, *if God does exist*, then exactly the same Freudian argument will show you that it is atheism that is the comforting delusion, the flight from facing reality, a projection of the desire not to have to meet God one day and give account for your life. For instance, Polish Nobel Laureate

Czesław Miłosz, who had reason to know, writes: "A true opium of the people is a belief in nothingness after death – the huge solace of thinking that for our betrayals, greed, cowardice, murders, we are not going to be judged."[54] Thus, if God does exist, atheism can be seen as a psychological escape mechanism to avoid taking ultimate responsibility for one's own life.

Lütz presses home the implication of his argument: *as to whether God exists or not, Freud can give you no help whatsoever.*[55] If atheists are going to use Freud, they must also give other grounds for rejecting the existence of God. Similarly, if Christians are going to use Freud, they must also give other grounds for believing in God. Freud alone does not help with the real question at stake: Does God exist or not?

I am well aware, of course, that the New Atheists claim that faith is not only a delusion; it is a pernicious delusion that has led to horrific violence and acts of terror like 9/11, an event that helped spark off the New Atheist protest. We shall look at this accusation in detail in Chapter 2. First, however, we need to think about the relationship of faith to science.

FAITH AND SCIENCE

As we have seen, the New Atheists regard faith as a peculiarly religious term (which it isn't) and they define it to be belief without evidence (which it isn't). This inevitably leads them to another serious error – thinking that neither atheism nor science involves faith. Yet the irony is that atheism is a "faith position", and science itself cannot do without faith. Dawkins' statement, quoted earlier, that "atheists have no faith",[56] seems doubly silly since, in common with all other scientists, he could not engage in science without *believing in (having faith in)* the rational intelligibility of the universe. Nor could he do science without *believing* in the evidence presented to him. He even says so himself, as we pointed out earlier: "Scientific *belief* [italics mine] is based upon publicly checkable evidence."[57] Faith, then, lies at the heart of science.

After all, the goal of science, as most scientists see it, is not to impose on the matter and workings of the universe our human sense of order; but to unveil and discover the universe's own order and intelligibility. That means, of course, that scientists have always had to *assume*, before they started their investigations, that the universe does have an inherent order and intelligibility. If they didn't believe that such order and intelligibility existed, scientific research would never discover them, and their work would be fruitless and pointless.

Physicist Paul Davies, though not a theist, says that the right scientific attitude is essentially theological: "Science can proceed only if the scientist adopts an essentially theological worldview." He points out that "even the most atheistic scientist accepts *as an act of faith* [italics mine] the existence of a law-like order in nature that is at least in part comprehensible to us".[58] Albert Einstein famously said:

> Science can only be created by those who are thoroughly imbued with the aspiration towards truth and understanding. This source of feeling, however, springs from religion. To this there also belongs the faith in the possibility that the regulations valid for the world of existence are rational, that is, comprehensible to reason. *I cannot imagine a scientist without that profound faith* [italics mine]. The situation may be expressed by an image: science without religion is lame, religion without science is blind.[59]

Richard Dawkins is allergic to believers in God citing Einstein, as if Einstein belonged to them. He makes a great fuss about it near the beginning of *The God Delusion*, saying that Einstein "was repeatedly indignant at being called a theist". Dawkins, although he classifies Einstein as an atheistic scientist,[60] appears to come down on the side of Einstein being a pantheist, because of his sympathy with Spinoza. Yet the very book that Dawkins cites as his source gives a very different impression.[61] Einstein himself explicitly stated: "I'm not an atheist and I don't think I can call myself a pantheist."[62] Therefore, though it is true that Einstein said that he did not believe in a personal God, Dawkins is clearly not entitled to claim him as an atheist.

Furthermore, we certainly don't find Dawkins urging us, as Einstein did, to recognize that:

> Everyone who is seriously involved in the pursuit of science becomes convinced that a spirit is manifest in the laws of the Universe – a spirit vastly superior to that of man, and one in the face of which we with our modest powers must feel humble. In this way the pursuit of science leads to a religious feeling of a special sort, which is indeed quite different from the religiosity of someone more naïve.[63]

The main point I wish to gain from citing Einstein, however, is that he evidently did not suffer from the New Atheist delusion that all faith is blind faith. Einstein speaks of the "profound faith" of the scientist in the rational intelligibility of the universe. He could not imagine a scientist without it. So, while Dawkins may not classify Einstein as a theist, he (Dawkins) must share in that profound faith that Einstein had – otherwise Einstein would probably not classify him (Dawkins) as a scientist.

This talk of faith in a scientific context jars with the New Atheists, since it just does not fit in with their idiosyncratic concept of faith. They are determined to keep the concept of faith out of science, with disastrous results. One example of this is an article by philosopher A. C. Grayling (whose misreading of the "doubting Thomas" story is, incidentally, a worthy companion to Baggini's). Grayling chose the title "No, science does not 'rest on faith'"[64] for his first article as a columnist in the *New Scientist*. Grayling does not seem to have read Einstein, let alone to have understood him. He rather appears to have swallowed the New Atheists' blind-faith-meme, hook, line, and sinker. He contrasts the scientific method with faith, as he understands it: "Making well-motivated evidence-based assumptions that are in turn supported by their efficacy in testing predictions is the very opposite of faith. Faith is commitment to belief in something either in the absence of evidence or in the face of countervailing evidence."

This sounds like Baggini all over again. Grayling's first assertion is correct, provided only that he begs the question by defining faith as he does in his second assertion. However, it is easy to think of a series of scenarios where the terms "belief" and "faith" are used in a positive sense. Scientists believe (have faith in) in Newton's laws[65] or the genetic basis for heredity, because they are backed by evidence based on observation and experimentation. And that faith in turn springs from their faith in the scientific method, one aspect of which Grayling, in complete self-contradiction, has just described as being the "opposite of faith". After all, as we saw earlier, making well-motivated, evidence-based *assumptions* is just how faith is normally exercised – think of how you get your bank manager to trust you; or the basis for your decision to board an aircraft.

Faith, therefore, is essential to science. Indeed, even after all their successes, if scientific research is thought to be still worth pursuing, scientists have to *believe in* the rational intelligibility of the universe as their fundamental *article of faith* or *basic assumption*. Scientists are all people of faith, in the sense that they *believe* that the universe is accessible to the human mind. And, as my teacher of quantum mechanics at Cambridge, Professor Sir John Polkinghorne, points out: "physics is powerless to explain its faith [note his explicit use of the word] in the mathematical intelligibility of the universe", for the simple reason that you cannot begin to do physics without believing in that intelligibility.

Furthermore, the behaviour of elementary particles presents us with quantum phenomena that, for the moment, outstrip our reason, intuition, and powers of imagination. Various theories are proposed; none is universally accepted. The same is true of human consciousness: no one yet understands it and no theory has produced general agreement. In this situation, for research to continue, it requires faith not only in the order and intelligibility of nature, but faith that nature's intelligibility will not peter out into unintelligible chaos (though, for all we know, a level of intelligibility might be involved that is higher than any we can grasp at present). Thus, faith in something that has not yet been proved still is, as it has always been, a prerequisite for scientific investigation of the universe. Shall we therefore accuse science of irrationality? Of course not!

FAITH, EVIDENCE, AND PROOF

The reader will have noticed that the word "proof" has not been used in this chapter until now. One reason for this is the confusion that exists about the meaning of proof. In my own field of pure mathematics, "proof" has a rigorous meaning, so that when one mathematician says to another "Prove it", they expect to be presented with a watertight argument proceeding from accepted axioms via accepted rules of logic to a conclusion that she can expect also to be accepted by all mathematicians. There is no degree of tentativeness – if you cannot prove the result rigorously, you do not publish.[66]

This does not mean, of course, that mistakes are never made; but these are usually weeded out very rapidly, especially if the result is of considerable interest. There are also problematic areas in certain extreme special cases as to what, precisely, constitutes a proof – can we, for instance, accept as valid a proof that involves 10,000 pages of argument and is only understood by a handful of experts?[67]

What is important for us here is that such mathematically rigorous proof is not available in any other discipline or area of experience, not even in the so-called "hard" sciences. There we find another, less formal use of the word "proof" akin to the use of the term by lawyers when they speak of "proof beyond reasonable doubt", by which they mean that there is evidence strong enough to convince a reasonable person that a certain claim is true. I shall try here not to use the word "proof" to avoid such ambiguities and will speak rather of the strength of evidence that warrants a given conclusion.

This does not mean, however, that everything is equally tentative, that we can be certain of nothing, or that we can come to no conclusions. On the contrary, although we cannot speak of absolute certainty, there are many situations in which we think that there is sufficient evidence for us to trust even our lives to other people – pilots and surgeons, for instance. I cannot mathematically "prove" to you that my wife loves me. However, with the cumulative evidence of over forty years of marriage, I would stake my life on it. There are things, then, in all of our lives that we regard as beyond reasonable doubt and we confidently place our faith in them.

FAITH IN GOD, AND THE HUMAN COGNITIVE FACULTY

In light of our analysis of the nature of faith, Michel Onfray's view seems as patronizing as it is false: "Better the faith that brings peace of mind than the rationality that brings worry – even at the price of perpetual mental infantilism."[68] It is a classic example of the universalized false antithesis that abounds in New Atheist literature. It is also an insult to some of the greatest (scientific) minds in the world. Are we really to think that Francis Collins, Director of the US National Institute of Health and former head of the Human Genome Project, is locked into a "perpetual mental infantilism"; that American Nobel prize-winning physicist William Phillips is somehow cerebrally challenged; that Sir John Houghton FRS, who was in succession Professor of Physics at Oxford, Director of the British Meteorological Office, and Head of the Nobel prize-winning Intergovernmental Panel for Climate Change (IPCC), is a deluded faith-head? According to the New Atheists they must be, for they are convinced Christians.

In the same vein as Onfray, Dawkins opines that scientists who believe in God are "the subject of amused bafflement to their peers in the academic community".[69] I must say that this is far from my experience; and in any case it is a strange way for a member of the scientific academy to talk about his fellows. There does not seem to be any realization on the part of the academics among the New Atheists that, by the same token, they also might be candidates for the amused bafflement of at least some of their colleagues, who may just be tempted to think that atheism sits ill with their professed scientific rationality. One of the great ironies is that it is not faith in God in general and Christianity in particular that sit ill with rationality and science; it is the New Atheism that ought to feel uncomfortable in their presence. By its reductionist explanation of all aspects of the universe in terms of unguided natural processes, the New Atheism cuts off at its root the very rationality on which science rests, and in which scientists must trust to come to their conclusions. To see this, let us ask the following question.

ON WHAT EVIDENCE DO SCIENTISTS BASE THEIR FAITH IN THE RATIONAL INTELLIGIBILITY OF THE UNIVERSE?

The first thing to notice is that human reason did not create the universe (unless we are extreme idealists – a position that has not endeared itself to many scientists). This point is so obvious that at first it might seem trivial; but actually it is of fundamental importance when we come to assess the validity of our cognitive faculties. Not only did human beings not create the universe, but we did not create our own powers of reason either. By using our rational faculties we can develop them; but we did not originate them. How can it be, then, that what goes on in our tiny heads can give us anything near to a true account of reality? How can it be that a mathematical equation, thought up in the human mind of a mathematician, can correspond to the workings of the universe out there? It was reflection on this idea that led Einstein to say: "The only incomprehensible thing about the universe is that it is comprehensible." Similar reflection stimulated physics Nobel Prizewinner Eugene Wigner to write a famous paper entitled "The Unreasonable Effectiveness of Mathematics in the Natural Sciences."[70]

The question we are addressing boils down to this: what authority, and, hence, what reliability or warrant has our reason? Are our cognitive faculties deliberately designed to enable us to discover, recognize, and believe the truth? Now I am well aware that some will at once choke on the word "designed", and I am also aware that atheists, by definition, deny any deliberate design by a creator. But even atheists believe that reason does have a proper function and purpose, in the same sense as, say, the heart does. The heart's proper purpose is to pump the blood round the body; whereas a cancerous growth has no proper purpose or function within the human body. It results from purposeless, chaotic growth.

Moreover atheists, when they assert that belief in the existence of God results from a misuse of reason, inadvertently reveal their belief that the faculty of reason is in this sense "designed" to fulfil the purpose of discovering the truth. If reason had no proper function, obviously no one could be accused of misusing it. But, as we saw above, many follow Freud's contention that all the apparently rational arguments put forward by believers for the existence of God are in fact driven and corrupted by a hidden, subconscious wish-fulfilment-mechanism: the desire to construct for themselves a crutch to help them through life's difficulties;[71] whereas reason, if uncorrupted, would achieve its proper purpose and discover the truth, namely atheism. Indeed, Richard Dawkins now makes the astonishing claim that religious belief comes about by a misfiring of evolution.[72]

The irony of the atheists' position becomes instantly apparent, however, as soon as one enquires about the origin of the human faculty of reason. Atheists hold that the driving force of evolution, which eventually produced our human cognitive faculties – reason included – was not primarily concerned with truth at all, but with survival. And we all know what has generally happened – and still happens – to truth when individuals or commercial enterprises or nations, motivated by what Dawkins calls their "selfish genes", feel themselves threatened and struggle for survival.

The New Atheists have signally failed to appreciate the sceptical implications of their view. They are essentially obliged to regard thought as some kind of neuro-physiological phenomenon. From the evolutionary perspective, the neurophysiology might well be adaptive – but why should one think for a moment that the beliefs caused by that neurophysiology would be mostly true? After all, as the chemist J. B. S. Haldane pointed out long ago, if the thoughts in my mind are just the motions of atoms in my brain – a mechanism that has arisen by mindless unguided processes, why should I believe anything it tells me – including the fact that it is made of atoms? In particular, what grounds are there to believe that naturalism is true? In other words, the New Atheists' unguided evolution undermines their naturalism.

Stephen Hawking seems not to have taken this into account when he wrote in *The Grand Design*: "The fact that we human beings – who are ourselves mere collections of fundamental particles of nature – have come close to an understanding of the laws governing us and our Universe is a great triumph."[73]

Atheist John Gray spells out the implications of this view: "Modern humanism is the faith that through science humankind can know the truth and so be free. But if Darwin's theory of natural selection is true this is impossible. The human mind serves evolutionary success, not truth."[74]

In light of this we might well ask: how can the New Atheists claim that it is, on the one hand, *rational* to believe in the theory that the evolution of our faculty of reason was not directed for the purpose of discovering the truth; and, on the other hand, *irrational* to believe that our faculty of reason was designed and created by our Maker to enable us to understand and believe the truth?

American philosopher Alvin Plantinga sums up the position:

If Dawkins is right that we are the product of mindless unguided natural processes, then he has given us strong reason to doubt the reliability of human cognitive faculties and therefore inevitably to doubt the validity of any belief that they produce – including Dawkins' own science and his atheism. His biology and his belief in naturalism would therefore appear to be at war with each other in a conflict that has nothing at all to do with God.[75]

That is, atheism undermines the very rationality that is needed to construct or understand or believe in any kind of argument whatsoever – let alone a scientific one. Atheism is ultimately nothing but one great self-contradictory delusion.

R. A. Collingwood once said that materialism[76] has the characteristic of "writing itself a large cheque on income it had not yet received". Reducing thought to nothing but neurophysiology is a prime example of this tendency, as inevitably it also leads to the demise of science, rationality, and belief in truth itself – it is ultimately nihilistic. That is the real price you have to pay for the New Atheism – a price that the New Atheists do not put on the sales ticket.

Putting this very important point the other way round, eminent German philosopher Robert Spaemann has pointed out that we are faced, not with the choice between God and science, as the New Atheists would have us to think, but with the choice either to put faith in God or to give up on understanding the universe. That is, if there is no God there can be no science. Spaemann is not suggesting that atheists cannot do science: that would be completely untrue. He is saying that, if we eliminate God, there is no rational basis for science. Indeed, there is no rational basis for truth. Science and truth are left without warrant.

By contrast, biblical theism is coherent in its explanation of why the universe is (scientifically) intelligible. It teaches that God is ultimately responsible as Creator, both for the existence of the universe and the human mind. Human beings are made in his image: the image of a rational, personal Creator; and that is why they can understand the universe, at least in part. It is not surprising, therefore, that there is a close link between this belief and the rise of modern science in the sixteenth and seventeenth centuries. Thus, thinking both critically and biblically is not the oxymoron that Dawkins imagines.[77] The oxymoron would seem rather to be trying to think both critically and "Dawkinsly".

SUMMARY

In this chapter we have attempted to understand why there is such confusion about the nature of faith. We have seen that the New Atheists essentially define as faith what most people would think of as blind faith; whereas the OED makes clear that faith and belief are cognate concepts intimately related to the question of substantiating evidence. That is, evidence-based faith is the normal concept on which we base our everyday lives.

We then found that the New Atheists' idiosyncratic definition of faith leads to them failing to appreciate the role of faith in science, and failing to see that at the heart of science is the *belief* that the universe is rationally intelligible. We went on to see that the New Atheists' view of the origin of the human cognitive faculty gives them no ground for the faith in science that they cannot do without. Indeed, their reduction of human thought to neurophysiology is ultimately nihilistic and destroys the possibility of truth, thus undermining the validity of all arguments including those of the New Atheists. The faith of the New Atheists turns out to have no evidential base. Their view, therefore, is a perfect example of their own (erroneous) notion of a "faith position". By contrast, the biblical view makes perfect sense of the fact that we can do science. The universe is (in part) intelligible to the human mind, since both trace their origins ultimately to the same Creator.

At this point the atheist faith strikes me as the very opposite of great. To quote a fine phrase of Christopher Hitchens out of context, the New Atheists are "assassins of the mind". Epistemically their atheism is blind, anti-science, and incoherent, even though emotionally its proponents seem unable to take this on board. However, if one still insists on taking the view that all faith is blind faith, then one should dismiss the New Atheism as well; since, like the old atheism, it is equally a matter of faith. It is ironic that the New Atheists are classic examples of the very thing that they despise: they are characterized by the blind faith that all faith is blind faith. It is also ironic that the New Atheists do not even see that they themselves are driven by faith, even as they seek to destroy it. They believe that the world is rational, that truth is important. They have faith that their own minds can understand the things they are talking about. They also have faith that they can convince us by their arguments. If they think that their view is not a faith or belief system, why do they try to give evidence to get the rest of us to *believe* it? All of this they do, failing blissfully to see that their atheism cuts the rational ground from under them on which they so much wish to stand.

The upshot of all this is that it is not faith in God that is the delusion. It is the New Atheist concept of faith that is a delusion in the precise sense they assign to that term: a persistent false belief held in the face of strong contradictory evidence. Against all the evidence (do they not even bother to consult dictionaries?) they irrationally reduce all faith to blind faith, and then subject it to ridicule.

Of course, that approach provides them with a very convenient way of avoiding intelligent discussion about real evidence. "People of faith" or "faith-heads" cannot have anything sensible to say, for, by definition, they have no evidence for their beliefs. So don't listen to them or engage them in discussion. It is very tempting to describe this attitude as intellectual laziness – or perhaps even delusional. Who, after all, turns out to be the real "faith-heads"?

The delightful irony of all this is that if we for a moment (but only for a moment) adopt the New Atheists' definition of faith as blind belief, then their atheism seems in prime position to be the only true faith around.

CHAPTER 2

IS RELIGION POISONOUS?

"The concept of 'God' invented as the antithesis of life – everything harmful, poisonous, slanderous, the whole hostility unto death against life synthesized in a gruesome unity."
Friedrich Nietzsche

"Religion poisons everything."
Christopher Hitchens

"The advantageous effect of religious belief and spirituality on mental and physical health is one of the best-kept secrets in psychiatry and medicine generally. If the findings of the huge volume of research on this topic had gone in the opposite direction and it had been found that religion damages your mental health, it would have been front-page news in every newspaper in the land."
Andrew Sims

At the 2007 conference entitled "Beyond Belief: Science, Religion, Reason, and Survival" mentioned in the previous chapter, physics Nobel Prizewinner Steven Weinberg said: "Religion is an insult to human dignity. With, or without it, you would have good people doing good things and evil people doing evil things. But for good people to do evil things, that takes religion." This impression that religion is harmful would appear to be spreading. According to the 2007 British YouGov poll cited in the Introduction, nearly half (42 per cent) of the 2,200 people taking part thought religion had a harmful effect, and only 17 per cent thought the influence of religion was beneficial, a figure rather strangely less than the 28 per cent who claimed to believe in God.[1]

Again, it is of interest to set these figures in the wider context of the ten-nation BBC poll of 2004, also mentioned earlier in the Introduction, entitled: "What the world thinks of God".[2] Thus, in the UK 29 per cent of people polled believed that the world would be better off if people did not believe in God, by contrast with the USA where just 6 per cent held this view.

There would seem to be a marked increase, therefore, between 2004 and 2007. John Humphrys comments on possible causes: "One reason might be the publicity attracted by a handful of mad mullahs and their hate-filled rhetoric."[3] This observation is in line with the assertions of the New Atheists, that fundamentalist Islam has tipped the scales in alerting the world to the dangers of religion. It certainly is all too easy to write a searing account of the atrocious behaviour attributable to adherents of various religions; as for instance Christopher Hitchens' chapter "Does religion make people better?"[4]

THE DANGER OF UNWARRANTED GENERALIZATION

However, the New Atheists undermine their own case in astonishingly naïve fashion by lumping all religions together indiscriminately, as if all religions were equally guilty of the charge of fomenting dangerous behaviour. One would not expect such unscholarly, crass oversimplification to come from authors who loudly praise their "scientific approach". In this connection it is to be noted that *Prospect* magazine, which had earlier voted Dawkins a world-class intellectual, described his book *The God Delusion* as "incautious, dogmatic, rambling and self-contradictory". After all, it does not take one to be at the cutting edge of academic research into religious thought, to see that classifying the peace-loving Amish with Islamic fundamentalist extremists is culpably and dangerously naïve. Indeed, anyone who knows anything at all about religions knows that they differ profoundly in their teachings and practices. Therefore, millions of moderate people of all religious persuasions will, rightly, strenuously object to being classified by the New Atheists along with violent extremists, even those of their own religious persuasion. After all, 9/11 is a rather strange launching pad for the New Atheist attack on Christianity.

At times Dawkins does appear to appreciate that there are real differences. Speaking of Islam, he says: "If you don't take it seriously and accord it a proper respect you are physically threatened on a scale that no other religion has aspired to since the Middle Ages."[5] At other times he warns that "even mild and moderate religion helps to provide the climate of faith in which extremism naturally flourishes".[6]

There is a deep irony in the New Atheists' failure to discriminate between religions; for they clearly expect everyone else to discriminate between atheists. They themselves, as self-confessedly peace-loving people, would not like to be arbitrarily classified with violent extremists of their own worldview persuasion, such as Stalin, Mao, and Pol Pot. Why, therefore, do the New Atheists not warn us that mild and moderate atheism might provide the climate of faith in which extreme atheism naturally flourishes, as it did in the twentieth century? If we were to apply the New Atheists' own oversimplifying technique to them, vehement protest would not be long in coming.

This rather blatant inconsistency, in expecting non-atheists to discriminate between atheists while the New Atheists themselves resolutely refuse to do the same with religious groups, does nothing to enhance the intellectual credibility of the New Atheist message. It even tempts one to apply Dawkins' dictum to them, and ignore everything else they say. However, that temptation must be resisted; since many serious-minded people are, rightly, deeply concerned at the deservedly bad reputation some religions have for being involved in patently evil activities. It is therefore important to address the issue in a temperate way. As Keith Ward suggests, the right question to ask is whether "this particular religion, at this stage of its development, is dangerous in this social context".[7]

It should be noted, however, that Sam Harris appears to have grasped the inadequacy of his colleagues' approach – possibly because he seems to have certain quasi-religious notions of his own. Consciously breaking ranks with Dawkins and the others, he calls on them to attend to the differences among the world's religions, giving as one of his main reasons for so doing:

These differences are actually a matter of life and death. There are very few of us who lie awake at night worrying about the Amish. This is not an accident. While I have no doubt that the Amish are mistreating their children, by not educating them adequately, they are

not likely to hijack aircraft and fly them into buildings. But consider how we, as atheists, tend to talk about Islam. Christians often complain that atheists and the secular world generally balance every criticism of Muslim extremism with a mention of Christian extremism. The usual approach is to say that they have their jihadists, and we have people who kill abortion doctors. Our Christian neighbours, even the craziest of them, are right to be outraged by this pretence of even-handedness, because the truth is that Islam is quite a bit scarier and more culpable for needless human misery, than Christianity has been for a very, very long time. And the world must wake up to this fact. Muslims themselves must wake up to this fact. And they can....

Harris continues:

Atheism is too blunt an instrument to use at moments like this. It's as though we have a landscape of human ignorance and bewilderment – with peaks and valleys and local attractors – and the concept of atheism causes us to fixate one part of this landscape, the part related to theistic religion, and then just flattens it. Because to be consistent as atheists we must oppose, or seem to oppose, all faith claims equally. This is a waste of precious time and energy, and it squanders the trust of people who would otherwise agree with us on specific issues.[8]

Quite so; and, if Harris's co-belligerents do not take this on board and learn to discriminate, they will cut no ice whatsoever. As Harris says, they will simply be wasting everyone's time and energy. Incidentally, it is quite something to see an atheist like Harris describe the typically atheist attitude as "a pretence of even-handedness", even though Harris's own visual metaphor of atheism, surveying "a landscape of human ignorance and bewilderment", ironically and myopically fails to take into account the possibility that his atheism might just be part of that landscape.

In his lecture Harris went as far as suggesting that the term "atheism" is so unhelpful that the New Atheists ought to drop it completely:

We should not call ourselves "atheists". We should not call ourselves "secularists". We should not call ourselves "humanists", or "secular humanists", or "naturalists", or "sceptics", or "anti-theists", or "rationalists", or "freethinkers", or "brights". We should not call ourselves anything. We should go under the radar – for the rest of our

lives. And while there we should be decent, responsible people who destroy bad ideas wherever we find them.

His naiveté is wonderful. What Harris does not seem to realize is that he, in common with everyone else, has a worldview. There is no neutral default position, where he or anyone else can sit in splendid neutrality destroying bad ideas. If Harris thinks that certain ideas are bad, then that is because he thinks that certain other ideas are good; and the sum total of those ideas forms his worldview. That worldview is naturalism – the belief that this world is all there is. Harris, unconsciously and wrongly, assumes that his worldview is the default position, and that it will eventually triumph as long as we simply employ reason to destroy bad ideas. He is utterly convinced that atheism has nothing to fear from reason. It simply does not occur to him that his atheism might itself be full of bad ideas that need to be destroyed in the name of reason. Worse still, his atheism might be false.

Of course, one has to have some sympathy with Harris, in the sense that it is so much easier to hurl labels at people than to discuss ideas; except that in this case it is hard to see that the appellations "atheist" or "naturalist" are mere labels, since they accurately describe the beliefs of those people thus labelled. Perhaps, then, Richard Dawkins is more honest in wearing his lapel badge with its red capital "A" drawing attention to his public stance as an atheist. And some New Atheist websites offer such badges for sale.

Attacking religion as such is nothing new. In an essay entitled "Has Religion Made Useful Contributions to Civilisation?" Bertrand Russell wrote: "My… view on religion is that of Lucretius. I regard it as a disease born of fear and as a source of untold misery to the human race."[9]

Now, it would not make sense for me as a Christian to pretend to be able to speak on behalf of other religions. It is clearly up to the adherents of any particular religion, if they so wish, to give their own answers to the accusations made against them by the New Atheists. In any case, a great deal of New Atheist attention is given to attacking Christianity.[10] Dawkins says explicitly that his main target is Christianity;[11] and Hitchens claims that his atheism is "a Protestant atheism",[12] making him almost eligible to be an honorary Irishman. Furthermore, Harris calls one of his books *Letter to a Christian Nation*.[13] I shall therefore concentrate on Christianity.

In their vehemence against God and the Christian faith, the New Atheists noticeably echo Friedrich Nietzsche who wrote in *The Antichrist*:

I condemn Christianity; I bring against the Christian Church the most terrible of all the accusations that an accuser has ever had in his mouth. It is, to me, the greatest of all imaginable corruptions; it seeks to work the ultimate corruption, the worst possible corruption. The Christian Church has left nothing untouched by its depravity; it has turned every value into worthlessness, and every truth into a lie, and every integrity into baseness of soul.[14]

HAS CHRISTIANITY SPAWNED VIOLENCE?

As a Northern Irishman, I am all too familiar with a certain brand of sectarian violence where a religious history has been used to fan the flames of terrorism (on both sides of the divide); although, as historians point out, a whole additional complex of political and social factors has been at work that makes analysis in terms of religion alone far too simplistic.

What, then, have I to say about this evil aspect of religion?

The first thing to say is that I roundly condemn and abhor it, every bit as much as the New Atheists. I do so, be it noted, as a Christian. For, although the New Atheists' charge against Christendom for its violence may well be justified, their charge is not valid against the teaching of Christ himself. Christendom is not the same as Christianity, as the Danish theologian and philosopher Kierkegaard pointed out. Christendom's violence was not Christian, for the simple reason that it was diametrically opposed to what Christ himself taught. People who engage in violent and cruel activities at any time, in Northern Ireland or the Balkans or anywhere else, while invoking the name of God, are certainly *not* obeying Christ when they do so, whatever they may say to the contrary. After all, the name "Christian" means a disciple or follower of Jesus Christ. Following Christ means obeying his commandments. And one of those commands was the explicit *prohibition* of the use of force to defend Christ or his message. That command has been very well known since it was issued at a point of high tension in the Gospel narrative, the arrest of Jesus in the Garden of Gethsemane.

Jesus taught his followers not to hate their enemies but to love them; and he acted accordingly when the armed crowd came with Judas to the Garden of Gethsemane to arrest him. In that historic encounter he specifically *forbade* his disciples to use violence. Jesus rebuked one of his disciples, Peter, who, untrained in swordsmanship, swung wildly with his sword and cut off the ear of the High Priest's servant, Malchus. "Put your sword back into its place," Jesus said, "for all who take the sword will perish by the sword."[15] He could not have made it more plain. To take the sword, gun, or bomb in Christ's name is to *repudiate* both Christ and his message. He will have none of it. Gunning for God, in the sense of taking a weapon into one's hands on God's behalf, is a contradiction of and an affront to the Christian message.

Pressing home this crucially important lesson, the historian Luke records that Jesus' reaction to Peter's attempt to defend him with a sword was to act at once to repair the ear that Peter had severed. Luke (a doctor) tells us that Jesus used his powers[16] to heal the man. Peter's sword slash had impaired the man's hearing. Christ gave that faculty back to him.[17] As always with Christ's miracles, the physical miracle is not arbitrary. It points to a deeper, yet very obvious, truth. Whenever people have taken to physical violence to defend Christianity (as they imagine), they have succeeded only in cutting off people's ears in more ways than the physical, so that Christ's real message is not heard. Clear evidence of this is the sad fact that New Atheism's intellectual elite are deaf to Christ's words, at least in part because of the behaviour of those disobedient to Christ.

So let it be said loudly and clearly – it will have to be loud to be heard above the caterwauling of the New Atheists – *Christ repudiated violence*. He would not allow force to be used to save him from false accusation, suffering, and even death.[18] He allowed himself to be arrested and led away to trial. To be charged with what? With fomenting acts of anti-state terrorism! It is indeed a strange irony that the very charge levelled against Christ is identical to the New Atheists' accusation against Christianity – incitement to violence.

One could wish that the New Atheists were as canny as Pilate. He did not take long to see how inconsistent and false the charge against Jesus was. As Roman Procurator, Pilate was ultimately responsible to Rome for civil order; and he was fully aware that the Jewish festivals in Jerusalem, particularly the Feast of Passover when thousands of pilgrims swelled the local population, were times of political tension.

He feared rebellion, so he took very seriously the charge of sedition brought against Jesus by the religious authorities led by the High Priest. Indeed, Pilate insisted on investigating the case himself. The accusers alleged that Jesus was inciting the populace to regard him as the Christ, the messianic king of the Jews; and that he was intent on fomenting a popular uprising against the imperial power of Rome. In their opinion, therefore, Jesus was guilty of treason against the Roman emperor – a capital charge under Roman law.[19]

The Christian apostle John gives us the detail of Pilate's interrogation of Jesus.[20] The first thing Pilate wanted to hear from the prisoner's own mouth was whether he considered himself to be the King of the Jews.

This question could not be answered with a simple yes or no; for the terms "king" and "kingdom" meant different things to different people. If "king" and "kingdom" were the labels that, left to himself, Pilate was putting on Christ – on his teaching and activity – then Pilate would understand the terms in a political sense. In this sense, Christ must deny that he was a king. Christ was not in political competition with the emperor Tiberius in Rome.

In another sense, however, Christ was "the King of Israel". A week earlier he had allowed himself to be acclaimed by the crowds as *the King who comes in the name of the Lord*. Thronged by followers, he had ridden into Jerusalem on a donkey, deliberately fulfilling an Old Testament prophecy describing the coming of Jerusalem's king.[21] If it was this incident that the Jewish religious authorities had reported to Pilate, Christ had no intention of denying it, nor the claim he had thereby made.

But the religious leaders had misinterpreted him. Christ was not, as they were now making out, the leader of an organized band of freedom-fighters, ready to fight to the death in a holy war in order to drive the Roman imperialists from their country (as a band of freedom-fighters attempted to do in the war of AD 66–70).

The only way Christ could answer was to explain to Pilate the nature of his kingdom and the power by which he would establish it. So he replied: "My kingdom is not of this world. If my kingdom were of this world, my servants would have been fighting, that I might not be delivered over to the Jews. But my kingdom is not from this world."[22]

Pilate would surely have earlier received the army officer's report, informing him of Christ's non-violent behaviour at his arrest in the

Garden of Gethsemane; so that it would now be clear that Jesus was telling the truth. But Pilate still had to make sure of exactly what Jesus was saying. After all, Jesus had just referred to his kingdom, which must imply that he did think of himself as a king. Could it be, then, that his refusal to let his followers fight to avoid arrest was merely a clever tactic? On being surprised by a squad of armed Roman soldiers, he could see that resistance was useless. If Pilate were to release Jesus now, given the right conditions, would he attempt to set up his kingdom by raising armed insurrection at a later date? Pilate probed further, for he could take no risks. "You are a king then?"

Jesus' answer put the matter beyond doubt. His non-violent stance in Gethsemane was not temporary pragmatism: it sprang from the very nature of his kingdom or rule. Its power to gain people's allegiance was, and could only be, truth. "You say that I am a king. For this purpose I have been born, and for this purpose I have come into the world, in order to bear witness to the truth. Everyone who is of the truth listens to my voice."[23] And one thing is clear about truth – you cannot impose it on people by force or violence. Religious fanatics and militant atheists have not always understood this.

"What is truth?" said Pilate, as he turned to leave. He was not necessarily being cynical. Truth, in the absolute sense in which Jesus obviously intended it, may not have been something in Pilate's estimation that had much to do with the military and political affairs in which he was involved. Truth was the kind of concept that occupied philosophers and religious-thinkers. Yet, however unclear Pilate may have been on what truth meant, it is apparent that he had seen enough evidence to convince him that the accused prisoner before him, who abjured violence and was concerned only with truth, was no political rival to the emperor. Pilate was now in no doubt that Christ posed no threat to Rome, so he publicly declared him innocent.

That was not the end of the matter, of course. The crowd and its leaders at once subjected Pilate to such intense emotional blackmail that he lost the courage to act consistently with his moral convictions. It was Pilate's moral cowardice, not Christ's guilt, which led to the crucifixion.

We are thus presented with an unfortunate multiple irony. First of all, the New Atheists' accusation against Christianity is precisely the same as the charge that brought Christ himself to trial – the charge of fomenting violence. Secondly, the charge against Christ was not brought by atheists but by highly religious people – the leaders of the religious community, of which Christ was himself a member.[24] Thirdly, Pilate, the supreme commander of the Roman occupying power, declared Christ innocent of the charge of religious incitement to violence.

It is, therefore, abundantly clear that Christ did not attempt to impose his message of truth by force, but in the interests of truth he openly and plainly condemned the kind of rigid, unthinking, exploitative religion that concentrated more on outward ritual and social advantage than an inner attitude of heart, involving a deep relationship with God, which expresses itself in love and service to fellow human beings. Here is a sample of what Jesus had to say to some of the religious leaders of his day:

> **"Woe to you, scribes and Pharisees, hypocrites! For you tithe mint and dill and cumin, and have neglected the weightier matters of the law: justice and mercy and faithfulness. These you ought to have done, without neglecting the others. You blind guides, straining out a gnat and swallowing a camel!**
>
> **"Woe to you, scribes and Pharisees, hypocrites! For you clean the outside of the cup and the plate, but inside they are full of greed and self-indulgence. You blind Pharisee! First clean the inside of the cup and the plate, that the outside also may be clean.**
>
> **"Woe to you, scribes and Pharisees, hypocrites! For you are like whitewashed tombs, which outwardly appear beautiful, but within are full of dead people's bones and all uncleanness. So you also outwardly appear righteous to others, but within you are full of hypocrisy and lawlessness."[25]**

The upshot of all this is that the New Atheists' claim to be committed to rationality and evidence-based thought does not square with their attitude to the history of the first century, which shows that they are seriously wrong in their assessment of the nature and history of Christianity. They inexcusably confuse the evils of renegade Christendom with the teachings of Christ, and thus think that violence is part and parcel of the Christian faith; whereas the Christian faith itself actually explicitly repudiates violence and religious exploitation. The New Atheists ought to be applauding Christ, not condemning him.

THE EXTENT OF THE VIOLENCE OF CHRISTENDOM

Now, in the interest of fairness, it would also be important to take a careful look not only at the teaching of Christ but also at the history of Christendom itself, since a great number of misapprehensions have grown up around that also. For instance, David Bentley Hart relates responses to a question posed in the *New York Times*: What is humanity's worst invention? One respondent, Peter Watson, wrote: "Without question ethical monotheism… This has been responsible for most of the wars and bigotry in history." It would seem that Watson has never heard of the twentieth century.

Yet blaming monotheism for most wars in history is a widespread popular view, as German philosopher and theologian Klaus Müller observes: "The thesis that there is a connection between monotheism and intolerance has been for a long time regarded as common sense even in prominent philosophical textbooks."[26] This thesis does not stand up to serious scrutiny. Religious persecution and intolerance are anything but peculiar to monotheistic cultures, as anyone with any grasp of world history should know.

However, we have been for so long bombarded with stories about the horrors of the Crusades, the Inquisition, and the persecution of witches, that any attempt to assess the extent of such evils may well be met with incredulity, if not with outright rejection. Nevertheless, it is important for us not only to point out that the New Atheists have got Christ's teaching wrong, but also that they are guilty of misrepresenting the subsequent history of Christendom. This has been shown most clearly by the comprehensive and magisterial work of the eminent historian Arnold Angenendt, *Tolerance and Violence*.[27] Angenendt's historical analysis has received press acclaim for its thoroughness and accuracy as "probably the most remarkable book on church history in recent years", and as a book that cannot be ignored by anyone "who wishes to engage in substantial discussion about the relationship between the crusader mentality and the Christian message of peace or that between inquisitorial severity and religious tolerance".[28]

The question is simply this: Is the "church militant" the "oldest and greatest criminal organisation in the world"?[29] It is quite striking, for instance, to learn that, from 1540 to the middle of the eighteenth century, the Spanish Inquisition was responsible for 827 executions, and the Roman Inquisition for 93.[30] Of course, there is no excuse even for one execution for a person's faith in God; but, as we shall see in the next chapter, the crimes of secular philosophies of the so-called enlightened twentieth century are far greater than the crimes of the Inquisition. It would seem fairly obvious that the New Atheists try to focus attention on the latter to divert it away from the former – a very foolish ploy, if they wish to convince anyone who has a rudimentary knowledge of history.

Now it is impossible in a short book like this to rehearse the encyclopedic details of Angenendt's research, but perhaps it has been sufficient for our purposes to record their existence to make interested readers aware of them.

VIOLENCE TO CHILDREN: DOES RELIGIOUS LABELLING CONSTITUTE CHILD ABUSE?

Richard Dawkins feels very strongly about religious attitudes to children: so strongly that he uses a metaphor that is calculated to shock. He asks: "Isn't it always a form of child abuse to label children as possessors of beliefs that they are too young to have thought about?"[31] He is protesting vigorously against the habit of calling a child a "Christian child" or a "Muslim child" or a "Hindu child", etc., simply because that is the religion of their parents. He says that they should be allowed to decide for themselves when they are old enough.

Dawkins might be surprised to know that I learned this from my parents. They took me to church; but they also taught me to be critical about what I heard, and to compare it with other worldviews. And in sectarian Northern Ireland, of all places on earth! Was it not Dawkins who wanted us to imagine with Lennon that wonderful world, in which there was "no Northern Ireland"? We know what he means; but he is wrong to think that everyone in Northern Ireland behaved as in his stereotypical image. My parents and many others I knew did not believe that a child is born a Christian, even if its parents are Christians. Indeed, they thought that this is one of the most important things to be clear about – that one does not become a Christian either by birth or by any ceremony or ritual performed on you as an infant.

The reason for this was that they took the New Testament seriously and saw there that we are not born children of God; one has to become a child of God by a personal act of trust in Christ as Lord. That act of trust is a free and unforced commitment based on evidence. That step cannot be made by an infant. My parents saw (as the New Atheists could see if they took the trouble to read what the New Testament says on the topic) that Christ's ordinance of baptism was given as a public symbol to express the Christian life on the part of those who had already received it: baptism was given not to generate that life in the first place. The order of events is clear: people believed and were baptized as a public confession, which meant, of course, that baptism represented a very public standing up and being counted for the faith.

At the risk of being provocative, I would add that there is a sense in which the New Atheists are putting their finger on one of the great confusions of Christendom: that infants, children, or indeed adults can be made Christians by ceremony – tragically, sometimes administered by force. As a result, many people think that a ceremony conducted on them in infancy has made them Christians, even though they admit to having no idea what personal faith in Christ means.

I therefore agree with Dawkins' statement that to say that a particular child is a child of Christian parents is not the same as saying that she is a Christian child. She may become a Christian child if she becomes a Christian; on the other hand she may decide the other way.

My parents did not ram their faith down my throat. They believed in encouraging their children to think through the issues for themselves and come to their own decision on the basis of available evidence. They would have been contemptuous of Dawkins' notion that religion "teaches us that it is a virtue to be satisfied with not understanding".[32] They believed the exact opposite. Indeed, the more I read Dawkins' and others criticisms of Christianity the more it becomes obvious that the boot is on the other foot – it is atheism that appears to make a virtue of not understanding what the Christian case is.

Whatever other religion Dawkins' remarks may apply to, they do not apply in any way to the Christianity my parents taught me from the Bible. Their home (and also that of my wife's parents) was full of discussion. Here were people who encouraged me to be intellectually inquisitive because they were like that themselves – not in spite of their Christian faith, but because of it. For them, the Bible was an inexhaustible source of fascinating things to think about; of questions to be discussed, as well as principles to live by. I, for one, owe my parents an immense debt for their real Christian love, a love that gave me space to think. And, let it be said, Christianity gave me and has given me a great deal more than atheism to think about.

Christian conviction cannot be produced by heredity, ceremony, or force. Indeed, Jesus Christ reserved some of his severest denunciations for religious people who caused offence to children. We all need to heed the warning that our teaching does not become indoctrination – whether it is religious or atheist, since the very same thing can be said about atheist teaching; although this side of it tends to be conspicuous by its absence in the canons of New Atheism's writings.

Now I am aware that others were not as fortunate as I was. I have seen firsthand the results of people who have been force-fed with religion and who were never allowed to have their own opinions. Not surprisingly, many abandoned religion at the first opportunity. For instance, in the German Democratic Republic force-fed atheism was the norm. Would the New Atheists call that mental child abuse? Or we might think of the Cultural Revolution in China, when parents could not tell their children about their faith, lest the children betray them to the authorities. Where does that fit in to New Atheist thinking? I would certainly like to imagine a world without that, and am delighted that at least part of the world has got rid of it.

I would plead with the New Atheists to be responsible in their use of terms – for terms can themselves be abused, with frightful consequences. Child abuse is an exceedingly serious offence that society justifiably abhors. It is surely not hard to see that applying such a term incautiously could be a step on a very dangerous and sinister road: a road that could lead eventually to the removal of some children from their parents because of alleged "religious abuse". If this is thought to be alarmist, let us listen to Dawkins again: "It's probably too strong to say the state should have the right to take children away from their parents," he told an interviewer. "But I think we have got to look very carefully at the rights of parents – and whether they should have the right to indoctrinate their children." That sounds ominously familiar. And what about indoctrination with atheism: is that the alternative? Should we "look very carefully at the rights of parents" to do this? Dawkins may need to re-read his own extra commandments in connection with children.[33]

HAS CHRISTIANITY DONE ANY GOOD?

Concentration on the deeds of those people who disobey Christ leads the New Atheists to compound their error, by failing to take account of the great good that has been done throughout the centuries by those who genuinely follow him. For instance, the New Atheists say little or nothing about the immense positive contribution that Christianity has made to Western civilization.

Terry Eagleton trenchantly sums up this blinkered attitude to history:

> **Such is Dawkins's unruffled scientific impartiality that, in a book of almost four hundred pages, he can scarcely bring himself to concede that a single human benefit has flowed from religious faith, a view which is as a *priori* improbable as it is empirically false. The countless millions who have devoted their lives selflessly to the service of others in the name of Christ or Buddha or Allah are wiped from human history – and this by a self-appointed crusader against bigotry. He is like a man who equates socialism with the Gulag.[34]**

Eagleton is by no means alone in his assessment. The leading German philosopher Jürgen Habermas, who calls himself a "methodological atheist", warns against an "unfair exclusion of religion from the public space in order not to cut secular society off from important resources for creating meaning".[35] He goes on to reference the biblical doctrine that all human beings are created in the image of God: "This *createdness* of the image expresses an intuition that can, in our context, say something to those who are religiously unmusical." Unlike the New Atheists, Habermas is in no doubt about the unique contribution of this biblical worldview to the basic prerequisites for civilized human flourishing:

> **Universalistic egalitarianism, from which sprang the ideals of freedom and a collective life in solidarity, the autonomous conduct of life and emancipation, the individual morality of conscience, human rights and democracy, is the direct legacy of the Judaic ethic of justice and the Christian ethic of love. This legacy, substantially unchanged, has been the object of continual critical appropriation and reinterpretation. To this day, there is no alternative to it. And in light**

of the current challenges of a post-national constellation, we continue
to draw on the substance of this heritage. Everything else is just idle
postmodern talk.[36]

That "everything else" thus includes much of the New Atheism which,
in its detachment from truth, really is no more than "postmodern
chatter". The irony is that Christianity originally gave the world
its universities that educated the New Atheists. It was Christianity
that provided the hospitals and hospices that care for them, and
that undergirds the freedoms and human rights which allow them
to disseminate their ideas. There are large tracts of the world where
they might just be reluctant to give their lectures; and it would not be
Christianity that would stop them.

David Aikman points out that Sam Harris also shares this incapacity
to see the contribution of Christianity, even in his own country:

Sam Harris ignores altogether the fact that America's Founders,
although sometimes openly sceptical of Christian orthodoxy, saw
political liberty itself as indissolubly linked to the virtues deemed to
be rooted in Christian ethics. As Thomas Jefferson, who said that he
could not find in orthodox Christianity "one redeeming feature", put
it himself: "God who gave us life gave us liberty. Can the liberties of
a nation be secure when we have removed a conviction that these
liberties are the gift of God?" Perhaps the Founders, who had studied
the constitutions of dozens of previously attempted republics, knew a
truth about theism when they saw it.[37]

Avoiding any serious attempt to come to grips with history in his
quest to show that religion does no good, Dawkins endeavours to
bring science to his aid by enlisting the results of the so-called "Great
Prayer Experiment". Many believers would share his scepticism
(that is, about the experiment; not necessarily about the deductions
Dawkins makes from it). They are not surprised that the living God,
revealed to us in the Bible, is not likely to be amenable to our testing
him by praying for some people and not for others, and trying to
measure the difference. The God who is the Creator of heaven and
earth (and not some figment of the imagination) is interested in
genuine prayer; and it is hard to see that prayer produced for such an
experiment could be genuine.

In fact, Dawkins' feeble attempt to bring science to bear on this issue leaves much to be desired, even in the eyes of his fellow atheists. Biologist David Sloan Wilson is forthright in his assessment:

When Dawkins' *The God Delusion* was published I naturally assumed that he was basing his critique of religion on the scientific study of religion from an evolutionary perspective. I regret to report otherwise. He has not done any original work on the subject and he has not fairly represented the work of his colleagues. Hence this critique of *The God Delusion* and the larger issues at stake.[38]

If atheists (or anyone else) wish to enlist science for their cause, it would surely be wise for them to find out what research has been done in this area. For someone who claims to put great store by scientific evidence, Dawkins displays culpable ignorance of the considerable body of research that has shown the positive contribution of Christianity to well being. For instance, contradicting Dawkins' contention that religion causes more stress through guilt than it relieves, Sloan Wilson cites the results of recent research carried out by himself and Mihaly Csikszentmihalyi:

These studies were performed on such a massive scale and with so much background information that we can compare the psychological experience of religious believers vs. nonbelievers on a moment-by-moment basis. We can even compare members of conservative vs. liberal protestant denominations when they are alone vs. in the company of other people. On average, religious believers are more pro-social than non-believers; feel better about themselves; use their time more constructively; and engage in long-term planning rather than gratifying their impulsive desires. On a moment-by-moment basis, they report being more happy, active, sociable, involved and excited. Some of these differences remain even when religious and non-religious believers are matched for their degree of prosociality.[39]

In this regard Daniel Batson of the University of Kansas makes a useful distinction between "intrinsic" religiosity – belief in God and motivation to attend church as an end in itself – and "extrinsic" religiosity, where religion and churchgoing are seen more as social activities that are often engaged in for personal gain. Unsurprisingly, perhaps, Batson found a correlation between the former group and compassion or reduced prejudice; whereas the latter group tended to be less helpful to others and show increased prejudice.[40]

Wilson deduces that "Dawkins' armchair speculation about the guilt-inducing effects of religion doesn't even get him to first base", and later adds:

> I agree with Dawkins that religions are fair game for criticism in a pluralistic society and that the stigma associated with atheism needs to be removed. The problem with Dawkins' analysis, however, is that if he doesn't get the facts about religion right, his diagnosis of the problems and proffered solutions won't be right either. If the bump on the shark's nose is an organ, you won't get very far by thinking of it as a wart. That is why Dawkins' diatribe against religion, however well-intentioned, is so deeply misinformed... At the moment, he is just another angry atheist, trading on his reputation as an evolutionist and spokesperson for science to vent his personal opinions about religion.

Nicholas Beale and John Polkinghorne point out that, ironically, Dawkins cannot even claim that evolution is on his side here:

> The claim that religious belief is harmful from an evolutionary point of view is simply false. Whether or not the tenets of (say) Christianity are true, there is overwhelming evidence that Christians have, on average, more children than atheists (surviving fertile grandchildren is really the acid test, but I don't know of any data on this). They also live longer, are healthier, and so on. The fact that there are individual counter-examples to this is beside the point: evolution works on populations and not on individuals. Such practical effects of practicing the Christian faith are at best only weak evidence for the truth of Christianity. But it is dishonest for evolutionary biologists to say "Christian belief is harmful" unless they make it crystal clear that what they mean is: Christian belief is beneficial from an evolutionary point of view, but I consider it harmful for other reasons.[41]

But that kind of clarity tends to be avoided. New Atheism needs a dense intellectual fog in order to survive – but then it is not notably short of prolific fog-generators.

You may be tired of my saying it, but it seems to me that repetition is needed in order to "heighten the consciousness" of the public to the signal fact that the New Atheists, who are loudest in their claims to be governed by the scientific approach, have evidently failed to engage with the real science that has been done on the topic of the benefits conferred by Christianity. Before Richard Dawkins wrote a book claiming that God is a delusion it would surely have been wise for him, since he is not a psychiatrist himself, to have consulted psychiatrists' views on the subject. I am not a psychiatrist either, so I did consult the relevant expert evidence. The result does not favour Dawkins' viewpoint at all.

Perhaps the most important work that has appeared recently on the whole question of the benefits or otherwise of religious belief in general, and of Christianity in particular, is the book *Is Faith Delusional?*[42] by Professor Andrew Sims, former President of the Royal College of Psychiatrists. Sims has done his research over many years and does not confine himself, like Dawkins, to commenting on one (flawed) experiment. His studied conclusion backs up the results of Wilson mentioned above. It is the following:

The advantageous effect of religious belief and spirituality on mental and physical health is one of the best-kept secrets in psychiatry and medicine generally. If the findings of the huge volume of research on this topic had gone in the opposite direction and it had been found that religion damages your mental health, it would have been front-page news in every newspaper in the land.

I might add that it would have been trumpeted most loudly by the New Atheists.

Sims cites as evidence the *American Journal of Public Health*'s major meta-analysis of epidemiological studies on the psychological effects of religious belief:

In the majority of studies, religious involvement is correlated with well-being, happiness and life satisfaction; hope and optimism; purpose and meaning in life; higher self-esteem; better adaptation to bereavement; greater social support and less loneliness; lower rates of depression and faster recovery from depression; lower rates of suicide and fewer positive attitudes towards suicide; less anxiety; less psychosis and fewer psychotic tendencies; lower rates of alcohol and drug use and abuse; less delinquency and criminal activity; greater marital stability and satisfaction... We concluded that for the vast majority of people

the apparent benefits of devout religious belief and practice probably
outweigh the risks.[43]

We read the New Atheists in vain to find even a hint of awareness of
this "huge volume of research". It would seem that their blind faith
that they are right trumps any evidence. Their vaunted commitment
to science is not quite all that it seems.

Sims raises a further important psychological matter that has been
ignored by the New Atheists. He points out that "delusion has become
a psychiatric word and always has overtones of mental illness". He
deduces: "The statement that all religious belief is delusion is both
erroneous and innately hostile." He gives an example of that hostility:
"The suggestion that faith is delusional does not help psychiatric
patients for whom their religious faith may be very important." Sims
concludes with the observation: "Although the content of delusion
may be religious, the whole of belief, of itself, is not and cannot be a
delusion."[44] What now of the "God delusion"?

AN ATHEIST WHO BELIEVES THAT AFRICA NEEDS GOD

The well-known *Times* columnist Matthew Parris, an atheist, is
convinced of the positive value of Christianity and says so in no
uncertain terms. In a widely discussed *Times* article he wrote: "As
an atheist I truly believe that Africa needs God: missionaries, not aid
money, are the solution to Africa's biggest problem – the crushing
passivity of the people's mindset." Parris explains:

Travelling in Malawi refreshed another belief, too: one I've been
trying to banish all my life, but an observation I've been unable to
avoid since my African childhood. It confounds my ideological beliefs,
stubbornly refuses to fit my worldview, and has embarrassed my
growing belief that there is no God.

Now a confirmed atheist, I've become convinced of the enormous
contribution that Christian evangelism makes in Africa: sharply distinct
from the work of secular NGOs, government projects and international
aid efforts. These alone will not do. Education and training alone
will not do. In Africa Christianity changes people's hearts. It brings a
spiritual transformation. The rebirth is real. The change is good.

I used to avoid this truth by applauding – as you can – the practical work of mission churches in Africa. It's a pity, I would say, that salvation is part of the package, but Christians black and white, working in Africa, do heal the sick, do teach people to read and write; and only the severest kind of secularist could see a mission hospital or school and say the world would be better without it.

Parris concludes:

Those who want Africa to walk tall amid 21st-century global competition must not kid themselves that providing the material means or even the knowhow that accompanies what we call development will make the change. A whole belief system must first be supplanted."
And I'm afraid it has to be supplanted by another. Removing Christian evangelism from the African equation may leave the continent at the mercy of a malign fusion of Nike, the witch doctor, the mobile phone and the machete.[45]

Parris, self-confessed atheist that he is, thus reaches a very different conclusion from that of the New Atheists. Yet Parris's article is credible. It has the ring of truth.

By contrast, Christopher Hitchens missed an obvious opportunity to point out that not all Christians are evil. He tells us that he cannot pass the White House or the Capitol, "without thinking of what might have happened were it not for the courage and resourcefulness of the passengers on the fourth plane, who managed to bring it down in a Pennsylvanian field only twenty minutes' flying time from its destination". What he omits to say is that one of the leaders of that brave group of passengers was Todd Beamer, an evangelical Christian.

Is all religion really the same, as the New Atheists allege? Are they going to classify the Todd Beamers of the world with suicide bombers? Keith Ward writes:

If there is a root of evil that became a terrifying force that almost brought the world to destruction in the first half of the twentieth century, it is the anti-religious ideologies of Germany and Russia, North Vietnam and North Korea. It takes almost wilful blindness to invert this historical fact, and to suppose that the religions that were persecuted and crushed by these brutal forces are the real sources of evil in the world.[46]

Air-brushing out the considerable evidence for the positive contribution of Christianity, and at the same time falsely blaming the evils of Christendom on the teaching of Christianity, does deep damage to the New Atheists' credibility. Such manifest distortions of history show that we are not dealing with the kind of objective and measured evaluation that we have every right to expect from prominent public intellectuals who claim the scientific high-ground. Indeed, it is hard to avoid the impression that we are not actually dealing with intellectuals at all, but with people so obsessed with their own agenda that they have lost touch with reality. After all, one does not have to be a genius to predict how the New Atheists would react against an all-out attack on science which, using their own methodology, piled example on example of the terrible things that science has done in and to our world (from weapons of mass destruction to the poisoning of the environment), in order to dismiss science as dangerous and immoral. In fact, there is surely much more justification for saying that science causes war, than to claim that monotheism causes war.

As ever, David Berlinski puts it succinctly. After citing Steven Weinberg's public statement, "For good people to do evil things, that takes religion", he points out that not one member of Weinberg's audience asked "the question one might have thought pertinent: Just who imposed on the suffering human race poison gas, barbed wire, high explosives, experiments in eugenics, the formula for Zyklon B, heavy artillery, pseudo-scientific justifications for mass murder, cluster bombs, attack submarines, napalm, intercontinental ballistic missiles, military space platforms, and nuclear weapons? If memory serves, it was not the Vatican."[47]

Noam Chomsky sees the New Atheist attitude as a turning away from reason: "I think the sharpest turn away from reason is among the educated intellectuals who advocate reason and blame others for turning away from it. If we can't even reach the level of applying to ourselves rational standards of the kind that we apply to others, our commitment to reason is very thin."[48]

In conclusion, it would therefore appear that Christopher Hitchens' allegation that "religion poisons everything" does not have reason on its side. Certainly, in the case of Christianity, his assertion is demonstrably false.

CHAPTER 3

IS ATHEISM POISONOUS?

"The abolition of religion as the illusory happiness of the people is required for their real happiness."
Karl Marx

"I do not believe there is atheist in the world who would bulldoze Mecca – or Chartres, York Minster or Notre Dame."
Richard Dawkins

"Cathedrals are too high for bulldozers. In the Soviet Union under Stalin and in the German Democratic Republic under Ulbricht they used explosives instead."
Richard Schroeder

It would be wonderful not only to imagine John Lennon's world without all the evils that have been attributed to religion, as Richard Dawkins calls us to, but also to live in such a world. All sensible people would surely agree with the New Atheists here. But then, if you will forgive me for stating the obvious, I am not John Lennon. I happen to be John Lennox, and I would like to ask you also to imagine a world with no atheism. No Stalin, no Mao, no Pol Pot, just to name the heads of the three officially atheistic states that were responsible for some of the worst mass crimes of the twentieth century. Just imagine a world with no Gulag, no Cultural Revolution, no Killing Fields, no removal of children from their parents because the parents were teaching them about their beliefs, no refusal of higher education to believers in God, no discrimination against believers in the workplace, no pillaging, destruction, and burning of places of worship. Would that not be a world worth imagining too?

Yet, as Pulitzer Prizewinner Marilynne Robinson observes, Dawkins finds atheism incapable of belligerent intent when he says: "Why would anyone go to war for the sake of an absence of belief?" Robinson continues:

> It is a peculiarity of our language that by war we generally mean a conflict between nations, or at least one in which both sides are armed. There has been persistent violence against religion – in the French Revolution, in the Spanish Civil War, in the Soviet Union, in China. In three of these instances the extirpation of religion was part of a program to reshape society by excluding certain forms of thought, by creating an absence of belief. Neither sanity nor happiness appears to have been served by these efforts. The kindest conclusion one can draw is that Dawkins has not acquainted himself with the history of modern authoritarianism.[1]

Christopher Hitchens is also aware of this issue: "It is interesting to find that people of faith now seek defensively to say that they are no worse than fascists or Nazis or Stalinists."[2] However, as Peter Berkowitz points out in *The Wall Street Journal*, it is Hitchens who is behaving defensively here. He is the one who unequivocally insists that religion poisons everything, and it is "he who holds out the utopian hope that eradicating it will subdue humanity's evil propensities and resolve its enduring questions".

Berkowitz adds perceptively:

> Nor is his [Hitchens'] case bolstered by his observation that 20th-century totalitarianism took on many features of religion. That only brings home the need to distinguish, as Mr Hitchens resolutely refuses to do, between authentic and corrupt, and just and unjust, religious teachings. And it begs the question of why the 20th-century embrace of secularism unleashed human depravity of unprecedented proportions.[3]

There is a deeper issue here. Hitchens tries to exculpate Stalin and Hitler by blaming their ideas on religion. But he can only do so by making the elementary mistake of failing to distinguish between nominal religion and a personal, living faith in God. Whatever these evil men were by label or background, they were atheists in practice. What they had in common was a utopian vision for the remaking of humanity in their own image; and in so doing they effectively created a substitute religion: "Those who in the name of science claim that we can overcome our imperfect human nature create a belief system *that functions like religion.*"[4] Huxley saw this long ago and was explicit about it; so did Haeckel in Germany. Michael Ruse is honest enough to admit that, for many, evolution seems to function in a similar way to an almighty creator.

The New Atheists think that science inevitably entails naturalism that eliminates religion, and they then use science to "arrogate to themselves moral authority over all creation including those of their species too dim to see the truth".[5] They alone think that they understand how to bring about collective salvation and redeem the human race. If Hitchens is going to call Stalin and Hitler religious because of their background or the religious overtones of what they say, then we might as well call Hitchens religious when he says he is a Protestant atheist.

John Gray, in his book *Black Mass*, makes a very important point:

The role of the Enlightenment in twentieth-century terror remains a blind spot in western perception... Communist regimes were established in pursuit of a utopian ideal whose origins lie in the heart of the Enlightenment... a by-product of attempt to remake life. Pre-modern theocracies did not attempt to do this... Terror of the kind practised by Lenin did not come from the Tsars.[6]

The New Atheists resort to desperate measures in their attempt to draw a line between the atrocities of Stalin, Mao, and Pol Pot, and the atheist philosophy they espoused. Indeed, in the course of my debate with him, Dawkins asserted that there was no pathway from atheists to their atrocities, comparable to that which exists from religious people to theirs. After all, he said to me, we are both atheists with respect to Zeus and Wotan and that clearly does not harm anyone – what a person does not believe in cannot harm anyone, can it?

Yes it can, when not believing in something entails a corresponding set of positive beliefs in something else that has the potential to inspire harm. The difference between not believing in Wotan and not believing in God is immense, because the former has no serious entailment that one can think of; but the denial of the existence of God has massive entailments – the whole of Dawkins' materialistic philosophy, in fact. That is why, as I pointed out to Dawkins in debate, that he has not bothered to write a 400-page book expounding a-Wotanism or a-Zeusism! But he has written such a tome on a-theism. Why so?

For he and the other New Atheists are not simply atheists, they are anti-theists. Not believing in God does not leave them in a passive, negative, innocuous vacuum. Their books are replete with all the positive beliefs that flow from their anti-theism. These beliefs form their credo, their faith – much as they like to deny that they have one. Indeed, their own definition of a Bright is "someone who has a naturalistic worldview". Dawkins is surely quoting Julian Baggini, with approval on the meaning of an atheist's commitment to naturalism, when he writes: "What most atheists do *believe* [italics mine] is that although there is only one kind of stuff in the universe and it is physical, out of this stuff come minds, beauty, emotions, moral values – in short the full gamut of phenomena that gives richness to human life." Just a little later in the text Dawkins says (no longer quoting Baggini or anyone else): "An atheist in this sense of philosophical naturalist is somebody who *believes* [italics mine] there is nothing beyond the natural, physical world, no supernatural creative intelligence lurking behind the observable universe…"[7] In light of his own statements, one wonders by what intellectual contortions Dawkins can persuade himself that his atheism is not a *belief* system – his faith shines out too clearly.

Dawkins is a thoroughgoing naturalist, indeed a materialist, in his philosophy. And to say, as he does, that there is "not the smallest evidence" that atheism systematically influences people to do bad things[8] is to tell us a lot more about himself than it does about history. This statement does not exactly encourage us to place much confidence in his judgment, especially when we add it to his observation describing all religion as evil (as discussed in our last chapter). He is, of course, wrong on both counts.

THE NEW ATHEIST ATTITUDE TO HISTORY ONCE MORE

And that is a most worrying matter. After all, it is not surprising that Dawkins has no time for theology – he is on record as calling into question its worthiness to be a university subject. But, whatever one may think of that, history is surely a very different matter. As a biologist, one of Dawkins' main interests is the history of life on earth; and he would be very quick to challenge those who disagreed with him on it. And yet, when it comes to broader matters of history, we find that he, in common with the other New Atheists, is characterized by a breathtakingly cavalier attitude. We have already seen the superficiality of the New Atheists' analysis of the history of Christianity; and now we are about to see the same weakness permeating their attitude to the history of the twentieth century.

Indeed the present writer, who has had the privilege of visiting the countries of the former communist world many times over the past thirty years, is simply flabbergasted by the naiveté and inaccuracy of Dawkins' assessment. Dawkins could not have got it more wrong if he had tried. I have often spoken with Russian intellectuals, some of them dissidents with impressive academic pedigrees, who have said to me something like: "We thought we could get rid of God and retain a value for human beings. We were wrong. We destroyed both God and man." My Polish friends are more blunt: "Dawkins has lost contact with the realities of twentieth-century history. Let him come here and talk to us, if he is really open to listening to evidence of the link between atheism and atrocity."

Yet Dawkins asserts blithely: "Individual atheists may do evil things but they don't do evil things in the name of atheism. Stalin and Hitler did extremely evil things, in the name of, respectively, dogmatic and doctrinaire Marxism, and an insane and unscientific eugenics theory tinged with sub-Wagnerian ravings."[9] Well, if Stalin and Hitler are to be criticized for being dogmatic, where does that leave the New Atheists? John Humphrys says that, when he produced the highly acclaimed 2006 series for BBC Radio, *Humphrys in Search of God*, one thing that struck him was that, of all the people he interviewed, the atheists were the most dogmatic. To paraphrase Peter Berkowitz,[10] Socrates defined an educated person to be someone who was aware of his own ignorance. The New Atheists show no awareness that their atheism, far from arising out of open inquiry, is the rigidly dogmatic premise from which their inquiries proceed, that colours all their observations, and determines their conclusions.

Moreover, they are entrapped in a dogmatism that is stiffened on this issue by lack of the basic knowledge that, for Marx, the foundation of all criticism was the criticism of religion. Hitchens actually (unconsciously?) echoes Marx, when he claims that: "The argument with faith is the foundation and origin of all other arguments, because it is the beginning – but not the end – of all arguments about philosophy, science, history, and human nature."[11]

In the Foreword to his doctoral thesis, Marx wrote:

Philosophy makes no secret of it. Prometheus' admission "I hate all gods" is its own admission, its own motto against all gods, heavenly and earthly, who do not acknowledge the consciousness of man as the supreme divinity.[12]

A man does not regard himself as independent unless he is his own master, and he is only his own master when he owes his existence to himself. A man who lives by the favour of another considers himself a dependant being. But I live completely by another person's favour when I owe to him not only the continuance of my life but also its *creation*, when he is its source.[13]

Marx held that "the abolition of religion as the illusory happiness of the people is required for their real happiness". Thus, atheism lies at the very heart of the communist agenda. This is why many people in the former communist world, with whom I have spoken about the assertions of the New Atheists, dismiss them as ludicrous. Have Dawkins, Hitchens, and Harris never read *The Black Book of Communism*, in which we find that "communist regimes... turned mass crime into a full-blown system of government", with a death toll calculated to be around 94 million, of which 85 million were accounted for by China and Russia alone?[14]

And what about Hitler? In his authoritative book entitled *Hitler's God: The German Dictator's Belief in Predestination and his Sense of Mission*,[15] historian Michael Rissmann records that Hitler thought of "God" as "the rule of natural law throughout the universe", and that "his [Hitler's] religiosity consisted of an attempt to equate predestination with the regularities established by science".[16] Rissmann also relates how Hitler on one occasion told those gathered in the Bunker that as a schoolboy he had already "seen through the lying fairy tales of a church with two gods".

Furthermore, Hitler expected Christianity to shrivel before the inexorable advance of science. In *Table Talk*[17] he is reported as saying: "When understanding of the universe has become widespread... then the Christian doctrine will be convicted of absurdity." His view of Christianity was very clear: "The reason why the ancient world was so pure, light and serene was that it knew nothing of the two great scourges: the pox and Christianity." Put that way it sounds familiar. Did one of the

New Atheists not express the very similar sounding opinion somewhere, that religion is like a "virus of the mind, similar to the smallpox virus but harder to eradicate"? There really is nothing new under the sun.

For Hitler, Christianity was "the heaviest blow that ever struck humanity"; it was "the first creed in the world to exterminate its adversaries in the name of love. Its key-note is intolerance." Hitler thus echoed Nietzsche, who called Christianity "the one great curse, the one great intrinsic depravity, the one great instinct for revenge for which no expedient is sufficiently poisonous, secret, subterranean, petty – I call it the one immortal blemish of mankind." Whatever category Hitler is put in, one thing is certain – he was both vehemently anti-Christian and anti-Jewish.

However, Dawkins eschews serious analysis and contents himself with what can only be described as very silly statements about both Hitler and Stalin. "Even if we accept that Hitler and Stalin shared atheism, they both also had moustaches, as does Saddam Hussein. So what?"[18] We might add, in a sudden flash of deep insight, that all three had noses in common with the rest of us. What kind of "reasoning" is this? We are talking, not of shared, general characteristics, but of the motivating ideology that drove Hitler, Stalin, and others to murder millions in their attempt to get rid of religion, whether Jewish or Christian or anything else. David Berlinski has put his finger on the real issue. He recalls one occasion:

Somewhere in Eastern Europe, an SS officer watched languidly, his machine gun cradled, as an elderly and bearded Hasidic Jew laboriously dug what he knew to be his grave. Standing up straight, he addressed his executioner. "God is watching what you are doing," he said. And then he was shot dead.

What Hitler did *not* believe, and what Stalin did *not* believe, and what Mao did *not* believe, and what the SS did *not* believe, and what the Gestapo did *not* believe, and what the NKVD did *not* believe, and what the commissars, functionaries, swaggering executioners, Nazi doctors, Communist Party theoreticians, intellectuals, Brown Shirts, Blackshirts, Gauleiters, and a thousand party hacks did *not* believe, was that God was watching what they were doing.

And as far as we can tell, very few of those carrying out the horrors of the twentieth century worried overmuch that God was watching what they were doing either.

That is, after all, the *meaning* of a secular society.[19]

Michel Onfray rates Feuerbach, Nietzsche, and Marx as the "luminaries who succeeded Kant". "Luminaries" seems a strange term to describe men whose atheistic philosophy fired the minds of a succession of tyrants, and in the twentieth century led to a great darkness that enveloped vast segments of the earth resulting in the murder of millions. Far more perished then than in the religious wars of all other centuries put together – inexcusable as they were also. Does Onfray seriously want us to think of Feuerbach, Nietzsche, and Marx as the first "Brights"?

Do the New Atheists really think that a truly secular society, in which religion had been abolished, would be less prone to violence than a society in which any form of religion was tolerated? This is an astonishing idea to hold, when the twentieth century's examples of such regimes have been the most intolerant and violent in all of history.

Nevertheless, the New Atheists' insistence on exonerating atheism precipitates their headlong rush across the boundaries of absurdity. Dawkins writes that he does not believe that there is an "atheist in the world who would bulldoze Mecca – or Chartres, York Minster or Notre Dame". This statement has received the response it deserves: "Cathedrals are too high for bulldozers. In the Soviet Union under Stalin and in the German Democratic Republic under Ulbricht they used explosives instead – for instance, to blow up the University Church in Leipzig in 1968." This is the apt rejoinder of Richard Schröder, now Professor of Philosophy in Berlin; formerly an SPD-Party leader, who grew up in the German Democratic Republic and therefore knows communism well.[20]

The mind boggles at the implications of Dawkins' statement. Has he really never read of the wanton destruction of churches in atheist countries, or of their forcible transformation into museums of atheism in order to obliterate religion, or into warehouses, cinemas, restaurants, and the like? After all, Stalin closed only about 54,000 churches; admittedly not all of them were blown up. And if Dawkins has read these things, why does he deny them so explicitly? And yet it is this same Dawkins who is prepared to risk drawing some kind of parallel between creationists and holocaust deniers.[21]

One also wonders whether the New Atheists have ever met men and women who have been tortured within an inch of death, or pumped full of psychiatric drugs, or spent years in prison, or all of these – simply because they were believers in God who did not fit in to an atheistic society, and had to be forcibly "cured". I feel fairly sure that they have not met too many atheists who have suffered like that at the hands of Christians.

I also suspect that they have never sat with a thirteen-year-old in the former German Democratic Republic, as I have done. She was the brightest child in the school, but had just been told that she could not have any more education since she was not prepared to swear public allegiance to the *atheistic* state. One is tempted to call that intellectual murder. It was committed many times – all in the name of atheism. Was that not even worse than bulldozing buildings? But according to Dawkins there is not the *smallest* evidence for this. Really? If this is the level of rational criticism of twentieth-century history that the New Atheists have to offer, they are well on the way to writing their own intellectual obituary.

It is with some relief that we come across atheists who have a much more balanced view of the historical situation. After charging religion with various crimes, Peter Singer and Marc Hauser write:

> **Lest we be charged with a blinkered view of the world, atheists have also committed their fair share of heinous crimes, including Stalin's slaughter of millions of people in the USSR, and Pol Pot's creation of the "killing fields" in which more than a million Cambodians were murdered. Putting these threads together, the conclusion is clear: neither religion nor atheism has a monopoly on the use of criminal violence.**[22]

They are, however, being far too generous to atheism.

In this connection it is also encouraging to see that Dawkins has admitted more recently (perhaps as a result of the influence of Sam Harris?) that:

> **There are no Christians, as far as I know, blowing up buildings. I am not aware of any Christian suicide bombers. I am not aware of any major Christian denomination that believes the penalty for apostasy is death. I have mixed feelings about the decline of Christianity, in so far as Christianity might be a bulwark against something worse.**[23]

It is a pity that he did not think this through before he wrote *The God Delusion*; but I am glad to see that he is saying it now.

IS THE NEW ATHEISM DANGEROUS?

The public at large is rightly concerned about the New Atheist propensity for calling into question widely held scholarly interpretations of history, in the interests of propagating an atheist ideological agenda. Such a tendency can so easily warp into an ugly totalitarianism. Of course, it is not hard to think of a reason why the New Atheists are so insistent on rewriting the history of the twentieth century by air-brushing out the role of atheism. They do not want it to occur to anyone to draw a parallel between their anti-religious agenda and the violent and cruel attempt of communism to obliterate religion from the face of the earth.

Unfortunately, some of them invite such comparisons. At the forum sponsored by The Science Network at the Salk Institute in La Jolla, California (mentioned in the Introduction), the tone of intolerance reached such a peak that anthropologist Melvin J. Konner commented: "The viewpoints have run the gamut from A to B. Should we bash religion with a crowbar or only with a baseball bat?"

I would hope that most of the New Atheists would distance themselves from this kind of inflammatory statement. After all, it sits ill with a movement that makes such an issue of religious violence. Furthermore, history teaches us that movements that begin with intellectual analysis and debate can end in intolerance and violence. In the nineteenth century Karl Marx developed his atheistic theories in the idyllic quietness of a library in London. One wonders what he would think now of what his words have led to. Ideas have consequences. Ideas can be explosive. It would therefore be unwise to forget that attempts to obliterate belief in God have been made before – and have only succeeded in obliterating human beings.

Was it not comrade Khrushchev who claimed that he would soon show to the world the last remaining Russian Christian? I wonder why I thought of this when I read Steven Weinberg's words at the Salk Institute conference, encouraging scientists to contribute "*anything we can do to weaken the hold of religion*". This hint of totalitarianism may only be a straw in the wind. But straws serve to show where the wind is blowing, and not so long ago that same wind blew in the direction of the Gulag.

I wish to stress once more that many of us who are not atheists share the New Atheists' antipathy to the patent evil that has been perpetrated in the name of religion. However, their atheistic programme, though superficially attractive to many, is potentially dangerous for exactly the same reasons that the New Atheists (with less justification) use against religion. For instance, Dawkins warns (against the evidence, in the case of Christianity at least) that "the teachings of moderate religion are an open invitation to extremism".[24] By the same token, might it not be wise for him to heed his own advice and also warn us that the teachings of moderate atheism may be an even more open invitation to extremism – an idea for which there is very strong evidence? After all, there is a noticeable straight line from the Enlightenment to the violence of the nineteenth and twentieth centuries.

But nonetheless the biblical diagnosis is that the human race is flawed by evil, a contention that is surely not surprising in light of our common experience, even though that contention is resisted by those whose minds are irrationally full of optimistic notions of "progress". John Gray insists, however:

> The cardinal need is to change the prevailing view of human beings, which sees them as inherently good creatures unaccountably burdened with a history of violence and oppression. Here we reach the nub of realism and its chief stumbling-point for prevailing opinion: its assertion of the innate defects of human beings. Nearly all pre-modern thinkers took it as given that human nature is fixed and flawed, and in this as in some other ways they were close to the truth of the matter. No theory of politics can be credible that assumes that human impulses are naturally benign, peaceable or reasonable.[25]

The source of that evil flaw is given in the following key statement by St Paul: "just as sin came into the world through one man, and death through sin, and so death spread to all men because all sinned".[26] We shall discuss this statement in more detail in Chapter 6.

John Gray, not an obvious friend of theism, writes:

> The totalitarian regimes of the last century embodied some of the Enlightenment's boldest dreams. Some of their worst crimes were done in the service of progressive ideals, while even regimes that viewed themselves as enemies of Enlightenment values attempted a project of transforming humanity by using the power of science, whose origins are in Enlightenment thinking. The role of the Enlightenment in twentieth-century terror remains a blind spot in western perception.[27]

It is certainly a blind spot in New Atheist perception, and it is not hard to see why: Dawkins' argument for banning the teaching of religion would logically lead even faster to banning the teaching of atheism because of the horrors it has provoked, even within the living memory of many people.

It is, after all, no small irony that a filmed discussion between the four leaders – Dawkins, Dennett, Harris, and Hitchens – is entitled *The Four Horsemen*: an undoubted allusion to the Four Horsemen of the Apocalypse, described in the book of Revelation as conquest, war, famine, and death.[28] One just wonders whether their choice of this epithet is another evidence of their ignorance of the book they attempt to rubbish? I hope so, for I find some of the statements of these horsemen rather chilling. For example, the following reprehensible statement by Sam Harris sounds like a harbinger of death: "Some propositions are so dangerous that it may even be ethical to kill people for believing them."[29] We might well ask whether it will be the New Atheists who in the end have the authority to decide what those deadly propositions are and who will execute the sentence?

The New Atheists do their best to show that violence, cruelty, and war lie at the heart of Christianity, but have nothing whatsoever to do with atheism. The supreme irony in this wildly intemperate assertion is that investigation of the teaching of Christ and the teaching of the aforementioned anti-religious ideologies of the twentieth century shows the exact opposite to be the case. The New Atheists' crusade will inevitably founder, because its false diagnosis leads to a solution that history has shown to be even worse than the problem they are trying to solve. But, since experience teaches us that we learn little from history, the New Atheism may not founder before it does a great deal of damage.

THE NEW ATHEISM IS NOT NEW

My debate with Christopher Hitchens, which opened the Edinburgh Festival in August 2008, was on the motion "The New Europe Should Prefer the New Atheism". In my final contribution to that debate I said something like the following:

There is actually nothing new about the New Atheism. For over forty years a version of it dominated Eastern Europe. And Eastern Europe decisively rejected it in 1989. Far from Christianity hindering the formation of the New Europe, as our motion suggests, it played a crucial role in creating the New Europe. President of the British Academy, Sir Adam Roberts, Professor of International Relations at Oxford, is a world authority on the Cold War and the role of religion in resistance movements. In a public lecture in Oxford that I attended, he pointed out that in 1989 the Christian churches in Leipzig played a crucial role in preventing the violence that would have given the German Democratic Republic an excuse to send in the troops and thus threaten Gorbachev's policy of allowing peaceful democracy to have its way. Sir Adam emphasized that if the churches had not acted as they did the outcome might well have been disastrous – there would have been no New Europe.

The very creation of the New Europe is thus an example of how genuine Christianity, in its insistence on the dignity of human beings made in the image of God, brings freedom. The New Atheism threatens to undermine those freedoms, as its communist predecessor did. Aleksandr Solzhenitsyn puts it well:

If I were asked today to formulate as concisely as possible the main cause of the ruinous Revolution that swallowed up some sixty million of our people, I could not put it more accurately than to say: Men have forgotten God; that's why all this has happened... if I were called upon to identify the principal trait of the entire twentieth century, here too, I would be unable to find anything more precise and pithy than to repeat once again: Men have forgotten God... To the ill-considered hopes of the last two centuries, which have reduced us to insignificance and brought us to the brink of nuclear and non-nuclear death, we can propose only a determined quest for the warm hand of God, which we have so rashly and self-confidently spurned. Only in this way can our eyes be opened to the errors of this unfortunate twentieth century and our bands be directed to setting them right. There is nothing else to cling to in the landslide: the combined vision of all the thinkers of the Enlightenment amounts to nothing.[30]

It is only because the wall created by the previous version of the New Atheism was pulled down that the New Europe exists today. Do we really want to build another wall?

CHAPTER 4

CAN WE BE GOOD WITHOUT GOD?

If God does not exist, everything is permissible.
Fyodor Dostoievski

The New Atheists are gunning for God not only on the scientific level, but also the moral level. Their attack has two prongs. Firstly, they fulminate against what they perceive to be the primitive, unacceptable, indeed, for them, abhorrent, morality of the Bible. Secondly, they claim that God is unnecessary for morality. They tell us that they are not rejecting morality as such – simply the traditional view that morality is somehow dependent on God. In short, their view is that we can be good without God.

Christopher Hitchens thunders about the "nightmare of the Old Testament"[1] and the "evil of the New Testament".[2] Richard Dawkins loves to shock audiences by reading aloud a blistering invective against the God of the Old Testament, describing him as "arguably the most unpleasant character in all of fiction".[3] Hitchens, in debate with me at the Edinburgh Festival, made no bones about his abhorrence of a God who, in his view, is a tyrant and a bully, always watching us. In his view, "God is not Great".

Now all of these New Atheist criticisms of God are clearly moral criticisms. That is clear even to their fellow atheists. In a brief section of his book devoted to Richard Dawkins, Michael Ruse writes: "Finally, and most importantly, there is the fact that Dawkins is engaged on a moral crusade, not as a philosopher trying to establish premises and conclusions but as a preacher, telling the ways to salvation and to damnation. *The God Delusion* is above all a work of morality."[4] Now, moral crusades must be squarely based on moral standards, otherwise it would not be possible to distinguish evil from its opposite. Indeed, in this particular case, those standards must be very lofty, since they are used to justify an extremely vehement intolerance of religion. We naturally are led to ask: where do such uncompromising standards come from, if God is not in the picture?

Leading ethicist Peter Singer articulates the implications of leaving God out of the picture as follows:

> Whatever the future holds, it is likely to prove impossible to restore in full the sanctity-of-life view. The philosophical foundations of this view have been knocked asunder. We can no longer base our ethics on the idea that human beings are a special form of creation made in the image of God, singled out from all other animals, and alone possessing an immortal soul. Our better understanding of our own nature has bridged the gulf that was once thought to lie between ourselves and other species; so why should we believe that the mere fact that a being is a member of the species *Homo Sapiens* endows its life with some unique, almost infinite value?[5]

Similarly, Singer's former student, now a professor at Oxford, Julian Savulescu, writes: "I believe that God's existence is irrelevant. What matters is ethical behaviour."[6]

The Russian novelist Fyodor Dostoievski disagreed. In his famous novel, *The Brothers Karamazov*, he put a statement into the mouth of Ivan that is usually quoted as: "If God does not exist, then everything is permissible." Now Dostoievski was not arguing that atheists were incapable of moral behaviour, of being good. That would simply be slanderously false. Indeed, many who claim to be Christians are at times put to shame by their atheist neighbours. The point Dostoievski is making is not that atheists cannot be good, but that atheism does not supply any intellectual foundation for morality.

The New Atheists take a different tack of course. Richard Dawkins cites the work of Harvard biologist Marc Hauser, who suggests that morality is hard-wired into human nature very much as language appears to be.[7] In collaboration with Peter Singer, Hauser found that there is no real difference in the way in which people of different faiths respond to moral dilemmas.[8] Dawkins argues that this finding is evidence that we do not need God in order to be good – or evil.

However, the hard-wiring of morality into human nature is entirely consistent with the biblical view that human beings are created in the image of God as moral beings. For this would mean that all human beings possess an innate sense of morality, whether or not they actually believe in God – which is precisely what we find. In other words, Christianity supports the findings of Hauser's research, but not the atheistic conclusions drawn from it. This argument – that the pool of common morality observed around the world in the most disparate ethnic groups is consistent with the existence of God – was presented long before Hauser's work, by C. S Lewis in his seminal work *The Abolition of Man.*[9]

However, there is a deeper consideration that diminishes the plausibility of Dawkins' view, which comes to light when we ask how atheism proposes to ground the concepts of good and evil. Logically speaking, there is only a limited number of possible sources on which to base morality. Traditionally, in the West, at least, God has been the transcendent ultimate guarantor and source of morality. If there is no God, then we are left with raw nature and society, or a mixture of both to source morality. It is here that the problems begin.

First of all, there is widespread acknowledgment on all sides that it is very difficult to get a base for morality in nature. Albert Einstein, in a discussion on science and religion in Berlin in 1930, said that our sense of beauty and our religious instinct are: "tributary forms in helping the reasoning faculty towards its highest achievements. You are right in speaking of the moral foundations of science, but you cannot turn round and speak of the scientific foundations of morality." According to Einstein, therefore, science cannot form a base for morality: "Every attempt to reduce ethics to scientific formulae must fail."[10]

Richard Feynman, also a Nobel Prize-winning physicist, shared Einstein's view: "Even the greatest forces and abilities don't seem to carry any clear instructions on how to use them. As an example, the great accumulation of understanding as to how the physical world behaves only convinces one that this behaviour has a kind of meaninglessness about it. The sciences do not directly teach good or bad."[11] Elsewhere he states: "Ethical values lie outside the scientific realm."[12]

Dawkins, also, has thought the same until recently: "It is pretty hard to defend absolute morals on anything other than religious grounds." He has also admitted that you cannot get ethics from science: "Science has no methods for deciding what is ethical."[13] However, it would appear that Dawkins has been persuaded to change his mind on this issue by Sam Harris's latest book, *The Moral Landscape: How Science Can Determine Human Values.*[14]

Holmes Rolston points out:

> Science has made us increasingly competent in knowledge and power, but it has also left us decreasingly confident about right and wrong. The evolutionary past has not been easy to connect with the ethical future. There is no obvious route from biology to ethics – despite the fact that here we are... The genesis of ethics is problematic.[15]

DAVID HUME AND THE "IS TO OUGHT" PROBLEM

One of the main reasons why the genesis of ethics from biology (or indeed, from any other aspect of nature) is problematic was pointed out long ago by the Scottish Enlightenment philosopher David Hume (1711–76). Here is the famous excerpt:

> I cannot forbear adding to these reasonings an observation, which may, perhaps, be found of some importance. In every system of morality, which I have hitherto met with, I have always remark'd, that the author proceeds for some time in the ordinary way of reasoning, and establishes the being of a God, or makes observations concerning human affairs; when of a sudden I am surpriz'd to find, that instead of the usual copulations of propositions, *is*, and *is not*, I meet with no proposition that is not connected with an *ought*, or an *ought not*. This change is imperceptible; but is, however, of the last consequence. For as this ought, or ought not, expresses some new relation or affirmation, 'tis necessary that it should be observ'd and explain'd; and at the same time that a reason should be given, for what seems altogether inconceivable, how this new relation can be a deduction from others, which are entirely different from it. But as authors do not commonly use this precaution, I shall presume to recommend it to the readers; and am persuaded, that this small attention wou'd subvert all the vulgar systems of morality, and let us see, that the distinction of vice and virtue is not founded merely on the relations of objects, nor is perceiv'd by reason.

Hume here observes that authors on moral philosophy often advance arguments for what *ought*[16] to be on the basis of factual statements about what *is*. They appear to derive imperative conclusions from indicative premises. According to Hume, this is just not possible.

Furthermore, in claiming that there was no rational basis for ethics in nature, Hume pointed out that, in the first place, nature tended to give conflicting signals and, secondly, and more importantly, to attempt to deduce ethics from nature was to commit a category mistake: observations of nature are first-order activities, whereas value-judgments are second-order; that is, they do not belong to the same category. In his opinion a statement was either true for logical reasons or empirical reasons, a disjunction commonly known as "Hume's Fork". Therefore, since he thought ethical statements could not be seen to be true for logical reasons, he held that they could only hold on the basis of experience. He thought, in fact, that sympathy was a key factor in human nature and that ethics depended on that sympathy. Hume thus sought in some way to ground ethics in human nature and psychology and so could be said to espouse a version of naturalism.[17] However, this does not succeed in avoiding the "is to ought" problem. He is still trying to get, as C. S. Lewis puts it, "a conclusion in the imperative mood out of premises in the indicative mood: and though he continues trying to all eternity he cannot succeed, for the thing is impossible".[18]

It is important to state at this point that I am not suggesting that science cannot help us to make ethical judgments. For instance, knowing about how much pain animals feel can help shape judgments on animal testing. But the judgment is made on the basis of a prior moral conviction, that pain and misery is a bad thing. Science can tell us that if you put strychnine in your grandmother's tea it will kill her. Science cannot tell you whether you ought or ought not to do so in order to get your hands on her property.

Sam Harris's attempt to get moral values from science does not escape this problem. There are two main reasons for this. The first has to do with the meaning of science. In the English-speaking world the word "science" normally means "the natural sciences". This usage contrasts with, for instance, the German usage of the parallel term "*Wissenschaft*", which includes not only the natural sciences but also the humanities – history, languages, literature, philosophy, and theology. That is, *Wissenschaft* is much closer in meaning to the Latin term "*scientia*", "knowledge", from which the word "science" is derived. Harris, in an interview with *The Independent*,[19] says that he is using "science" in the broader sense of "rational thought" – that is, in the sense conveyed by *Wissenschaft*. But if that is the case, then there is no problem in "deducing" morality from "science" since theology is a perfectly rational activity – although, of course, Harris cannot concede this and maintain his stance.

Harris then links another sleight of hand (or, rather, of mind) to this as follows: "We simply must stand somewhere. I am arguing that, in the moral sphere, it is safe to begin with the premise that it is good to avoid behaving in such a way as to produce the worst possible misery for every one."[20] Thus Harris *begins* by assuming a *moral* conviction *then* brings his science to bear on deciding on whether a given situation conforms to it. That is a very different matter from what is implied by the subtitle of his book: *How Science Can Determine Human Values.*[21]

There is more to say. In his *New York Times* review of Harris, Kwame Anthony Appiah asks: "How do we know that the morally right act is, as Harris posits, the one that does the most to increase well-being, defined in terms of our conscious states of mind? Has science really revealed that? If it hasn't, then the premise of Harris' all-we-need-is-science argument must have non-scientific origins."[22]

Biologist P. Z. Myers elaborates:

> I don't think Harris's criterion – that we can use science to justify maximizing the well-being of individuals – is valid. We can't. We can certainly use science to say *how* we can maximize well-being, once we define well-being... although even that might be a bit more slippery than he portrays it. Harris is smuggling in an unscientific prior in his category of well-being.[23]

Harris's response to this is illuminating:

> To use Myer's formulation, we must smuggle in an "unscientific prior" to justify any branch of science. If this isn't a problem for physics, why should it be a problem for a science of morality? Can we prove, without recourse to any prior assumptions, that our definition of "physics" is the right one? No, because our standards of proof will be built into any definition we provide.[24]

Quite so; but if the unscientific prior is a *moral* assumption, then Harris cannot claim to deduce morality from science. By the same token, we note that Harris cannot rule out the prior assumption of God.

Harris has not avoided Hume after all.

Nevertheless, such attempts to defy Hume have been and are constantly being made, particularly to try to find a pathway from biology to ethics. Historically, since the time of Darwin, these efforts have been made in essentially two waves. There was, first of all, the period of what has come to be thought of as traditional evolutionary ethics, now called "Social Darwinism";[25] although it was really developed by Herbert Spencer (1820–1903), whose explicit aim was to establish a "scientific" morality. The theory was characterized by a great confidence that evolution gave a direction to progress: evolution was progress and therefore could, in some sense, ground ethics as that kind of behaviour that advanced progress.[26]

The second "sociobiological" wave started in the middle of the last century, with the molecular biological revolution inaugurated by the discovery of DNA with all its implications for genetics and heredity. By contrast with the first wave, some at least of its major scientific promoters (though not all) insist that the new understanding of the mechanisms of inheritance leaves no room for any idea of progress in which to ground ethics. We shall discuss some of the implications of this below.

SOCIAL DARWINISM

Michael Ruse describes the essence of traditional evolutionary ethics succinctly: "One ferrets out the nature of the evolutionary process – the mechanism or cause of evolution – and then one transfers it to the human realm, arguing that that which holds as a matter of fact among organisms holds as a matter of obligations among humans."[27] Ruse himself points out the move from "is to ought" lies at the heart of the methodology of Social Darwinism – and yet it does not seem to trouble anybody: "traditional evolutionary ethicists seem to be supremely untroubled by charges of fallacious reasoning. They are even inclined to agree that the move from is to ought is fallacious:[28] save only in this one case!"[29]

Ruse asks reasonably why they are so confident about making this move that David Hume claims is impossible. Could there be a missing premise? His answer is that there is indeed a missing premise: social Darwinians believe that evolution has a direction, that it spells progress, ever upward, ever onward, getting better and better. We see this attitude in Spencer, Haeckel, Fisher, and Julian Huxley. In that sense, they are humanists and regard human beings with their intellectual powers as evolution's supreme product so far. For them human beings were very special and, because of their capacities, clearly superior to all non-human animals. Peter Singer might well have accused them of speciesism! Ruse sums up the position: "Evolution leads to good and to things of great value. Hence it is the source of our moral obligations." Ruse is far from happy with the traditional view, and we shall look at his own take on the matter later.

The contemporary attitude to evolutionary moral progress is much more complicated and mixed. We find some, like E. O. Wilson, still championing such progress; and others, like John Gray, saying that it is Wilson's very Darwinism that proves that such progress is a fantasy. One of the reasons for this divided picture is that there are certain dark aspects of the ways in which social Darwinism is perceived to have been applied; and another is the effect of the revolution in molecular biology.

The idea of taking what happens in nature and applying it to human societies has had a far from happy history. Alfred Russell Wallace, co-discoverer with Darwin of the principle of natural selection, was one of the first to discuss the social implications of that principle. In 1864 he wrote that selection would cause rationality and altruism to spread – a process that would lead to utopia but in the course of which "savage man" would "inevitably disappear in encounters with Europeans whose superior intellectual, moral and physical qualities make them prevail 'in the struggle for existence and to increase at his expense'".[30]

Darwin did not address the social implications of his theory in *The Origin of Species*, leaving that to his later book, *The Descent of Man and Selection in Relation to Sex*. There he drew social and ethical implications from the twin principles of "the struggle for survival" and Spencer's notion of "the survival of the fittest" as applied to the development of the moral side of human nature. He and some of his contemporaries thought that these twin principles not only could satisfactorily explain the origin of species; they could also safely predict the future development of the various races of mankind. Echoing Galton he wrote: "At some future period, not very distant as measured by the centuries, the civilized races of man will almost certainly exterminate and replace the savage races throughout the world."[31] Again: "The more civilized so-called Caucasian races have beaten the Turkish hollow in the struggle for existence. Looking to the world at no very distant date, what an endless number of lower races will have been eliminated by the higher civilized races throughout the world."[32]

From a contemporary perspective the inaccuracy of this view, to say nothing of its political incorrectness, is striking, to say the least. Indeed one cannot help reflecting that, even in Darwin's day, it might not have been easy to convince the "Turkish", the "lower", and "the savage" races – as he called them, that his evolutionary principles formed a sound basis for moral values. It goes without saying that the application of this kind of "scientific" thinking to Jews, Gypsies, the handicapped, and other unwanted minorities proved no hindrance to the Nazi "Final Solution".

The net result of this and other developments (for example, attempts at eugenics) was to discredit the Social Darwinist approach, so that by 1944 Richard Hofstadter could write: "Such biological ideas as 'the survival of the fittest'… are utterly useless in attempting to understand society… The life of man in society… [is] not reducible to biology and must be explained in the distinctive terms of cultural analysis."[33]

In this connection, it is worth quoting John Horgan's *Globe and Mail* review of Sam Harris's attempt to derive ethics from science in *The Moral Landscape*. Horgan, it should be noted, regards Harris as one of his "favourite religion-bashers":

> **My second, more serious objection to Harris's thesis[34] stems from my knowledge of past attempts to create what he calls a "science of human flourishing". Just 100 years ago, Marxism and eugenics struck many reasonable people as brilliant, fact-based schemes for improving human well-being. These pseudo-scientific ideologies culminated in two of the most lethal regimes in history, the Soviet Union and Nazi Germany.**
>
> **Harris repeatedly insists that we shouldn't rule out the scientific revelation of an objectively true, universal morality, just because it isn't possible yet. As long as this achievement is possible in principle, he says, we shouldn't worry that it still isn't possible in practice. But we live in the world of practice, where even the smartest, best-informed, best-intentioned people make terrible mistakes. I therefore fear the practical consequences of a scientific movement to derive a universal morality.[35]**

After all, scientists' concern for humanity's well-being has not always been benign.

SOCIOBIOLOGY[36]

The discovery of the structure of DNA by Crick and Watson in Cambridge in 1953 ushered us into a new world; and it was not long before some of the leading scientists, in particular Nobel Prizewinners Crick and Monod, were indicating publicly what were for them the moral and ethical implications of this revolutionary new understanding of the genetic basis of life.

In particular, Jacques Monod claims that contemporary evolutionary theory leaves us with a universe free of ultimate purpose and moral obligation, so that there is no route from biology to ethics. Monod was convinced that Hume was right – that "ought" could not be deduced from "is": "Pure chance, absolutely free but blind, is at the very root of the stupendous edifice of evolution with the result that man at last knows that he is alone in the unfeeling immensity of the universe… Neither his destiny nor his duty have been written down." His view is based on his perception of the relationship between the "is to ought" problem and evolutionary theory:

One of the great problems of philosophy is the relationship between the realm of knowledge and the realm of values. Knowledge is what "is" and values are what "ought" to be. I would say that all traditional philosophies up to and including communism have tried to derive the "ought" from the "is". This is impossible. If it is true that there is no purpose in the universe, that man is a pure accident, you cannot derive any ought from is.[37]

Note the assumption, "if there is no purpose in the universe". It is evident that if there is no personal Creator responsible for the universe, then the universe and human life are accidental products of impersonal, mindless, and therefore aimless, natural processes – what other possibility is there? Gray is stark: "In monotheistic faiths God is the final guarantee of meaning in human life. For Gaia,[38] human life has no more meaning than the life of slime mould."[39]

The very concept of meaning itself is therefore an inevitable casualty of Monod's view. Singer expresses it: "Life as a whole had no meaning. Life began, as the best available theories tell us, in a chance combination of molecules; it then evolved through random mutations and natural selection. All this just happened; it did not happen for any purpose."[40] And biologist and historian of science William B. Provine also agrees with Monod that man's duty is not written down: "No inherent moral or ethical laws exist, nor are there absolute guiding principles for human society. The universe cares nothing for us and we have no ultimate meaning in life."[41]

At the popular level, the same message is communicated to the public. For, example, Alasdair Palmer, Scientific Correspondent of *The Sunday Telegraph*, likewise assures his readers:

> **It is not just the religious explanation of the world that is contradicted by the scientific explanations of our origins. So, too, are most of our ethical values, since most of them have been shaped by our religious heritage. A scientific account of mankind has no more place for free-will or the equal capacity of each individual to be good and act justly than it has for the soul.[42]**

To Monod, the implications for ethics are plain. First he pours contempt on what he sees as the basis for morality: "The liberal societies of the West still pay lip-service to, and present as a basis for morality a disgusting farrago of Judaeo-Christian religiosity, scientistic progressivism, belief in the natural rights of man and utilitarian pragmatism." Next he argues that man must set these errors aside and accept that his existence is entirely accidental. He "must at last awake out of his millenary dream and discover his total solitude, his fundamental isolation. He must realise that, like a gypsy, he lives on the boundary of an alien world; a world that is deaf to his music and as indifferent to his hopes as it is to his suffering and his crimes."[43]

We are clearly dealing here with an extreme form of materialistic reductionism[44] that views human beings as nothing but their genes. The logical implication, then, is that morality must be based on the genes; though apparently the prime, indeed the sole, purpose of the genes is not to produce further human beings, but to reproduce themselves – a strategy is written into the genetic code in every cell in our bodies and brains. Generations of human beings are merely machines or vehicles for reproducing what Dawkins calls "selfish genes".

But in what sense, then, is it possible to base morality on human genes? Michael Ruse joins Edward O. Wilson to explain how they think it can be done: "Morality, or more strictly our belief in morality, is merely an adaptation put in place to further our reproductive ends. Hence the basis of ethics does not lie in God's will… In any important sense, ethics as we understand it is an illusion fobbed off on us by our genes to get us to co-operate."[45]

But, if a person is nothing but his/her genes, and these genes control his/her moral behaviour, how could s/he ever be blamed for doing wrong, or praised for doing right? In any case, what sense would that make if the concept of morality is a genetically induced illusion? One cannot resist the temptation to think that it is a very strange kind of *ethics* that is founded on such an *unethical* trick as deception by an illusion to get our cooperation! And why stop there: what reason is there then to think that this theory is not itself a genetically generated illusion?

Gray finds irony in the fact that Monod, in spite of his radical materialistic interpretation of life as written in the genes, espouses the idea that humanity is a uniquely privileged species:

Like many others, Monod runs together two irreconcilable philosophies – humanism and naturalism. Darwin's theory shows the truth of naturalism: we are animals like any other; our fate and that of the rest of life on Earth are the same. Yet, in an irony all the more exquisite because no one has noticed it, Darwinism is now the central prop of the humanist faith that we can transcend our animal natures and rule the Earth.[46]

But then there is another even more delicate irony that Gray himself appears not to have noticed. His philosophy, he admits, undermines truth: "Modern humanism is the faith that through science humankind can know the truth – and so be free. But if Darwin's theory of natural selection is true [sic!] this is impossible. The human mind serves evolutionary success, not truth."[47] But what about Gray's own mind, when it leads him to write of philosophy over the past 200 years: "It has not given up Christianity's cardinal error – the belief that humans are radically different from other animals."[48] One must suppose, according to Gray, that his writing this sentence "serves evolutionary success". Well, it certainly would appear to serve the success of evolutionary theory, if it were true. But then Gray has undermined the very concept of the truth, and so has removed all reason for us to take him seriously. Logical incoherence reigns once more.

Monod's book is entitled *Chance and Necessity*. For Gray, it is precisely chance and necessity that prove that the idea that morality wins out in the end is a pretence. Indeed for him, morality is very largely a branch of fiction and consists simply of: "those prejudices which we inherit partly from Christianity and partly from classical Greek philosophy". The case really is: "At bottom we know that nothing can make us proof against fate and chance."[49]

EVOLUTION AND ALTRUISM[50]

One aspect of human social and moral behaviour that evolutionary theory has always found difficult to account for is altruism. This is a problem, since such behaviour would seem to make it harder, not easier, for the race to survive on evolutionary terms. For the sake of the argument we assume that, since evolution was always working to promote the survival of the species, it might somehow cause human beings to attach a moral significance to acts and practices that promoted the survival of the race. But then we would, for the very same reason, expect evolution to produce moral aversion to anything that made survival more difficult or less likely.

In light of this, it is very difficult to see how a mindless evolutionary process could explain the deep-seated ubiquitous moral conviction that we have a *duty* to support those very people who, in the nature of things, are most liable to inhibit, or even to threaten, evolutionary "progress" – the weak, the handicapped, the ill, the aged. And not only those of our own family, tribe, or race, but of people generally; even though supporting them will involve a serious drain on our resources and make the survival of the race more difficult. To argue that the instinctive desire to survive leads the healthy to support the weak and the ill in the hope that, when the healthy become weak and ill themselves, others will support them, is not convincing. Such mutual compassion is highly commendable; but it is definitely not necessary for the survival of the race. If that survival were the *sole* aim of evolution, as the claim runs, evolution would never produce a sense of moral duty to spend resources on the handicapped, the weak, the ill, and the aged. We have already noted the confusion into which Dawkins is led, when he tries to account for altruism by rebellion against the selfish genes.

Sociobiologists, led by Wilson, nevertheless think that they have found answers to this, "the central theoretical problem for socio-biology",[51] by studying the social habits of non-human groups of animals, and comparing them with the behaviour patterns of humans. They start by observing that the idea, "nature is red in tooth and claw", is highly inaccurate; and that in fact many examples of cooperation have been noted in animal (and of course human) behaviour. Cooperation of one organism with another to serve its own survival interests is called *biological altruism*, a technical expression that does not carry moral overtones. Thus, biological altruism is not to be confused with genuine moral altruism. The key question, then, is: what is the relationship between biological altruism and genuine moral altruism? We give Ruse's answer: "Literal, moral altruism is a major way in which advantageous biological cooperation is achieved", and in order to achieve it, "Evolution has filled us full of thoughts about right and wrong, about the need to help our fellows, and so forth."[52]

But this is not an explanation of where these thoughts come from, or what the basis of their "morality" is. In fact it would appear from this that Ruse is essentially admitting failure to ground morality in evolution. Prominent evolutionary biologist Francisco Ayala points out in the same symposium that what Ruse (and Wilson) are saying is that it is "not that the norms of morality can be grounded in biological evolution, but that evolution predisposes us to accept certain moral norms, namely, those that are consistent with the 'objectives' of natural selection".[53] And let us not forget that all of this is subsumed under a morality that is an illusion, fobbed off on us by our genes. The confusion seems almost complete. What resistance can the authors offer to us applying their own logic to themselves, and concluding that their theories are a genetically induced illusion?

Ayala goes on to draw attention to Wilson's view of the function of morality: "Human behaviour – like the deepest capacities for emotional response which derive and guide it – is the circuitous technique by which human genetic material has been and will be kept intact. Morality has no other demonstrable function." As Ayala points out, it looks as if the naturalistic fallacy is being committed. Not only that, but one way of reading this (one surely far from Wilson's mind) is that it is saying that the only function of a moral code is to preserve genes; and therefore could be understood as a justification for racism or genocide, "if they were perceived as the means to preserve those genes thought to be good or desirable, and to eliminate those thought to be bad or undesirable".[54] The upshot of all this is that attempts to ground ethics in biology seem as doomed as the efforts to construct a perpetual motion machine.[55]

Richard Dawkins nonetheless tries desperately[56] to construct some semblance of a basis for morality in general and altruism in particular by saying that, even though man is nothing but his genes, he can somehow rebel against his genes when they would lead him to do wrong: "We are built as gene machines... but we have the power to turn against our creators. We, alone on earth, can rebel against the tyranny of the selfish replicators."[57]

We use the word "desperately" advisedly, for at the beginning of the very same book Dawkins says: "We are survival machines – robot vehicles blindly-programmed to preserve the selfish molecules known as genes."[58] But then he appears to retreat from this position in the final chapter of the book: "For an understanding of modern man, we must begin by throwing out the gene as the sole basis of our ideas on evolution";[59] and gives us as his grand conclusion the encouragement to rebel against a genetic tyranny.

But how can we rebel, if we are nothing but our genes? If there is no non-material, non-genetic, element or force within us, what is there in us that could possibly have the capacity to rebel against our genes and behave morally? Nowhere does Dawkins tell us about the origin of such a capacity or when it appeared. And where would we ever get any objective moral principles to guide us in that rebellion? Dawkins gives us no answers.

The attempt to derive morality from genes is reminiscent of the futile attempts to derive morality from instinct, as C. S. Lewis pointed out.

Suppose you are sitting in your home one evening, when you hear outside a terrified shriek for help. You immediately feel an instinctive urge to go to the rescue of whoever is in need. But then the contrary instinct of self-preservation surfaces and urges you not to get involved. Now, how shall you decide which of these two instincts to obey; in other words, what your *duty* is? It is clear that whatever it is that tells you what you *ought* to do, when your instincts are delivering conflicting advice, cannot itself be an instinct.[60]

THE ABOLITION OF MORALITY

The greatest irony in this saga is that it is Dawkins himself who confirms Dostoievski's dictum, by delivering the death blow not only to the attempt to get a gene-based morality, but to the concepts of good and evil themselves on which morality is based. He writes:

> In a universe of blind physical forces and genetic replication, some people are going to get hurt, other people are going to get lucky and you won't find any rhyme or reason in it, nor any justice. The universe we observe has precisely the properties we should expect if there is, at the bottom, no design, no purpose, no evil and no good. Nothing but blind, pitiless, indifference. DNA neither knows nor cares. DNA just is. And we dance to its music.[61]

One would presume that these are carefully crafted words, representing the author's considered opinion. Their implications for morality, or more accurately for the lack of it, are profound. Dawkins explicitly denies the very existence of the categories of good, evil, and justice in the name of a deterministic interpretation of the function of DNA. His naturalistic atheism leads him, quite logically, to conclude that not only is there no basis for morality, but that ultimately there is no such thing as morality.

Dawkins wishes us to imagine a world without religion. But just imagine his deterministic world of blind physical forces and genetic replication. In such a world we would have no other option than to say that the suicide bombers in New York and Washington on September 11, 2001, the schoolboy who murdered half of the teachers in his school in Erfurt, Germany in April 2002, the London tube and bus bombers of July 2005, and a seemingly endless list of others, were simply dancing to their DNA. The architects of genocide in the killing fields of Cambodia, Rwanda, and Sudan were, likewise, following the dictates of their own inbuilt genetic programmes. How, then, could anyone blame them for what they did? Indeed, in such a deterministic world, the word "blame" would itself have no meaning.

And if some people felt that abusing or cutting babies to pieces was their idea of fun, would that simply be them dancing robotically to their DNA? If this is the case, then none of us can help being, what some people misguidedly call, morally evil. Indeed, the very categories of good and evil are annihilated into meaninglessness.

They simply do not apply to a population of biologically pre-programmed robots.[62]

It is not hard to imagine the consequences of teaching such nihilistic ideas to young people, whose sense of responsibility is already being eroded by contemporary Western culture to the extent that the tragic toll of vicious juvenile knifings and shootings is mounting rapidly in country after country. To tell them that their behaviour is nothing but a dance to the music of their DNA, with the implication that they have no responsibility for their behaviour or its consequences, would be a recipe for social catastrophe. Do we really want to throw petrol on the fire?

SUMMING UP

If there is no eternal base for values external to humanity, how can Dawkins', Hitchens', or anyone else's standards be anything but limited human conventions: ultimately meaningless products of a blind, unguided evolutionary process? Thus, far from delivering an adequate explanation for morality, this particular New-Atheistic acid dissolves it into incoherence.

Dostoievski long ago saw that the high cost of rejecting God was the destruction of morality. Sartre was so impressed with this insight that he made Dostoievski's argument the starting point of his existentialist philosophy. Sartre wrote:

> **The existentialist... thinks it very distressing that God does not exist, because all possibility of finding values in a heaven of ideas disappears along with Him; there can no longer be an *a priori* Good, since there is no infinite and perfect consciousness to think it. Nowhere is it written that the Good exists, that we must be honest, that we must not lie; because the fact is we are on a plain where there are only men. Dostoievski said; "If God didn't exist, everything would be possible." That is the very starting point of existentialism. Indeed, everything is permissible if God does not exist, and as a result man is forlorn, because neither within him nor without does he find anything to cling to. He can't start making excuses for himself.[63]**

David Berlinski adds a sharp twist to the implications of Dostoievski's *Brothers Karamazov*:

> **What gives Karamazov's warning – for that is what it is – its power is just that it has become part of a most up-to-date hypothetical syllogism:**
>
> **The first premise:**
> **If God does not exist, then everything is permitted.**
>
> **And the second:**
> **If science is true, then God does not exist.**
>
> **The conclusion:**
> **If science is true, then everything is permitted.**[64]

The New Atheists increasingly appear to be "soft atheists" who have not really begun to understand the implications of their own atheistic beliefs. "Hard" atheists like Nietzsche, Camus, and Sartre would ask the New Atheists how they can rationally justify their absolute-sounding commitment to timeless values without implicitly invoking God. They would say that this is impossible: the existence of absolute values demands God. They might also say that the New Atheists are well aware of this, since their deterministic world, in which human behaviour is nothing but a dance to the tune of DNA, has no more moral significance than the dance of the bees.

In spite of Dawkins' statement just quoted, by and large, the New Atheists do not appear to have taken on board the fact that their atheism removes from them not only their liberal values, but also any moral values whatsoever. *Consequently, all of the New Atheists' moral criticisms of God and religion are invalid not so much because they are wrong but because they are meaningless.* If such a denial of ethics is the heart of the God-delusion hypothesis it does not take a rocket scientist to see where the delusion really lies. After all, if DNA neither knows nor cares and we dance to its music, how is it that most of us both know and care?

CHAPTER 5

IS THE GOD OF THE BIBLE A DESPOT?

"No one takes their morality from the Bible."
Richard Dawkins

"Universalistic egalitarianism, from which sprang the ideals of freedom
and a collective life in solidarity, the autonomous conduct of life and
emancipation, the individual morality of conscience, human rights
and democracy, is the direct legacy of the Judaic ethic of justice and
the Christian ethic of love. This legacy, substantially unchanged, has
been the object of continual critical appropriation and reinterpretation.
To this day, there is no alternative to it. And in light of the current
challenges of a post-national constellation, we continue to draw on the
substance of this heritage. Everything else is just idle postmodern talk."
Jürgen Habermas

The conclusion of the last chapter is simply this: the invective of the
New Atheists against the morality of the Bible is invalid, since their
atheism gives them no intellectual base for moral evaluation of any
sort. Their criticism is as meaningless as they say the universe is. We
could, therefore, reasonably discard all they have to say. Yet this would
not be a helpful approach to the matter; for their criticisms appeal to
many as having some validity in light of the common morality we
all share as created in the image of God, whether or not we believe
in him. Thus, it is inadequate simply to dismiss the atheist objections
on the grounds that they cannot logically ground their morality. We
must now consider, therefore, the content of what they have to say.

The first thing that strikes many about the New Atheist moral assessment of Christianity is its lack of balance. For instance, I mentioned earlier that Christopher Hitchens, in our debate at the Edinburgh Festival, made no bones about his abhorrence of a God who, in his view, is a tyrant and a bully, always watching us. Apart from anything else, describing God as someone who is constantly watching you is a sad caricature. Sad because, as I pointed out to Hitchens at the time, one might as well describe marriage as, "living with someone else who is constantly watching you". That jaundiced view would leave out all that is wonderful about the deepest of all human relationships, just as Hitchens' caricature of God leaves out the wonder of the deepest of all relationships, that of a human being with his or her Creator. The New Atheists appear not to have noticed that God is portrayed in the Old Testament as a God of compassion, of love, of mercy, and as companion, shepherd, and guide as well as a God of justice and judgment. Compassion and mercy are not noted characteristics of either tyrants or bullies. Nor is the notion that God watches us to be construed negatively, as we shall see.

The New Atheists do a hatchet job on the God of the Bible. This is just about as useful for rational discussion as the hatchet job that can easily be done with much more justification on science, if you have a mind for it (and some do). It is not hard to bring science into disrepute by concentrating on its involvement in the production of bombs, mines, weapons of mass destruction, poisons, pollution, deforestation, desertification, etc. The New Atheists would be the first to protest against such distortion, if science were the topic.

Yet their ill-tempered onslaught bristles with hostility rather than even-handed scholarly analysis – which might just strike one as somewhat ironic for a *moral* critique, let alone an intellectual one. The net result is patent superficiality. We cannot consider every example in this book; but one particularly glaring instance is Dawkins' engagement with the biblical teaching on altruism. He dives in with: "Christians seldom realise that much of the moral consideration for others which is apparently promoted by both the Old and the New Testaments was originally intended to apply only to a narrowly defined in-group."[1] It seems to have completely escaped his research methodology that the reason Christians "seldom realise" lies in the fact that it is completely false. One wonders how many Christians he consulted in order to come to his conclusion, since most of them could easily have helped him avoid making such a clumsy and uninformed blunder.

Dawkins then authoritatively informs us that: "'Love thy neighbour' didn't mean what we now think it means. It meant only 'Love another Jew'."[2] This statement tells us a great deal about Dawkins' complete abandonment of any pretence at scholarly thoroughness when it comes to investigating topics outside his competence. If he had taken five minutes to look at the biblical text, instead of simply culling the ignorance of non-theologian John Hartung, he would surely not have made himself look so ridiculous. The Hartung-Dawkins "exegesis" is based on Leviticus 19:18: "You shall not take vengeance or bear a grudge against the sons of your own people, but you shall love your neighbour as yourself." It is clear that Dawkins (or Hartung?) was so convinced of the correctness of his interpretation that he did not bother to read the rest of Leviticus 19. He would have discovered a little further on the explicit injunction that loving one's neighbour was *not* intended to be confined to an in-group: "When a stranger sojourns with you in your land, you shall not do him wrong. You shall treat the stranger who sojourns with you as the native among you, and you shall love him as yourself, for you were strangers in the land of Egypt."[3]

Not content with misconstruing Leviticus, Dawkins now informs us that Jesus was himself a "devotee of the same in-group morality".[4] As we have just seen, this in-group morality was not taught in the Old Testament. Nor was Jesus one of the devotees of such a fictitious morality. This is not a matter of conjecture. On one occasion Jesus was asked what was meant by the word "neighbour" in the Old Testament dictum "Love your neighbour as yourself." He replied with the Parable of the Good Samaritan, the whole point of which was to show that neighbourliness transcended ethnic boundaries.

Perhaps Dawkins can be forgiven for not knowing Leviticus; but he can scarcely be forgiven for displaying an equally abysmal ignorance of one of the most famous parables in all of literature. Such is the mess that Dawkins has got himself into, by failing to check the facts and by restricting himself to a single and non-expert source – the medical doctor and part-time social anthropologist John Hartung, whose speciality, perhaps unsurprisingly, is anaesthetics. A brief internet perusal of Hartung's views on the Jewish people would lead one to shy away very rapidly from lending credibility to any assessment of biblical documents he might make. I know what Dawkins would think if I obtained all my information about Darwin from a theologian, an expert on Chinese philology, or maybe even an anaesthetist.

Such a misreading of Scripture on a fundamental yet elementary issue is hardly calculated to inspire confidence in any other pronouncement Dawkins might make on biblical teaching. There is no doubt that moral questions do arise in connection with the Bible that need to be addressed; but it will not help us in the least if that analysis is based on unscholarly, ill-informed, and incorrect views of what the Bible actually has to say.

The New Atheists are surely aware, but they omit to say, that the Bible teaches that God is not only a God of awesome creatorial genius and power, but a God of compassion, mercy, justice, beauty, holiness, and love, who cares for his creation and for human beings as part of it. According to the Bible, human beings are special: every man and woman is made in the image of God and therefore has infinite value. The importance of this teaching cannot be over-emphasized, since it lies behind and energizes the values that most of us hold to be inviolable – in particular, our Western concepts of the value of each individual human life, of human rights, and of gender equality.

The eminent European lawyer Dr Ernst-Wolfgang Böckenförde was underlining this fact, when he made the following observation that has received a great deal of discussion: "The secular state lives from normative assumptions that it cannot itself guarantee."[5] It is for this reason that atheist intellectual Jürgen Habermas calls for secular society not to cut itself off from important resources by failing to retain a sense of the power of articulation of religious language: "Philosophy has reasons to remain open to learn from religious tradition."[6] Habermas makes it clear that the biblical idea of human beings as created in the image of God belongs to the genealogy of human rights.

History confirms this view. In his detailed discussion, historian Arnold Angenendt points out, for instance, that the early church fathers condemned slavery on the basis that no one made in the image of God should be bought with money. In the Middle Ages, Burchard von Worms said that anyone who killed a Jew or heathen person had blotted out both an image of God and the hope of future salvation. In the seventeenth century, John Milton said that "all men are free born because they are in the image of God".[7]

NEW ATHEIST MORALITY: THE NEW TEN COMMANDMENTS

The importance of biblical moral teaching for ethics receives a rather unexpected and unintended confirmation by the New Atheists themselves; although, to be fair, they put a different interpretation on it, as we shall see. In his section on "The Moral Zeitgeist"[8] Richard Dawkins observes[9] that most people, religious or not, subscribe to more or less the same general moral principles,[10] and he suggests that these ethics should be codified in a "New Ten Commandments" (NTC). His chosen list of commandments is taken from a web blog.

1. Do not do to others what you would not want them to do to you.

2. In all things, strive to cause no harm.

3. Treat your fellow human beings, your fellow living things and the world in general with love, honesty, faithfulness and respect.

4. Do not overlook evil or shrink from administering justice, but always be ready to forgive wrongdoing freely admitted and honestly regretted.

5. Live life with a sense of joy and wonder.

6. Always seek to be learning something new.

7. Test all things; always check your ideas against the facts, and be ready to discard even a cherished belief if it does not conform to them.

8. Never seek to censor or cut yourself off from dissent; always respect the rights of others to disagree with you.

9. Form independent opinions on the basis of your own reason and experience: do not allow yourself to be led blindly by others.

10. Question everything.[11]

Now the first thing that strikes us about this list is that, although they contain no reference to God, of course, these New Ten Commandments have much in common with the biblical Ten Commandments (BTC), which we list for comparison:

1. You shall have no other gods before me.

2. You shall not make for yourself a carved image – any likeness of

anything that is in heaven above, or that is in the earth beneath, or that is in the water under the earth.

3. You shall not take the name of the Lord your God in vain.

4. Remember the Sabbath day, to keep it holy.

5. Honour your father and your mother.

6. You shall not murder.

7. You shall not commit adultery.

8. You shall not steal.

9. You shall not bear false witness against your neighbour.

10. You shall not covet your neighbour's house; you shall not covet your neighbour's wife, nor his male servant, nor his female servant, nor his ox, nor his donkey, nor anything that is your neighbour's.

The Ten Commandments have what we might think of as two dimensions: a vertical dimension to do with relationships between humans and God (1–4), and a horizontal dimension concerned with relationships between humans and their fellows (5–10). The New Ten Commandments have only the horizontal dimension in view.

Comparing the lists, the first four of the NTC roughly correspond to the last six of the BTC. The last five of the NTC relate to processes of reasoning, questioning, testing, and opinion forming, and are not, strictly speaking, moral injunctions at all, apart possibly from NTC 8. They are on the one hand a clear expression of the Enlightenment spirit that New Atheism wishes to foster – God replaced with (human) reason. And yet on the other hand we see at once that most of the sentiments expressed, like NTC 1–4, are also to be found in the Bible. Let's have a brief glance at them:

NTC 5. Live life with a sense of joy and wonder.
The Bible is replete with encouragement to be joyful – "A joyful heart is good medicine";[12] *and the coming of Christ into the world is heralded in the famous words "I bring you good tidings of great joy".*[13] *These words form part of a well-known Christmas carol which, we are reliably informed by none other than himself, Richard Dawkins is happy to sing.*[14] *So at least some of his joy would appear to come directly from Christianity.*

NTC 6. Always seek to be learning something new.
The early Christians were known as "disciples" – the word means
"learner". It is of the essence of true Christianity always to be seeking to
learn something new, to keep mentally fresh and vigorous. Christopher
Hitchens recalls[15] how he gave the address at his father's funeral in
Portsmouth, choosing as his text Philippians 4:8: "Finally, brethren,
whatsoever things are true, whatsoever things are honest, whatsoever
things are just, whatsoever things are lovely, whatsoever things are of
good report: if there be any virtue, and if there be any praise, think on
these things". One of the reasons Hitchens gives for choosing that text
is "for its essentially secular injunction." However, this is essentially a
Christian injunction, based on the fact that God is no killjoy (peace be to
the atheist bus campaign). God positively encourages us to get interested
in everything that is true, honest, just, lovely, and good.

NTC 7. Test all things; always check your ideas against the facts,
and be ready to discard even a cherished belief if it does not conform
to them.
But that is exactly what the Christian apostle Paul instructs all
Christians to do.[16] Atheists do not have a monopoly on avoiding
gullibility. All of us need to heed that warning.

NTC 8. Never seek to censor or cut yourself off from dissent; always
respect the rights of others to disagree with you.
Openness to dissent and upholding the right of others to disagree with
us is the meaning of true tolerance; and we need to be reminded of it
in an age of hypocritical and dangerous political correctness that says
that we must not disagree with anyone in case they would be offended.
Historically, the concept of true tolerance is grounded in the value of
human beings as made in the image of God. I welcome the fact that the
New Atheists profess tolerance to be one of their core beliefs. I must
confess, though, that it sounds rather empty, in light of the intolerance of
religious belief that characterizes so many of their statements. It sounds
as if they don't even take their own commandments very seriously.

NTC 9. Form independent opinions on the basis of your own reason
and experience: do not allow yourself to be led blindly by others.
It was none other than Jesus Christ who warned us about the blind
leading the blind.[17]

NTC 10. Question everything.
This is very similar to NTC 8. One of the very striking things about the teaching of Jesus in the Gospels is the frequency with which he asked questions and stimulated others to ask them.

This brief survey shows at once that the basic morality that Dawkins approves of is broadly Christian in terms both of its moral injunctions regarding our attitudes to others and its advice. In light of this, Dawkins' statement elsewhere (in the same book), that "no one takes their morality from the Bible",[18] is unconvincing. After all, the bulk of his own stated morality is, in the main, biblical; and he has just told us that "most people, religious or not, subscribe to the same moral principles". I can only think, therefore, that what he must mean by this is that there are some moral attitudes in the Bible that he finds unacceptable. That is a rather different matter that we must now consider; but it must not be allowed to obscure the fact that Dawkins, like most other people – in the West at least – is deeply indebted to the Bible for his morality.

ISSUES OF OLD TESTAMENT MORALITY

The fact that the New Atheists' morality, as expressed above, corresponds with that found in the Bible, however, is eclipsed for them by certain things that they find unacceptable, particularly in the Old Testament: the invasion of the Canaanites by Israel, the institution of slavery, and various judicial penalties, in particular that of stoning for adultery.

Moreover, since New Atheist criticism of the Old Testament is based on moral values that are themselves essentially found in that same Old Testament, the questions that the New Atheists raise also trouble many Christians. Take the invasion of Canaan, for instance. According to the Old Testament, Joshua, a commander of the forces of Israel, was instructed by God through Moses to attack the Canaanite tribes that occupied the land. Moses commanded the Israelites: "And when the Lord your God gives them over to you, and you defeat them, then you must devote them to complete destruction. You shall make no covenant with them and show no mercy to them."[19] The result was: "So Joshua and all his warriors came suddenly against them... and

fell upon them… They struck them until he left none remaining."[20]
This action appears to violate the biblical commandment to love the stranger, and to be inconsistent with the existence of a God who is said to be compassionate and loving.

This incident raises the wider problems of the existence of moral evil, pain, and suffering. Quite apart from the Canaanites, innocent people still suffer horribly, and many are killed every day in many parts of the world, both as a direct result of the evil of others and in consequence of natural disasters and disease.

I hasten to say at once that the twin problems of evil and pain are the most difficult that Christians (but not only Christians) face – both theoretically and practically. These are, after all, the reasons that many give for jettisoning belief in God altogether. It would be wholly wrong, however, to imagine that the New Atheists are the first to have thought of these objections, although sometimes that is the impression given. Serious minds have wrestled with the problem of evil since the dawn of history. All of us still do. Indeed, is there anyone of us who is not affected by them?

Let me be personal for a moment. In the same year as my own life was saved at the last moment by skilful medical intervention, my sister lost her (just) married 22-year-old daughter through a malignant brain tumour. If I thank God for my recovery, what shall I say to my sister? Or to my brother who, some years ago, was nearly killed and permanently injured by a terrorist bomb in Northern Ireland? Yet, my niece who died was a Christian; her husband has not lost his faith in God; neither has my sister, nor my brother. So there must be something to be said by those that suffer, rather than merely by those who philosophize about it. We shall need to listen to them.

THE CANAANITE INVASION AND ITS MORAL CONTEXT

Of course some will say: why do we need to think about the Canaanites at all? After all, this invasion took place centuries before Christianity started, and so is scarcely relevant to the confrontation between the New Atheism and Christianity.

Well, it is true that the invasion of Canaan is by definition historically pre-Christian. It is also true that there are important distinctions between the Old Testament and the New. For instance, ancient Israel was a theocracy – a physical nation that, according to the Bible, was chosen by God as a major and special witness for him in the world. There is no such nation today; for, as we have seen, Christ pointed out to Pilate that his kingdom was not of this world, so that his servants did not fight. For this reason the specifically Christian injunctions are very different from some found in the Old Testament.

However, although there are clear discontinuities between the Old and the New Testament, it is equally clear that there are continuities. In particular, the Bible teaches that there is only one God. There are not two: one in the Old Testament and one in the New Testament. Nor are there two sets of moral commandments. In one form or another, each of the Ten Commandments, apart from the Sabbath law, is repeated in the New Testament for Christians. Thus, the New Atheists are justified in regarding the Old Testament depiction of the nature of God as relevant to the discussion.

One point we should clear out of the way, before looking at the specifics of the invasion of Canaan, is this. Just because an incident is recorded in the Bible, it does not mean that God (or anyone else) necessarily approves of it. What took place is sometimes simply recorded without moral comment. On other occasions, like King David's adultery with Bathsheba, the incident is first related, and the (negative) moral comment comes later.

However, this is *not* the case with the invasion of Canaan. It is not related in some obscure part of the Bible without moral comment. The very reverse is the case. In fact, the instructions to Israel, concerning what was to be done to the Canaanites when Israel entered the land, are to be found in one of the major books in the Old Testament devoted to matters of ethics, morality, and justice; indeed to the very moral laws that we have just been discussing. It is the book of Deuteronomy. It is this book that says that God "executes justice for the fatherless and the widow, and loves the sojourner, giving him food and clothing".[21] To put the point even more sharply: the Bible does not seem to be embarrassed in juxtaposing a discussion of the lofty morality of "love your neighbour as yourself" with the command to invade the Canaanites, even though this action seems to conflict with the Bible's own understanding of justice.

The reason for this lack of embarrassment is that, according to Deuteronomy, *the action taken against the Canaanites was morally justifiable.*[22] The ground is explicitly given: "Because of the wickedness of these nations the Lord is driving them out from before you."[23]

Now before we simply dismiss this, as the New Atheists do, as an example of whitewashing what is nothing but brutal ethnic cleansing, we should notice several things.

Firstly, the action contemplated is exceptional in terms of the biblical record as a whole. In this same book (Deuteronomy, chapter 20) the rules of war that are to characterize Israel are set out. For their time they are remarkably humanitarian. For instance, men were excused military duty if they had just become engaged, bought a house, planted a vineyard, or even if they were just fearful (20:5–8). In addition, war was only justifiable as a last resort. In the first instance the army was commanded to sue for peace wherever possible (20:10). And when they did go to war, it is noteworthy that women and children were to be spared; and the army was not permitted to engage in wanton destruction of the trees. Lord Jonathan Sacks, the Chief Rabbi of the United Hebrew Congregations of the Commonwealth, points out that the books of Leviticus and Deuteronomy contain the world's first environmental legislation.[24]

Moreover, Deuteronomy, like Leviticus, does not teach Dawkins' mythical "in-group" morality. It contains specific instructions to ensure the fair and just treatment of foreigners ('sojourners', as the Bible calls them). Indeed, in a section devoted to the impartiality of God's judgment, we actually find an explicit injunction to *love* foreigners. The text says of God that: "He executes justice for the fatherless and the widow, and loves the sojourner, giving him food and clothing. Love the sojourner also, since you were sojourners in Egypt."[25] The fact that the invasion of Canaan does not appear at first sight to have been characterized either by the normal rules of war or by these customary positive attitudes to aliens, shows that it was a very exceptional occurrence indeed.

Secondly, the invasion of Canaan is regarded as a judgment of God on the evils of these nations. "Every abominable thing that the Lord hates they have done for their gods, for they even burn their sons and their daughters in the fire to their gods."[26] That is, these tribes went in for a particularly cruel and brutal form of idolatry that not only violated the first three of the Ten Commandments but also involved that most horrific of all pagan rites, child sacrifice, one of the most degrading practices that has ever existed.

Thirdly, God had been patient with the tribes engaged in these evil practices for several centuries. Indeed, in the famous vision that Abraham had concerning his posterity, he was told that his descendants would spend 400 years in a land that "is not theirs" (Egypt) before they would be brought into the land of the Amorites. The reason given is that "the iniquity of the Amorites is not yet complete".[27] In other words, the invasion of Canaan coincided with the judgment of God on the sheer evil of a group of tribes that had been brewing for centuries.

Fourthly, the invasion was not to be based on any assumed feeling of national moral superiority. In fact, the people of Israel were explicitly told of the dangers of such an attitude: "Do not say in your heart after the Lord your God has thrust them out before you, 'It is because of my righteousness that the Lord has brought me in to possess this land'; whereas it is because of the wickedness of these people that the Lord is driving them out before you."[28]

Fifthly, the nation of Israel was not to regard itself as God's favourites who could do no wrong. Moses explicitly warned them that the very same judgment that fell on the Canaanites would fall upon them, if they themselves got involved in similar cruel idolatries. "And if you forget the Lord your God and go after other gods and serve them and worship them, I solemnly warn you today that you shall surely perish. Like the nations that the Lord makes to perish before you, so shall you perish because you would not obey the voice of the Lord your God."[29] History confirms to us that this is exactly what happened. The ten northern tribes of Israel disobeyed God's injunctions and were taken captive by Assyria; and later Judah followed suit and was overcome by Babylon – just as Moses and the prophets had predicted.

It follows that it is simplistic and inaccurate to regard the invasion of Canaan as ethnic cleansing by a war-thirsty antagonist. It also follows that, if we are to criticize the invasion of Canaan by the Israelites, we must by the same token take the same attitude to the subsequent invasions of Israel by the Assyrians and Babylonians.

However, there is another consideration. I have already drawn attention to the fact that, for Christians, it is the Bible's own understanding of justice that leads to questions about the morality of the invasion of Canaan. Could it just be that our difficulty with the biblical statements on this topic is that we misunderstand their meaning? Could it be that Deuteronomy is not embarrassed to juxtapose a high morality of protection of the weak and defenceless, for the simple reason that the action taken did not violate that morality? If that is the case, we next need to ask: how exactly would

Joshua have understood the command to "utterly destroy" the Canaanites?

Let us consider first another phrase that seems to be all-inclusive. Think, for instance, of the meaning of the phrase "all Israel" in the following examples: "These are the words that Moses spoke to all Israel beyond the Jordan";[30] "When all Israel comes to appear before the Lord";[31] "Now Samuel died. And all Israel assembled and mourned for him";[32] "Then the king, and all Israel with him, offered sacrifice".[33]

It is surely clear that the phrase "all Israel" should not be interpreted in the literalistic sense of "every single person in Israel without exception". For instance, many Israelites would not have been able to attend the ceremonies mentioned because of other duties, some would have been ill, and so on. In other words, the phrase is to be interpreted in the natural sense of "a substantial representation". We use this kind of language today: "All of London came to the Princess of Wales' funeral." We know exactly what this means: no one would think of interpreting it literalistically.

How, then, should we understand these commands to eliminate everyone without apparent exception? One obvious approach is to ask whether there is any evidence in the rest of the biblical account as to what actually took place. There is. If we read the book of Joshua we find that Joshua struck down every person in the towns of Debir and Hebron with the sword. However, in the succeeding book of Judges, Judah and Benjamin are said to have conquered those very same cities. But what would that mean, if the cities had already been completely exterminated by Joshua? On this basis, Nicholas Wolterstorff[34] argues that the expression "struck down all the inhabitants with the edge of the sword" is a formulaic phrase (for instance, it occurs seven times in Joshua 10). He argues that it is a literary convention that should be understood in conjunction with the fact that Joshua (as reported in Judges) did not literally wipe out the entire population of the cities with which he did battle.

Wolterstorff concludes that the commands to "utterly destroy" or "strike down all inhabitants with the sword", etc. are to be interpreted as "score a decisive victory over"; and did not therefore imply that the Israelites violated their normal rules of war by eliminating the defenceless.

One swift response to this will be: even if Wolterstorff is right, there have been and are still multitudes of innocent and defenceless people who have suffered monstrous evil at the hands of their fellow human beings in all kinds of horrific circumstances. The weight of this objection is surely felt by all. We shall consider it presently.

To sum up so far, then: according to the Bible the invasion of Canaan was carried out for moral reasons, and constituted divine judgment on the evil of the Canaanite tribes. This evil was so malign that it would bring down judgment not only on the Canaanites, but also on the Israelites if they compromised with it.

Here we reach the heart of the difficulty, as many see it. Judgment. First of all, there is the whole concept of divine judgment; secondly, there is the nature of the specific judgment that involves taking away human life; and finally, the fact that admittedly imperfect human beings are entrusted to carry out that judgment.

We are also justifiably suspicious of the motives of leaders who feel called by God to rid the world of evil. And anyway, is idolatry really that serious? How can God, if there is a God, contemplate such judgments, let alone command for them to happen? Do these actions constitute firm ethical grounds for abandoning faith in God and joining the New Atheists? Does the atheist view make better moral sense in the end?

These questions can easily generate a lot of deep emotion that makes discussion of them almost impossible. However, we must face them with as much sensitivity as we can muster.

THE JUDGMENT OF GOD

The central issue, then, is the judgment of God and its ramifications. It is important to be clear from the outset that, contrary to popular opinion, this topic is not confined to the Old Testament, just as the topic of the love and compassion of God is not confined to the New. Indeed, it is the Old Testament prophet Isaiah that people frequently quote to encapsulate their longing for a world in which there is no more war: "Nation shall not lift up sword against nation, neither shall they learn war any more."[35]

When it comes to the matter of judgment, the New Testament is, if anything, more solemn than the Old in its description of a final assize that is eternal in its implications. The fact is that, according to both Old and New Testaments, there is to be a final judgment at which human behaviour will be impartially evaluated. It is the claim of the New Testament that Christ is to be the judge.[36] That final assessment will proceed on the principle of judgment by peer: it is humans that are to be judged; it will therefore be a perfect human who will be entrusted with the judging.

Such claims are more than enough to send atheists into orbit, since they reject out of hand the existence of a final judgment, to say nothing of Christ's claim to be the judge. For atheism, by definition death ends all; and so there is no judgment to be feared. Remember the bendy bus message: "There's probably no God, now stop worrying…" That element in the atheist message is very ancient. It certainly goes back as far as the Epicurean philosophy, so well expressed in the Latin poet Lucretius's famous poem "*De Rerum Natura*".[37] In his poem, Lucretius takes up the ideas of the atomists Democritus and Leucippus, and argues that, because the atoms of the body disperse irretrievably on death, there can be no life after death: "Nothing at all will have the power to affect us or awaken sensation in us." He preaches this as a charter of freedom: freedom from the threat of a final judgment.

This "freedom" remains a key element in the New Atheism. As we mentioned earlier in this chapter, many atheists deeply resent the idea of a God who is watching over people, since they think that this is an expression of tyranny, and they wish to be free. However, the notion of God watching over us actually makes a great deal of sense, which the New Atheists, with their *a priori* conviction that God is a tyrant, do not seem to realize. Yet they ought to. Would they wish to live in a country where there was no police force watching over the people? Would they be prepared to fly across the Atlantic from an airport that had no security screening? I think not. For it is common human experience that we need people to watch over us. Of course, some people are tyrants – as dictatorships both of the right and left have proved. But such terrifying watchers of others are often precisely those who do not believe that there is a *God* watching them, a point made so powerfully by David Berlinski's story of the murder of the elderly Jew by the SS, related in Chapter 3.

The following abstract, from a research article on psychology, is telling:

We examined the effect of an image of a pair of eyes on contributions to an honesty box used to collect money for drinks in a university coffee room. People paid nearly three times as much for their drinks

when eyes were displayed rather than a control image. This finding provides the first evidence from a naturalistic setting of the importance of cues of being watched, and hence reputational concerns, on human cooperative behaviour.[38]

Incidentally, the poster displaying the watching eyes was placed directly above the honesty box.

In his essay "Human Nature in History", the eminent Cambridge historian Herbert Butterfield comments on the importance of some kind of supervision:

The historian begins, then, with a higher estimate of the status of personality than thinkers in some other fields, just as Christianity does when it sees each individual as a creature of eternal moment. Having made this splendid start, however, the historian proceeds – like the tradition of Christian theology itself – to a lower view of human nature than the one commonly current in the twentieth century... It seems to me, however, that in regard to the relations between human nature and the external conditions of the world, the study of history does open one's eyes to a significant fact... if you were to remove certain subtle safeguards in society many men who had been respectable all their lives would be transformed by the discovery of the things which it was now possible to do with impunity; weak men would apparently take to crime who had been previously kept on the rails by a certain balance existing in society; and you can produce a certain condition of affairs in which people go plundering and stealing, though hitherto throughout their lives it had never occurred to them even to want to steal. A great and prolonged police strike, the existence of a revolutionary situation in a capital city, and the exhilaration of conquest in an enemy country are likely to show up a seamy side of human nature amongst people who, cushioned and guided by the influences of normal social life, have hitherto presented a respectable figure to the world.

Butterfield's conclusion from this is that "the difference between civilisation and barbarism is a revelation of what is essentially the same human nature when it works under different conditions." And he adds: "One point is fundamental, however. Nobody may pretend that there has been an elimination of the selfishness, and self-centredness of man."[39] If in a well-run city, he argues, crime has significantly reduced, because the police have successfully restrained it, no one would argue that there is no longer any need for the police. Without them basic human nature would resume its criminal activity.[40]

One of the most memorable instances of this was the great lightning-induced power shortage in New York on the night of 13 July 1977, which left the city completely without electric power. Its first effect was that people could neither see, nor be seen. It was the complete state of "nobody is watching you". It spelt anarchy. People went on the rampage, looting stores, and then setting them alight to destroy any evidence. In one five-block stretch in Crown Heights, seventy-five stores were looted, thirty-five blocks of Broadway were destroyed; and in the mayhem 550 police were injured, and 4,500 looters arrested. Well-known behavioural psychologist Ernest Dichter said: "It was just like *Lord of the Flies*. People resort to savage behaviour when the brakes of civilisation fail."[41]

There are other areas where the brakes appear to be failing – for instance, in our attitude to the environment. Obtaining international agreement has proved extremely difficult, and some leading scientists are beginning to suggest that religion may have an important role to play. No lesser figures than E .O. Wilson, pioneer of sociobiology, and Lord May, former President of the Royal Society – neither of them a religious man – have called for an alliance of science and religion to combat the destruction of the biosphere.

Speaking about the failure to coordinate measures against such destruction, Lord May went so far as to suggest that, even though authoritarian religion had undermined attempts to achieve global cooperation on climate change, religion itself may have helped to protect human society from itself in the past, and it may be needed again. What is fascinating is the aspect of religion that Lord May feels important in this context: "Given that punishment is a useful mechanism, how much more effective it would be if you invested that power not in an individual, but in an all-seeing, all-powerful deity that controls the world." He felt that such a system would be "immensely stabilising in individual human cultures and societies." Thus, in his view, "a supernatural punisher may be part of the solution".[42]

The existence of "bad eggs" in a police force does not make us think that there can be no such thing as a decent and just policeman, magistrate, or judge. Yet it is just this kind of argument that the New Atheists are making about God. They imagine that a God of justice and judgment cannot simultaneously be a God of mercy, love, and compassion. What they fail to grasp, however, is that a God who did not judge Canaanite (or any other) evil would not be a God of mercy, love, and compassion.

Lucretius and the New Atheists rejoice that there is no God, and that death is the end. Their joy is premature and remarkably superficial. They fail to see that if there is no final judgment, then there is no such thing as *justice*. It is a tragic, yet obvious, fact that the vast majority of people do not get justice in this life; and since, in the atheist view, there is no life after death, there can be no final assessment after death – so these multi-millions will never get justice.

It is for that reason that a very different note is struck in the book of Psalms, where the thought of coming judgment is an occasion for song:

> **"Let the heavens be glad, and let the earth rejoice; let the sea roar, and all that fills it; let the field exult, and everything in it! Then shall all the trees of the forest sing for joy; before the Lord, for he comes, for he comes to judge the earth. He will judge the world in righteousness, and the peoples in his faithfulness."[43]**

God's judgment was not feared, but longed for by those who suffered. It was welcomed, because it promised the solution to the long-standing problem of justice. The influential Marxist intellectual Max Horkheimer saw this clearly and said so. Unlike the New Atheists, he feared that there might *not* be a God, since in that case there would be no justice. Justice and judgment are inseparable.

When I mentioned this matter to Dawkins in our debate in Oxford, he responded that it was important to campaign for justice in this life. I agreed. Of course we should campaign for justice in this life, and Christians have not been slow to do so. Witness, for instance, the campaign to abolish slavery, or the Herculean work of Christian medical missions. However, I went on to say that it was not a question of either having justice in this life or in the next. Even if we did ever reach the point (and history tends to indicate that we humans never shall) that justice was done on the earth, it would be of no value to the vast majority who have already died without obtaining justice.

However, Dawkins' words ring hollow, in light of his published view that *there is no such thing as justice*. What would be the point of campaigning for justice, even in this life, if justice doesn't exist? Yet, in the very same paragraph where Dawkins states that there is at bottom no good and no evil (and thus no morality), he also informs us that there is, in fact, no justice. Here is the full quote once more, with the relevant words italicized:

> In a universe of blind physical forces and genetic replication, some people are going to get hurt, other people are going to get lucky and you won't find any rhyme or reason in it, *nor any justice*. The universe we observe has precisely the properties we should expect if there is, at the bottom, no design, no purpose, no evil and no good. Nothing but blind, pitiless indifference. DNA neither knows nor cares. DNA just is. And we dance to its music.[44]

Neither justice nor morality then! This is the nearest that Dawkins gets to the kind of "hard" atheism of which Friedrich Nietzsche would have approved. David Bentley Hart writes (of Nietzsche):

> His famous fable of the madman who announces God's death is anything but a hymn of atheist triumphalism. In fact, the madman despairs of the mere atheists – those who merely do not believe – to whom he addresses his terrible proclamation. In their moral contentment, their ease of conscience, he sees an essential oafishness; they do not dread the death of God because they do not grasp that humanity's heroic and insane act of repudiation has sponged away the horizon, torn down the heavens, left us with only the uncertain resources of our will with which to combat the infinity of meaninglessness that the universe now threatens to become.
>
> Because he understood the nature of what had happened when Christianity entered history with the annunciation of the death of God on the cross, and the elevation of a Jewish peasant above all gods, Nietzsche understood also that the passing of Christian faith permits no return to pagan naiveté, and he knew that this monstrous inversion of values created within us a conscience that the older order could never have incubated. He understood also that the death of God beyond us is the death of the human as such within us. If we are, after all, nothing but the fortuitous effects of physical causes, then the will is bound to no rational measure but itself, and who can imagine what sort of world will spring up from so unprecedented and so vertiginously uncertain a vision of reality?
>
> For Nietzsche, therefore, the future that lies before us must be decided, and decided between only two possible paths: a final

nihilism, which aspires to nothing beyond the momentary consolations of material contentment, or some great feat of creative will, inspired by a new and truly worldly mythos powerful enough to replace the old and discredited mythos of the Christian revolution (for him, of course, this meant the myth of the *Übermensch*).

Perhaps; perhaps not. Where Nietzsche was almost certainly correct, however, was in recognizing that mere formal atheism was not yet the same thing as true unbelief. He writes: "Once the Buddha was dead, people displayed his shadow for centuries afterwards in a cave, an immense and dreadful shadow. God is dead: – but as the human race is constituted, there will perhaps be caves for millennia yet where people will display his shadow. And we – we have yet to overcome his shadow!"[45]

Nietzsche and Dawkins are right, of course – provided only that their atheism is true. If there is no judgment after death, then it is a matter of elementary logic that the vast majority of victims of injustice will never have their legitimate grievances put to rights. Not only that: their tormentors, the perpetrators of evil, will mostly get away with their crimes. The terrorist who murders thousands of people, or the dictator who destroys millions, simply has to put a gun to his head if he feels threatened. On the atheist view, the suicide bombers of 9/11 will never face justice.

No God, no shadow of God; and so no purpose, no justice, no evil, and no good. This, then, is the brave new world to which the New Atheist bus is inexorably driving us. This is the price that has to be paid for endorsing their philosophy: the admission that the very deep sense of justice embedded in the human psyche is sheer illusion.

Earlier in this chapter I said that the problem of evil and suffering is the most difficult that we face. The atheist "solution" is to deny the existence of God. But what, exactly, have they solved by taking this route? They certainly have got rid of the intellectual problem: evil for them is just part of the way the world is. Indeed, what they might now be hard put to explain is why there is any good at all, let alone so much of it. Why are they protesting against evil, since they don't actually believe that it exists?

But atheism has not got rid of the suffering and the evil. They are still there. Moreover, atheism's "solution" to the problem of evil has got rid of something else – hope. Atheism is a hope-less faith. Indeed, by removing hope, atheism can be seen to make the suffering much worse.

We have reached a strange juncture in our argument. Atheism imagines that it has got rid of the problem of evil; yet as a Christian I face the problem. On the other hand, atheism has got rid of hope; yet I as a Christian have hope, even in the face of suffering and evil. Not only that but, according to Christianity, criminal fanatics, terrorists, and the like are not forever going to get away with their evil. Human conscience and desire for justice are not a delusion. It is the atheism that denies ultimate justice that is the delusion.

But how can we know that this is true? How can we know that death is not the end, and that there is to be a final judgment when perfect justice will be done in regard to every injustice that has ever been committed, from the beginning of human history to its end? We can know on the basis of the historical, bodily resurrection of Jesus Christ from the dead.

The resurrection, it should be noted, is a central pillar of Christianity. The first history of the growth of the Christian church, the Acts of the Apostles, records the famous occasion on which the Christian apostle Paul addressed the philosophers at Athens in their Areopagus School, on their inconclusive musings about God. Among his hearers were some Epicurean philosophers who, as we have seen, were forerunners of the New Atheists, in that their materialistic atomistic belief rendered notions of a final judgment ludicrous. Paul told them: God "has fixed a day on which he will judge the world in righteousness by a man whom he has appointed; and of this he has given assurance to all by raising him from the dead."[46] The Christian apostle Paul connected the final judgment with the resurrection of Jesus because it is the supreme evidence that Jesus is to be the final judge.

Laughter rang out around the court, from the Epicureans in particular. But not only from them, for, although the notion of survival of the soul was a respectable doctrine to some of the Platonists who were present, no one, just no one, believed that a body could physically "stand up again".[47] But then, as now, there were others who were sufficiently interested to hear more; and there were some men and women who were convinced by Paul's presentation – among them Dionysius, a member of the Areopagus, and Damaris.

Not surprisingly, the New Atheists find the resurrection as laughable as their Epicurean antecedents did. At the culmination of the "God Delusion" debate in Alabama, when I mentioned the resurrection,

Richard Dawkins responded in amazement at what he thought was my naiveté: "So we come down to the resurrection of Jesus Christ. It's so petty; it's so trivial; it's so local; it's so earthbound; it's so unworthy of the universe."

I found this an astonishingly illogical outburst, for the naiveté was not mine. If Dawkins had simply affirmed his belief that Jesus did not rise from the dead, I would have understood it. However, to say that the resurrection is petty, trivial, and earthbound is to betray a profound failure to grasp what the resurrection is and what it implies. Petty, trivial, and earthbound are exactly what the resurrection isn't – if it happened. It is atheism, with its oblivion at death, that makes us earthbound, petty, and trivial. If Jesus rose from the dead, it demonstrates that he is very much not earthbound but God the Creator incarnate. As for "unworthy of the universe", the question should be: is the universe worthy of him?

THE CRUNCH

We have now reached the crunch issue. If death ends everything then the biblical worldview is false; and, since there is therefore no ultimate justice for anyone, any further discussion of the destruction of the Canaanites (or of anyone else, for that matter) is pointless. However, if death is not the end, and there is to be a final and fair judgment, then matters appear in a very different light.

But did Jesus rise from the dead? Many will say – and perhaps this is what Dawkins had in mind – that the resurrection is not worth considering, since: a) miracles are impossible, as Enlightenment philosopher David Hume pointed out a long time ago; and, b) there is not enough evidence, as Bertrand Russell once said.

These are such important issues that we shall devote the next two chapters of the book to them. However, before we do that, we must consider the Christian response to the problem of moral evil in light of the death and resurrection of Jesus.

The litany of unmitigated evil in our world seems never ending. Day by day thousands of innocent people die, among them many infants and children. The objection is that, if there is a God, he must therefore take ultimate responsibility for their deaths. The question is: how could one possibly believe in a God like that?

My answer is: I couldn't, if I thought that death was the end and that there was no ultimate justice. However, I believe that death is not the end, and that *God is a God of compensation*. The resurrection of Jesus Christ demonstrates that there is to be a final assessment at which God will not only be just, but will also be seen to be just. It also validates the biblical claim that there is an eternal realm where there is no pain, no death, and no hunger: a world that is filled with the joy of the immediate presence of God and of Christ, its king. Yes, I am talking about heaven – and I haven't forgotten that I am a scientist.

C. S. Lewis once wrote words that are as apposite today as when he wrote them:

A book on suffering which says nothing about heaven is leaving out almost the whole of one side of the account. Scripture and tradition habitually put the joys of heaven into the scale against the suffering of earth, and no solution of the problem of pain which does not do so can be called a Christian one. We are very shy nowadays of even mentioning heaven. We are afraid of the jeer about "pie in the sky"... but either there is "pie in the sky" or there is not. If there is not, then Christianity is false, for this doctrine is woven into its whole fabric. If there is, then this truth, like any other, must be faced...[48]

And so must its implications. The pioneer Christian apostle, Paul, wrote: "For I consider that the sufferings of this present time are not worth comparing with the glory that is to be revealed... For I am sure that neither death nor life... nor height nor depth, nor anything else in all creation, will be able to separate us from the love of God in Christ Jesus our Lord."[49] These are not the words of an armchair philosopher but of a man who had seen and experienced life at its rough end, unjustly suffering frequent beatings and imprisonment, and experiencing much deprivation and hardship.

At times I try to imagine what that glorious realm is like, and the question arises within me: if the veil that now separates the seen and the unseen world were to be parted for a moment, and we could see how God has treated, say, the myriads of innocent children who have suffered from the horrendous evil perpetrated by immoral governments, war lords and drug barons, or who have been the innocent victims of natural disasters, is it just possible that all our concerns about God's handling of the situation would instantly dissolve?

But we cannot yet see that realm; and so we are left with many ragged ends, many burning problems of injustice. In light of them, another question looms large: is there, nevertheless, enough reason to trust God with the ultimate outcome? Indeed, did it really have to be like this in the first place? Surely a God who is all-powerful could have prevented all this horrendous evil and suffering, simply by creating human beings incapable of doing evil?

Well, he could surely have made *beings* like that. But they would not have been *human* beings, would they? Let me try to explain. An essential and wonderful part of being human is that we have been endowed with the capacity to love. Love involves saying "yes" rather than "no" to another, and would be rendered meaningless if the capacity to choose between those two alternatives did not exist. In other words, the ability to love is intimately linked with the possession of what we call "free will". We are aware, of course, that the freedom implied is not unlimited: we are not free to do everything. For instance, I am not free to run at 60 miles per hour! Nevertheless, for a being to be free to say yes, it must be free to say no; to be free to love, it must be free to hate; to be free to be good, it must be free to be evil.

God could have removed the potential for hatred and evil at a stroke by creating us as automata, mere machines doing only that which we were programmed to do. But that would have been to remove all that we ourselves value as constituting our essential humanity. There is inevitably a built-in risk with creating beings with real powers of choice. We humans should know that, since we do something similar when we have children. We know that any children we generate could grow up to love us; we also know that they could turn out to reject us. Why, then, have children? For most of us, the hope and desire for the love of children far outweighs the risk of their rejection of us.

We would not wish our children to be degraded to machines. Nor will God similarly degrade human beings. It is worth just pointing out in passing that there is a strong current of atheistic thought that does just that – it degrades human free will to an illusion.

C. S. Lewis wrote: "If God thinks this state of war in the universe a price worth paying for free will – that is, for making a live world in which creatures can do real good or harm and something of real importance can happen, instead of a toy world which only moves when He pulls the strings – then we may take it that it is worth paying."[50]

Why? What reason is there to think it is worth paying? Is the price not obviously too high?

I believe the answer lies in another, supremely costly, suffering – the cross of Christ.

THE MEANING OF THE CROSS OF CHRIST

Let me try, first of all, to explain one aspect of that answer by means of an experience I had some years ago when teaching in Eastern Europe at the time of the Cold War. I joined a group of visitors to be shown around a large synagogue. As we entered, I fell into conversation with a woman from South America, who told me she was there to try to gain some idea of her identity – perhaps to find out something about some of her relatives who had perished in the Holocaust. In the synagogue there was a special exhibition devoted to the festivals that were part of the calendar of the nation of Israel: from Passover to the Feast of Tabernacles. A rabbi was explaining these festivals, which are still celebrated today; and I was doing my best to translate for my new acquaintance. Concentrating on that task, I did not at first notice the mock-up of a doorway that stood in the centre of the exhibition. But when the rabbi reached that point in his tour, I saw not only the doorway but also the ugly words that stood above it: "*Arbeit macht frei*" (work makes free). It was a mock-up of the main gate to the Nazi death camp at Auschwitz – a place that I have visited several times. Behind it, that is, through this door in the synagogue, there were photographs of the horrific medical experiments carried out on children by the infamous Dr Josef Mengele in the death camp. At that juncture my acquaintance suddenly moved into the doorway and put out her arms to touch both sides of it. She said: "And what does your religion make of this?" – earlier she had discovered that I believed in God.

She spoke loudly enough for several others to pause and look in our direction. What was I to say? What could I say? She had lost her parents and many relatives in the Holocaust. I had young children at the time and could scarcely bear to look at the Mengele photographs, because of the sheer horror of imagining my children suffering such a fate. I had nothing in my experience or in my family history that was remotely parallel to the horror that her family had endured.

But still she stood in the doorway waiting for an answer. This is what I eventually said: "I would not insult your memory of your parents by offering you simplistic answers to your question. What is more, I have young children and I cannot even bear to think how I might react if anything were to happen to them, even if it were far short of the evil that Mengele did. I have no easy answers; but I do have what, for me at least, is a doorway into an answer."

"What is it?" she said.

"You know that I am a Christian. That means – and I know it is difficult for you to follow me here – that I believe that Yeshua[51] is the messiah. I also believe that he was God incarnate, come into our world as saviour, which is what his name "Yeshua" means. Now I know that this is even more difficult for you to accept. Nevertheless, just think about this question – if Yeshua was really God, as I believe he was, what was God doing on a cross?

"Could it be that God begins just here to meet our heartbreaks, by demonstrating that he did not remain distant from our human suffering, but became part of it himself? For me, this is the beginning of hope; and it is a living hope that cannot be smashed by the enemy of death. The story does not end in the darkness of the cross. Yeshua conquered death. He rose from the dead; and one day, as the final judge, he will assess everything in absolute fairness, righteousness, and mercy."

There was silence. She was still standing, arms outstretched, forming a motionless cross in the doorway. After a moment, with tears in her eyes, very quietly but audibly, she said: "Why has no one ever told me that about my messiah before?"

There are no simplistic answers to the hard questions thrown up by human suffering. The answer that Christianity gives is not a set of propositions or a philosophical analysis of the possibilities – it is, rather, a Person who suffered.

But it is not simply a Person who suffered to show solidarity with us in our suffering. It went far deeper than that. The unique claim of Christianity is that, on the cross, Jesus suffered something very much worse than crucifixion – he suffered to atone for sin. As the old hymn says, "He died that we might be forgiven."

New Atheism, however, finds that concept reprehensible...

CHAPTER 6

IS THE ATONEMENT MORALLY REPELLENT?

"You shall call his name Jesus, for he will save his people from their sins."
St Matthew

"For even the Son of Man came not to be served but to serve, and to give his life as a ransom for many."
St Mark

"Ask yourself the question: how moral is the following? I am told of a human sacrifice that took place two thousand years ago, without my wishing it and in circumstances so ghastly that, had I been present and in possession of any influence, I would have been duty-bound to try and stop it. In consequence of this murder, my own manifold sins are forgiven me, and I may hope to enjoy eternal life."
Christopher Hitchens

Richard Dawkins correctly recognizes that the atonement is the "central doctrine of Christianity", but he regards it as "vicious, sado-masochistic and repellent".[1] The sad thing about this reaction is that atheism, by its very definition, has absolutely nothing to offer here. It leaves us in a broken world without a glimmer of ultimate hope. Yet, in spite of the hopelessness of their position, many prominent atheists content themselves with crude, dismissive, and puerile caricatures of the very message that, for centuries, has brought hope, forgiveness, peace of mind and heart, and power for living to multitudes of ordinary men and women.

This is a decidedly unimpressive stance on the part of those who keep telling us that they are interested in rational thought and the assessment of evidence. Dismissing ideas by caricature is a hallmark of lazy superficiality. And yet caricatures can sometimes help us pinpoint underlying misunderstandings.

So let us look at some of the caricatures to see what can be learned from them. Dawkins first objects that the "Christian focus is overwhelmingly on sin sin sin sin sin sin sin. What a nasty little preoccupation to have dominating your life."[2] But sin, though it certainly can be very nasty, is not a little preoccupation: it is a major preoccupation that dominates the world. It is the root cause of tyrannies, wars, genocide, murder, exploitation, financial crises, injustice; of international, societal, and family breakdown; of incalculable unhappiness due to lying, cheating, slander, bullying, stealing, domestic violence, and every form of crime, and so on and on and on and on and on and on and on. What is overwhelming (to use Dawkins' word) is the horrendous destructiveness of sin, daily forcing us to admit the bitter fact, as written long ago, that "the wages of sin is death".[3]

The New Atheists have to face sin every bit as much as the rest of us. Any philosophy, such as theirs, that trivializes or ignores sin is sheer fantasy. It is also dangerous fantasy. For history is littered with disastrous attempts to establish an earthly paradise without facing human sin – and those attempts have usually added immeasurably to the burden of human misery and suffering.

For theologian Nicholas Lash of Cambridge, Dawkins' complaint raises the suspicion that Dawkins has not read very widely in the early church fathers. Lash cannot resist a bit of irony:

How lamentable of the Fathers to have been preoccupied with the damage done by human beings to themselves, to others, and to the world of which we form a part, through egotism, violence and greed; through warfare, slavery, starvation! What a wiser atheist than Dawkins might at least agree to be a terrifyingly dark tapestry of inhumanity, Christians call "sin", knowing all offences against the creature to be disobedience against the Creator.[4]

The fact is that the Christian message has something both unique and profound to say about this matter of sin. I suspect that the real reason for the superficiality of much atheist reaction is not that they do not see sin as a problem. It is because they have no solution. It is also because the very word "sin" instinctively raises spectres in their minds that threaten their naturalistic worldview: it makes them think of God, of Christ, of his death on the cross, of his resurrection. Their instinct is correct; for sin, in the first place, has to do with our relationship with God – its disruption and repair.

What is more, to say with Dawkins that the Christian focus is "overwhelmingly" on sin is entirely to misunderstand the seriousness of the situation. Most of us, if we got cancer, would find that fact at once becoming the central focus of our lives. Furthermore, we would expect the overwhelming focus of our doctors and consultants to be on that cancer, in the hope of curing the disease and restoring us to health, so that our focus could then be directed, no doubt "overwhelmingly", elsewhere.

Sin is like a cancer: it eats up the possibility of real peace, joy, and happiness. The reason Christianity has so much to say about it is not because of morbid preoccupation. It is because Christianity offers us both a realistic diagnosis of the problem of human sin, and a solution to it that brings new, satisfying, and meaningful life with it. Atheism offers neither.

ORIGINAL SIN

In particular, Richard Dawkins vehemently disagrees with the doctrine of atonement:

But now the sado-masochism, God incarnated himself as a man, Jesus, in order that he should be tortured and executed in *atonement* for the hereditary sin of Adam. Ever since Paul expounded this repellent doctrine, Jesus has been worshipped as the *redeemer* of all our sins. Not just the past sin of Adam: future sins as well, whether future people decided to commit them or not!... I have described atonement, the central doctrine of Christianity, as vicious, sado-masochistic and repellent. We should also dismiss it as barking mad, but for its ubiquitous familiarity which has dulled our objectivity. If God wanted to forgive our sins, why not just forgive them, without having himself tortured and executed in payment...? Progressive ethicists today find it hard to defend any kind of retributive theory of

punishment, let alone the scapegoat theory – executing an innocent to pay for the sins of the guilty. In any case (one can't help wondering), who was God trying to impress? Presumably himself – judge and jury as well as execution victim. To cap it all, Adam, the supposed perpetrator of the original sin, never existed in the first place: an awkward fact – excusably unknown to Paul but presumably known to an omniscient God (and Jesus, if you believe he was God?) – which fundamentally undermines the premise of the whole tortuously nasty theory. Oh, but of course, the story of Adam and Eve was only ever *symbolic*, wasn't it? *Symbolic?* So, in order to impress himself, Jesus had himself tortured and executed, in vicarious punishment for a symbolic sin committed by a non-existent individual? As I said, barking mad, as well as viciously unpleasant.[5]

A similar sentiment is expressed in the following statement that appears at the end of a Christmas essay on the King James Version of the Bible: "Let's celebrate the 400th anniversary of this astonishing piece of English literature. Warts and all – for I have not mentioned… the Pauline obscenity of every baby being born in sin, saved only by the divine scapegoat suffering on the cross because the Creator of the universe couldn't think of a better way to forgive everybody."[6]

Though saddened by such crude misrepresentation, I am not surprised at it. For it has been so from the beginning. The message of the crucified Christ, as Paul pointed out in the very earliest days of Christianity, was and still is: "a stumbling block to Jews and folly to Gentiles".[7] By their mockery the New Atheists unwittingly prove those words to be true – an observation that gives me no pleasure.

Dawkins covers a wide range of topics in the above quote: the atonement, theories of punishment, forgiveness, and the historical origin of sin; and we shall address all of them in due course. The logical place to start is with the question of sin. The New Atheists do not understand the Christian message of the cross and salvation, because they do not understand the seriousness of human sin. They mock the former because they have trivialized the latter. However, when we cease to make light of sin, we discover that it infects all of us. Sin is universal.

The existence of a profound flaw in human nature has been recognized since time immemorial. The famous Dr Johnson was once asked by his biographer, James Boswell, what he thought of original sin. Johnson replied: "With respect to original sin, the inquiry is not necessary, for whatever is the cause of human corruption men are evidently and confessedly so corrupt, that all the laws of heaven and earth are insufficient to restrain them from crimes."[8]

In a masterpiece of succinct expression, G. K. Chesterton got it exactly right when, in answer to the question of what was wrong with the world posed by the *London Times*, he wrote the following justifiably famous letter:

Dear Sir,
I am.
Yours faithfully,
G. K. Chesterton

In the medical arena, a disease has to be faced and understood before it can be cured. Superficial diagnoses lead to superficial solutions. Symptoms have to be distinguished from root cause. A headache is a symptom. Its root cause could be anything from influenza to a brain tumour. It is only when you grasp the seriousness of brain tumours that you can begin to understand why a complex operation is necessary that may put you through a great deal of discomfort. There is no point in treating a brain tumour with aspirin.

Similarly, in order to understand the solution that Christianity offers to the problem of human sin, we need to grasp the radical nature of the biblical diagnosis of sin: that the human race itself is "fallen", fundamentally flawed by evil. Now, this stark statement should not be understood to mean that all humans are as bad as they could possibly be. Far from it. For, in spite of being flawed by evil, we human beings retain many of the noble features that stem from our original unflawed creation by God. This is indicated in Christ's remark: "If you then, who are evil, know how to give good gifts to your children, how much more will the heavenly Father give the Holy Spirit to those who ask him!"[9]

It is a self-evident fact that men and women of all faiths or none know how to give good gifts to their children; to have loving paternal instincts, and often care for others far beyond the confines of their families. Indeed, it is an important part of the biblical worldview to develop compassion, to promote and encourage efforts on the part of scientists, physicians, surgeons, psychiatrists, nurses, educationalists, economists, politicians, and others to alleviate the ills and sufferings that afflict humanity.

But nonetheless, the biblical diagnosis is that the human race is flawed by evil, a contention that is surely not surprising in light of our common experience. The source of that evil is given in the following key statement by St Paul: "sin came into the world through one man, and death through sin, and so death spread to all men because[10] all sinned".[11] This says, firstly, that we have all inherited a nature that is fallen, sinful, and mortal. Secondly, we have all individually sinned. Sin is universal. We note that Paul says "sin" entered the world and not "sins", for he is thinking not of particular sins, but of sin as a principle. It is an attitude consisting of a deep-seated egotism, where the human creature asserts his own will against that of the Creator.

Not surprisingly, the New Atheists mock such ideas of "original sin", by dismissing the Genesis account as a primitive symbolic aetiological myth. However, it should be noted in passing that most scientists assert that *Homo sapiens* sprang from a common ancestor (surely it must have been two?). Nor does anyone appear to dispute that all descendants of those two have inherited their genes, and therefore their nature. So it might be rather unwise to dismiss the biblical account out of hand – after all, no other account seems realistically to face human nature as we actually experience it. For instance, the notion that the moral Zeitgeist is improving,[12] in that human beings are gradually evolving to the state where their intellectual nature governs their animal nature, does not look very convincing in light of the monstrous evil of our most recent century. Interestingly, in conversation with me and Larry Taunton, the Director of the Fixed-Point Foundation that organized my debates, Christopher Hitchens, by contrast with other New Atheists, forthrightly admitted that man is unquestionably evil. Let us therefore be patient, and see what the Bible actually has to say.

The story of the Garden of Eden is one of the most famous stories in all of literature. It is also one of the most profound. It relates how the Creator placed the first humans in a garden paradise that was full of promise and interest. They were free to enjoy the garden and explore it and the regions around it to their hearts' content. However, one fruit was indeed forbidden them by God – the "tree of the knowledge of good and evil". Yet, far from diminishing the status of humanity, that prohibition was essential to establish the unique dignity of humans as moral beings. The biblical story here defines the irreducible ingredients that constitute humans as moral beings and enable them to function as such. In order for morality to be real, humans must have a certain degree of freedom, as we saw in the preceding chapter. So, they were free to eat all that was in the garden. But there must also be real moral choice between right and wrong. There must therefore be a moral boundary. So, one fruit was forbidden. God told them that in the day they ate it they would surely die.

This ancient story then relates how the serpent-enemy misrepresented God, suggesting that God was taunting human beings, first by placing them in a magnificent environment with its beautiful trees and luscious fruit, and then forbidding them to eat that fruit. The enemy also insinuated that God wished to limit human freedom by not letting the humans become as God.[13] The deception worked.

The "original" sin that infected the human race from its very start was a revolt of the human spirit against the God who created it; a revolt that changed the attitude of the creature to his Creator, to other humans and to the creation around him; a revolt that has given us the New Atheists. As soon as the first humans took the forbidden fruit, they experienced shame, unease, and, above all, alienation from God. The death of their relationship with God would inevitably be followed, but not immediately, by physical death. The man and woman who had enjoyed the joy and friendship of God now felt that God had become their enemy, and they fled to hide from him.[14]

We humans have likewise been fleeing ever since. There has lurked in the human heart the suspicion that God, if he exists at all, is innately hostile to us. He forbids us the enjoyment of natural pleasures, and represses us psychologically. He restrains us from developing our full human potential. Hitchens, in common with untold numbers of others, has swallowed this father of all misrepresentations. It permeates his thinking. As we saw earlier he imagines that God is a tyrant and a bully, and he complains: "It is useless to object that Adam seems to have been created with insatiable discontent and curiosity and then forbidden to slake it…"[15]

This attitude is as irrational as it is false. After all, does it really make sense to think that our Creator, who has equipped us among other things with the capacity to love others, is himself against us? Even a superficial glance at the text of Genesis shows that Hitchens' complaint rests on severe distortion. God certainly created Adam to be curious, but not discontented. The first humans were not prevented from slaking their curiosity. The very reverse: they had a whole world of possibilities at their feet. God encouraged them to engage in the fascinating task of naming things – in their case, the animals – a task that is of the very essence of science. God wanted them to explore his universe and to discover the treasures of his wisdom.

As for the "forbidding", it is to be noted that only one thing was forbidden (contrary to the impression Hitchens gives); and that particular fruit was forbidden, not to restrict humanity but so that they could develop a relationship of trust with the Creator. They really could choose whether to trust the Creator and believe his word, or to grasp at what they imagined would come to them by asserting their independence of him.

The biblical diagnosis is that we have inherited a nature that is sinful, and then have proceeded to sin on our own account. We are on all sides influenced and pressurized by the prevailing ethos of a fallen world. As the New Testament puts it, "All have sinned, and fall short of the glory of God."[16] However, this seems grossly unfair to many people. They say, "We did not ask to be born from a race that has been damaged at its root. Why should we be condemned as a result of what somebody else originally did?" The answer to this reasonable objection is given in a subsequent statement by St Paul in the very same letter: "For as by the one man's disobedience the many were made sinners, so by the one man's obedience the many will be made righteous."[17]

Because we were not personally responsible for the entry of sin into the world, we are not personally in a position to rectify the whole situation. That is why the salvation offered for human sin in the New Testament makes sense, because it (alone) is commensurate with the scale of the problem. If we were made sinners by what some other person did, rescue and redemption is offered to us freely on the very same terms: through what Another Person has done, *rather than by what we ourselves can do.*

Many people seem to find this immensely important principle of vicarious suffering difficult to grasp, and, as a result, misunderstanding abounds. One reason for that misunderstanding is another repercussion of human alienation from God: the widespread notion that religion can be used to merit God's acceptance, by the piling up of good deeds. As if religion, or any other activity on the part of a creature, could merit acceptance by the Creator, when the reality is that everything of good that any of us has or can do ultimately comes from him. In consequence, many people think that "salvation", if it means anything at all, is simply some sort of moral code that we have to keep to earn God's acceptance, like "loving your neighbour as yourself".

The Christian message is the direct opposite of this popular view. In Christianity "salvation" means exactly that: action on the part of God to rescue those who could not help themselves. At its heart is the magnificent doctrine of the grace of God. It says that, if they will, all can be "justified [i.e. be put right with God] by his grace as a gift, through the redemption that is in Christ Jesus... we hold that one is justified by faith apart from works of the law ... to the one who does not work but believes in him who justifies the ungodly, his faith is counted as righteousness".[18]

In particular, acceptance with God does not depend on attainment of a standard of perfection that is humanly impossible to attain.[19] Salvation, as the New Testament repeatedly says, is given by God's grace as a gift: "It is the gift of God, not a result of works, so that no one may boast."[20] However, like all gifts, it has to be accepted. It is not automatic;[21] it involves repentance and putting our trust in God as a deliberate act of our will. The logic of this is important: since the original rebellion involved lack of trust and grasping at independence from God, the way back inevitably involves repenting[22] of that attitude, trusting God and learning to depend on him. The way back starts, therefore, by our facing the seriousness of our position, repenting, and accepting from Christ the gift of salvation that we could not earn or provide for ourselves.

To sum up then. Just as the human race was infected by sin at the beginning by its founding father's disobedience to God; so we, individually, can be forgiven, reconciled, and accepted by God. This cannot be done through our efforts at obedience – even at their best they are imperfect and inadequate – but by the obedience of another, that is Christ. Putting that another way: just as we received a fallen, sinful nature from Adam, we can receive from God, through repentance and trusting Christ, his unfallen, eternal life – and with it all the potential to live in harmony with and for him.

IS SUBSTITUTIONARY ATONEMENT IMMORAL?

The New Atheists take great exception to what they call the scapegoat theory of atonement – "executing an innocent to pay for the sins of the guilty".[23] In fact, Richard Dawkins thinks that the doctrine of the atonement is "barking mad". It is interesting to see the reason he gives: "If God wanted to forgive our sins, why not just forgive them, without having himself tortured and executed in payment?"[24] Why not, indeed?

Because this is a moral universe, and dealing with sin is a non-trivial moral problem. A moment's contemplation of the sorry moral landscape that is human history ought to convince us of this fact. Dawkins' superficial reaction comes from a failure to understand what is involved in forgiveness. Let us try to think this through. The word most used in the New Testament for "forgiveness" is the Greek "*aphesis*", which means "release" or "let go". In these terms, Dawkins is asking, "Why can't God just let it go?" The answer has to do with human guilt.

It is a common human experience that guilt chains us to the past. Suppose I park my car illegally. I am deemed guilty of an infringement of traffic laws and incur a penalty in the form of a fine. The law demands that I should be punished. The fine has to be paid; and the law will insist that it is paid. I cannot just forget about it. The courts will certainly not "just let it go". More crucially, the courts will not just "let go" serious crimes. If there were no punishment for such crimes, the world would descend into anarchy as the message got out that *crime did not matter*.[25] Robert McAfee Brown says: "One cannot allow, as a human axiom, a position such as that of the philosopher-poet Heinrich Heine, 'God will forgive, that's what He's here for.'"[26]

There is another reason why God cannot "just let it go". Think of a woman whose marital happiness has just been ruined by the discovery of her husband's unfaithfulness. She is deeply hurt, her domestic world shattered. Forgiveness in this situation will involve *two* distinct processes. First there is the woman being able *inwardly* to "let it go" so as to limit the damage to herself as far as possible. Making progress here may be very difficult and take a long time and the good counsel of friends. But then there is the matter of her husband, and her active *outward* forgiveness of him. Suppose that she gets to the point where she is willing to forgive her husband. What then? True forgiveness here is conditional on her husband's repentance. If she "just lets it go" it amounts to saying "it doesn't matter" – which could be interpreted as effectively condoning the sin. Failure to separate these two aspects of forgiveness has often led to a great deal of unnecessary pain, when well-meaning friends have urged the victim of wrongdoing to "forgive, because it is your duty", even though there is no sign of repentance on the part of the perpetrator.

At this point there is a common objection: "But didn't Jesus pray for forgiveness for the soldiers that crucified him?" Indeed he did. But we should notice the grounds on which he prayed: "Father, forgive them *for they know not what they do* [italics mine]."[27] Greek scholar Professor David Gooding explains:

> This prayer, uttered in a moment of fearful pain, on behalf of those who were causing the pain, has rightly moved the hearts of millions and become the ideal which has taught countless sufferers not to yield to blind retaliation, but to seek the good of even their enemies... It detracts nothing, however, from the glory of Christ's prayer to point out that it was prayed on behalf of the soldiers who in all truthfulness did not know what they were doing. False sentiment must not lead us to extend the scope of his prayer beyond his intention. To pray forgiveness for a man who knows quite well what he is doing and has no intention of either stopping or repenting would be immoral: it would amount to condoning, if not conniving at, his sin. Christ certainly did not do that.[28]

Sin matters. If my sin doesn't matter, then I don't matter in the end. If your child is murdered and the law does not bother to arrest, try, and sentence the perpetrator, the law is saying, in effect, that your child does not matter. The courts cannot "just let it go". Such an attitude would spell the end of all morality and all hope of justice. It would inevitably lead to anarchy. So, if the legal system were to adopt the view that Dawkins seems to think God should take, it would be an offence to our moral conscience. But God will never accept that our lies, greed, theft, adultery, violence, murder, etc. do not matter. He takes our sin seriously, not because he hates us but because he loves us. His universe is a moral universe; and as its supreme moral governor he, a holy and perfect God, must deal justly with human sin. It is sin that ruins life and happiness. It is sin that brought human death into the world. The more we are aware of the holiness of God and our own shortcomings, weaknesses, failures, transgressions, and sinfulness, the more we can appreciate the gulf that separates us from God, and the connection there is between sin and death.

In our hearts we know that this makes sense – it fits in with our innate sense of justice and fairness. Yet it creates an obvious problem for each one of us. If God were to deal justly with me, where would I stand? I cannot break the guilt that chains me to my past. God cannot simply let it go, if he is to be just and I am to retain any significance as a moral being. There is a penalty to be paid, there is cost involved, and I cannot pay it. The heart of the Christian good news is that *God, in Christ, has paid that penalty on the cross*. As a result, God can justly forgive and accept all who repent and trust in Christ for salvation.

Hitchens, who appears to have more insight on the matter than Dawkins, still has a major difficulty here. He writes:

> **I can pay your debt, my love, if you have been imprudent, and if I were a hero like Sydney Carton in *A Tale of Two Cities* I could even serve your term in prison or take your place on the scaffold. Greater love hath no man. *But I cannot absolve you of your responsibilities. It would be immoral of me to offer, and immoral of you to accept* [italics mine]. And if the same offer is made from another time and another world, through the mediation of middlemen and accompanied by inducements, it loses all its grandeur and becomes debased into wish-thinking or, worse, a combination of blackmailing with bribery.**[29]

As he subsequently makes clear, Hitchens' last point here is a reference to the reprehensible commercialization of religion that has developed from (and serves to propagate) the false notion that acceptance with God can be gained by merit, ceremonies, or monetary contributions of various kinds. It is important to note that, long before Christopher Hitchens, Christ himself protested vigorously at such exploitation, with all of its attendant misrepresentations of God.[30] For such exploitation, whatever it calls itself, is not true Christianity. True Christianity knows no self-aggrandizing middlemen and no inducements of the sort Hitchens mentions – there is no blackmail or bribery. What Christianity teaches is: "there is one God and one Mediator between God and men, the man Christ Jesus, who gave himself a ransom for all."[31]

What does this mean? We can start with what Hitchens seems to accept, even though he expresses it somewhat tongue in cheek.

If a person gets into difficult financial circumstances then all of us understand what it means for someone else to step in and pay off that debt – indeed, many of us will at some time have been that someone else! We all know how sin (for instance, theft, greed, etc.) can get us into this kind of debt. We also understand the payment of a penalty, a fine, or a ransom to free a hostage. This kind of debt envisages a payment to someone. There are other kinds of "payment", of course, that do not involve debt. We might say that Sydney Carton paid the (ultimate) price for taking the place of Darnay in *The Tale of Two Cities*.[32] That price was very real, but there was no one to whom he paid it. Hitchens (like the rest of us) can understand and respect noble sacrifice of this ultimate kind. The principle of vicariousness – one taking the place of another – is something with which we are all familiar at some level.

Hitchens now reaches his moral impasse: "I cannot absolve you of your responsibilities. It would be immoral of me to offer and immoral of you to accept." His point is that one human being cannot absolve the sins of another human being. Hitchens is not the first to raise this issue. It was put to Jesus himself by the religious experts of the time. The scribes were shocked and angered when Jesus said to a paralysed man, "your sins are forgiven."[33]

The point has real substance. If I have seriously wronged and damaged you, when you get me to court what would you think if the judge said to me "I forgive you"? You would have every right to protest: "Wait a minute, this is absurd. Even though you are the judge, you cannot forgive this man. It is me he has wronged, not you. It is my prerogative to forgive and mine alone."

One of the most famous books to deal with this matter in depth is *The Sunflower* by Simon Wiesenthal.[34] It tells a deeply moving story of how Wiesenthal, while incarcerated in a concentration camp in Ukraine, was taken by a hospital orderly into a room where a young Nazi soldier was dying. The soldier, who was unknown to Wiesenthal, told him that he had taken part in a horrific SS atrocity in the city of Dnepropetrovsk – blowing up a house full of Jewish families and shooting them as they tried in vain to leap to safety. The Nazi begged Wiesenthal, as a representative Jew, to forgive him.

Wiesenthal listened and then departed without a word. When he subsequently related the incident to some friends in the camp, one of them, Josek, stayed behind to talk privately. "'Do you know," he began, "when you were telling us about your meeting with the SS man, I feared at first that you had really forgiven him. You would have had no right to do this in the name of people who had not authorized you to do so. What people have done to you yourself, you can, if you like, forgive and forget. That is your own affair. But it would have been a terrible sin to burden your conscience with other people's sufferings... What he has done to other people you are in no position to forgive."

Wiesenthal, who subsequently went through great uncertainty as to the rightness of his decision, ends his book by saying: "The crux of the matter is, of course, the question of forgiveness. Forgetting is something that time alone takes care of, but forgiveness is an act of volition, and only the sufferer is qualified to make the decision."

In common with Hitchens and the ancient scribes who challenged Jesus' right to forgive the sins of the paralysed man, Wiesenthal naturally assumes a situation in which the participants, let's call them X, Y, and Z, were merely human; in which case it is clear that X could not forgive the sins that Y had committed against Z.

What makes all the difference in the case of Jesus is that *he wasn't just another human being*. He could bear other people's sins, as a true mediator, because he was both God and man. He was human but never merely human: he was none other than God incarnate. And sin is ultimately against God. Now the New Atheists choke at this and reject it out of hand. But they should notice that it is their rejection of the incarnation that is responsible for their failure to see any significance in the cross. The cross and the incarnation are inseparable.

At the beginning of the story of the incarnation, Joseph, the husband of Mary, Jesus' mother, was told: "Do not fear to take Mary as your wife, for that which is conceived in her is from the Holy Spirit. She will bear a son, and you shall call his name Jesus, for he will save his people from their sins."[35] From the beginning, therefore, Jesus' very name bore witness to the fact that he was to be the sin-bearer. The prophet John the Baptist announced Jesus to the nation with the dramatic words: "Behold, the Lamb of God, who takes away the sin of the world!"[36]

For centuries the nation of Israel had been taught the seriousness of sin by having to kill a lamb to atone for their sin. This procedure vividly taught them at a basic level what experience constantly underlines – that sin enslaves, it is ultimately a killer, and therefore needs to be atoned for. The death of animals never really dealt with the problem, of course, as the Bible itself recognizes.[37] The prophet John announced that Jesus was the reality that the sacrificial lambs foreshadowed: Jesus was the real Lamb who could actually atone for sin. The imagery was unmistakeable. Jesus would one day die for his people's sin.

Jesus confirmed this by saying of himself: "The Son of Man came not to be served but to serve, and to give his life as a ransom for many."[38] At the Last Supper in Jerusalem, when he instituted the ceremony by which his first disciples and all subsequent believers should remember him, he chose bread and wine as eloquent symbols of his death: "This is my body, which is given for you. Do this in remembrance of me... This cup that is poured out for you is the new covenant in my blood."[39]

Incidentally, this completely refutes the widespread but erroneous idea that it was St Paul who "spoiled Christianity" by introducing the Jewish notion of vicarious suffering that was foreign to Christ's intentions. For, the communion service was deliberately designed, not by Paul but by Christ himself, to give people an unmistakeable reminder of why he died: his body given and his blood shed, for our sins. Paul understood its significance in exactly the same way as the Gospel writers. In what most scholars accept as one of the earliest and most important statements of the Christian message, Paul wrote, "For I delivered to you as of first importance what I also received: that Christ died for our sins in accordance with the Scriptures, that he was buried, that he was raised on the third day in accordance with the Scriptures".[40] The death of Christ for sin was not an innovation by Paul, or indeed of the Gospel writers. It was predicted in the Old Testament, for instance in the famous words of the prophet Isaiah regarding the suffering servant messiah: "He was wounded for our transgressions; he was crushed for our iniquities; upon him was the chastisement that brought us peace, and with his stripes we are healed."[41]

According to the New Testament, then, it took nothing less than the incarnation and the death of the Son of God on the cross in order for God to effect reconciliation between man and God. The message is this:

In Christ God was reconciling the world to himself, not counting their trespasses against them, and entrusting to us the message of reconciliation. Therefore, we are ambassadors for Christ, God making his appeal through us. We implore you on behalf of Christ, be reconciled to God. For our sake he made him to be sin who knew no sin, so that in him we might become the righteousness of God.[42]

Does anyone fully understand this? No – and that should not surprise us. If the cleverest of scientists do not fully understand things like energy, light and gravity, how could anyone ever hope to fathom this most profound of all events in the history of the universe – the crucifixion of God incarnate? There is inevitably a deep mystery surrounding the cross. Yet the rich biblical terminology – ransom, justification, reconciliation, etc.[43] – gives us sufficient insight to grasp the adequacy of the salvation that Jesus came to bring. It is very deep – but so is the problem with which it deals. It is also unique. Christ does not compete with any other religion, philosophy, or way of life here; for the simple reason that no one else has ever done what he has done, nor can or does offer us what he offers – forgiveness and peace with God, that depend not on our merit but on our trust in the grace and gift of God.

Contemporary New Atheist mockery will no more diminish what Christ did on the cross than did the mockery of those who were involved in his trial and crucifixion twenty centuries ago. Such mockery is nothing new. The historian Luke records: "Herod with his soldiers treated him with contempt and mocked him… the rulers scoffed at him, saying, 'He saved others; let him save himself, if he is the Christ of God, his Chosen One!' The soldiers also mocked him, coming up and offering him sour wine and saying, 'If you are the King of the Jews, save yourself!'"[44]

Even one of the two brigands[45] crucified with Jesus "railed at him, saying, 'Are you not the Christ? Save yourself and us!'" But saving himself is precisely what Jesus could not do, if he was the saviour he claimed to be. C. S. Lewis writes: "'He saved others, himself he cannot save' is a *definition* of the Kingdom. All salvation, everywhere and at all times, in great things or in little, is vicarious."[46]

The other brigand did not join in the jeering that was all around him. He had been thinking, inasmuch as a man in such excruciating agony could think. He sensed there was something going on around him that was a travesty of justice. He felt so strongly about it that, overcoming his pain, he rebuked his fellow criminal on the other cross for his mockery. "'Do you not fear God?" he said, "You got the same sentence as he did, but in our case we deserved it; we are paying for what we did. But this man has done nothing wrong.'"[47] Greek scholar Professor David Gooding takes up the story and explains how it gives profound insight into the nature of forgiveness:

> The first malefactor was suffering the consequence of his misdeeds in the form of temporal punishment inflicted by the government. For all his pain there was with him apparently no fear of God, no confession of guilt before God, no expression of repentance, no request even for divine forgiveness. He was prepared to believe that Jesus was the Messiah if he would do a miracle and release him from the temporal punishment that was the consequence of his crimes. When Jesus made no attempt to do that, he cursed him and his religion as a cheat. But to save people simply from the temporal consequences of their sins, without first bringing them to repentance and reconciliation with God, would be no true salvation at all. It would but encourage people to repeat their sins under the impression that any ugly or inconvenient consequences could and would be miraculously removed by a fairy godmother. No paradise could be built on such an irresponsible attitude to sin.
>
> It was different with the second malefactor. Reflection on the fact that Christ was innocent and yet was suffering along with the guilty convinced his conscience that there must be in the world to come a judgement in which the injustices of this world are put right. That in turn awoke in his heart a healthy fear of God, which led him to repentance and a frank acknowledgement of his sinfulness. Even the temporal punishment inflicted by the state, he owned, was well deserved and he made no request for a miracle to be done to let him off the consequences of his sins (see 23:40–41). Again reflection on the fact that Christ was suffering innocently led him to believe that he was indeed Messiah the King; and that if he was Messiah, and there was a God who cared about justice, then all he had heard about the resurrection must be true: Messiah would be raised from the dead and "come in his kingdom".

Perhaps it was hearing Christ's prayer to his Father to forgive the soldiers who crucified him; perhaps it was an instinct born of the Holy Spirit; but whatever it was that caused it, there arose in his heart the faith to realise that while there was no question of his being released from the temporal consequences of his crimes, there was every possibility of his being delivered from the wrath of God and from the eternal penalty of sin. With that there also came a deep change within his heart. He no longer wanted to be a rebel; he wanted nothing more than to be allowed to become a subject of the King in his eternal kingdom, if the King would have him. "Jesus," he said, "remember me when you come in your kingdom" (23:42).

The King's reply granted not only immediate forgiveness but also spelled out for the dying malefactor, and for all who repent and believe, what forgiveness involves: immediate and complete acceptance with God; the assurance that upon death he would be received directly into the presence of the King, without any interval he would be "with Christ"; and admission to paradise where there shall be no more pain, crying, sin or curse (22:43). "Today," said Christ, "you shall be with me in paradise." A rebel had been converted: is not that the true work of a king?"[48]

CHAPTER 7

ARE MIRACLES PURE FANTASY?[1]

"A miracle is a violation of the laws of nature; and as a firm and unalterable experience has established these laws, the proof against a miracle, from the very nature of the fact, is as entire as any argument from experience as can be imagined."
David Hume

"Generations of Humeans have... been misled into offering analyses of causation and of natural law that have been far too weak because they had no basis for accepting the existence of either cause and effect or natural laws... Hume's scepticism about cause and effect and his agnosticism about the external world are of course jettisoned the moment he leaves his study."
Anthony Flew

The vehement reaction of the New Atheists against miracles springs from the fact that they are convinced that miracles "violate the principle of science".[2] In his debate with Jay Richards at Stanford, Christopher Hitchens asked Richards if he believed that Jesus was resurrected from the dead. When Richards replied in the affirmative, Hitchens then asked if he believed that Jesus Christ was born of a virgin. Richards again said that he did. "I rest my case," Hitchens responded. "This is an honest guy, who has just made it very clear [that] science has nothing to do with his worldview."[3] To this I would in turn respond that Hitchens has just made it clear that understanding what science can and cannot do is not one of his strengths.

The same is true of Richard Dawkins. My debate with him in Oxford was on the question "Has Science Buried God?" The debate was staged in the Oxford Museum of Natural History, a place certainly famous for a previous debate there in 1860 between Thomas Henry Huxley and Bishop Samuel Wilberforce, on Charles Darwin's *Origin of Species*. That debate is now commemorated with the *Darwin Plinth*, placed at the main entrance to the museum in 2010. On the way in to the debate through that entrance I had a sudden recollection that the building had an interesting history connected with Christianity; but I could not quite focus, with the pre-debate pressure. I mentioned it tentatively to Dawkins in the debate; he said no, there was no connection. But he was wrong. In fact, the building was the project of Sir Henry Acland, Regius Professor of Medicine in the University, whose aim was to bring all aspects of science together around a central display area. In an 1858 lecture Acland explained that the reason for the building's construction was to give people the opportunity to learn of the natural world, and obtain the "knowledge of the great material design of which the Supreme Master-Worker has made us a constituent part". Not only that, but a considerable proportion of the money given towards the museum's construction budget came out of profits made by the Oxford University Press from its success in printing Bibles!

As I reflected on this afterwards I realized that there was a wonderful irony here. (I wish I had thought of it at the time, but such is the brilliance of hindsight!) Dawkins was supposed to be presenting the case that science has buried God – in a building constructed specifically to show that science showed the glory of God; and in his opening statement he identified me as an Oxford mathematician who believed in miracles! I should have thought that this might reasonably be taken as evidence that science has *not* buried God.

Dawkins was mocking me for believing what he considers to be ridiculous, but his mockery is hollow. Mockery is not an argument. It is an attitude, and it does no credit to the person who employs it in this connection. If there is a God who created the universe, then surely there is no difficulty in believing that he could do special things. Of course, whether he has actually done so on a specific occasion is a different matter. Francis Collins, who does believe in the miracles of Jesus, remarks wisely:

It is crucial that a healthy scepticism be applied when interpreting potentially miraculous events, lest the integrity and rationality of the

religious perspective be brought into question. The only thing that will kill the possibility of miracles more quickly than a committed materialism is the claiming of miracle status for everyday events for which natural explanations are readily at hand.[4]

For that reason I shall concentrate on the miracles recorded in the New Testament.

There is an important distinction to be made between miracles and supernatural events. Miracles (genuine miracles, that is) are supernatural events; but not all supernatural events are miracles in the strict sense. For instance, the origin of the universe and its laws, though a supernatural event, should probably not be subsumed under the rubric of miracle. Strictly speaking, miracles concern events that are exceptions to recognized laws. As such they clearly *presuppose* the existence of the normal course of things. It follows, then, that it does not really make sense to think of the creation of the normal course of things as a miracle.

We note here that Richard Dawkins confesses he does not know what caused the origin of the universe; but he believes (yes, his faith is shining out once more) that one day there will be a naturalistic explanation of it. As he said in our Oxford debate, he does not need to resort to magic to explain the universe. However, in the press conference after the debate, he responded to a question from Melanie Phillips, a journalist and author, by saying that he believed the universe could have just appeared from nothing. "Magic," she said. Presently she reported that Dawkins had told her afterwards that an explanation for the universe in terms of LGM (little green men) made more sense than postulating a Creator. Anything but God, it would seem.

The Christian gospel is based squarely on a miracle. It was the miracle of the resurrection of Christ that started it going, and that same miracle is its central message. Indeed, the basic qualification of a Christian apostle was to be an eyewitness of the resurrection.[5] C. S. Lewis expresses the situation precisely: "The first fact in the history of Christendom is a number of people who say they have seen the Resurrection. If they had died without making anyone else believe this 'gospel', no Gospels would ever have been written."[6] According to the early Christians, then, without the resurrection there simply is no Christian message. Paul writes: "If Christ has not been raised, then our preaching is in vain and your faith is in vain."[7]

DAVID HUME AND MIRACLES

It is here that the Christian gospel conflicts with the widely held notion that science has rendered miracles impossible. Christopher Hitchens pointed this out to me in our debate in Alabama, citing the Scottish Enlightenment philosopher David Hume as having said the last word on this.

Hitchens was referring of course to a famous essay Hume wrote, in which he said:

A miracle is a violation of the laws of nature; and as a firm and unalterable experience has established these laws, the proof against a miracle, from the very nature of the fact, is as entire as any argument from experience as can be imagined... It is no miracle that a man, seemingly in good health, should die on a sudden: because such a kind of death, though more unusual than any other, has yet been frequently observed to happen. But it is a miracle that a dead man should come to life; because that has never been observed, in any age or country. There must, therefore, be a uniform experience against every miraculous event; otherwise the event would not merit that appellation.[8]

Hume is actually advancing two arguments here, although they overlap.

1. The argument from the uniformity of nature:

   a. Miracles are violations of the laws of nature.

   b. These laws have been established by "firm and unalterable" experience.

   c. Therefore, the argument against miracles is as good as any argument from experience can be.

2. The argument from the uniformity of experience:

   a. Unusual, yet frequently observed, events are not miracles – like a healthy person suddenly dropping dead.

   b. A resurrection would be a miracle because it has never been observed anywhere at any time.

   c. There is uniform experience against every miraculous event; otherwise it would not be called miraculous.

It is interesting that Hume here selects resurrection as an example of a miracle. The fact is that atheists universally recognize that the supernatural would have to be involved in the "standing up"[9] of a body again.

THE ARGUMENT FROM THE UNIFORMITY OF NATURE – HUME'S SELF-CONTRADICTORY POSITION

Hume denies miracle, because miracle would go against the uniform laws of nature. But elsewhere he denies the uniformity of nature! He famously argues that, just because the sun has been observed to rise in the morning for thousands of years, it does not mean that we can be sure that it will rise tomorrow.[10] This is an example of the *Problem of Induction*: on the basis of past experience you cannot predict the future, says Hume. But if that were true, let us see what it implies in particular. Suppose Hume is right, and no dead man has ever risen up from the grave through the whole of earth's history so far; by his own argument he still cannot be sure that a dead man will not rise up tomorrow. That being so, he cannot rule out miracle. What has become now of Hume's insistence on the laws of nature, and its uniformity? He has destroyed the very basis on which he tries to deny the possibility of miracles.

The same argument would work just as well backward in time, as forward. For instance, the fact that no one has been observed to rise from the dead in the past thousand years is no guarantee that there was no resurrection before that. To illustrate this, we might say that uniform experience over the past three hundred years shows that kings of England are not decapitated. If you knew this, and were faced with the claim that King Charles I was decapitated, you might refuse to believe it, because it goes against uniform experience. You would be wrong! He *was* beheaded. Uniformity is one thing; absolute uniformity is another.

In any case, if according to Hume we can infer no regularities, it would be impossible even to speak of laws of nature, let alone the uniformity of nature with respect to those laws. And if nature is not uniform, then using the uniformity of nature as an argument against miracles is simply absurd.

In light of this fundamental inconsistency, I find it astonishing that Hume's argument has been responsible to a large extent for the widespread contemporary view (at least in the Western world) that we have a straightforward choice between mutually exclusive alternatives: either we believe in miracles, or we believe in the scientific understanding of the laws of nature; but not both. For instance, Richard Dawkins claims: "The nineteenth century is the last time when it was possible for an educated person to admit to believing in miracles like the virgin birth without embarrassment. When pressed, many educated Christians are too loyal to deny the virgin birth and the resurrection. But it embarrasses them because their rational minds know that it is absurd, so they would much rather not be asked."[11]

It cannot, however, be as simple as Dawkins thinks; since there are highly intelligent, eminent scientists, such as Professor Phillips (Physics Nobel Prizewinner 1998), Professor John Polkinghorne FRS (Quantum Physicist, Cambridge), and the current Director of the National Institute of Health and former Director of the Human Genome Project, Francis Collins (to name just three) who, though well aware of Hume's argument, nevertheless publicly, and without either embarrassment or any sense of irrationality or absurdity, affirm their belief in the supernatural, and in particular in the resurrection of Christ, which they regard as the supreme evidence for the truth of the Christian worldview.

This shows that it is clearly no necessary part of being a scientist that one should reject either the possibility (or the actuality) of miracles. To see why such scientists do not feel threatened by Hume, we shall now look more closely at his notion that miracles constitute "violations of the laws of nature".

MIRACLES AND THE LAWS OF NATURE

It has been one of the impressive achievements of science, not only to describe what goes on in the universe but also to discover the laws that govern its workings. Since Hume defines miracles to be violations of those laws, it will be important for us to understand what scientists think those laws are. Scientific laws are not simply descriptions of what happens, although they are at least that. They arise from our perception of the essential processes involved in any given phenomenon. That is, the laws are giving us insight into the internal logic of a system, in terms of the cause and effect relationships of its constituent parts.

It is here that we run up against a surprising self-contradictory element in Hume's position, for Hume denies the very cause and effect relationships that are involved in formulating these laws! He says: "All events seem entirely loose and separate. One event follows another; but we never can observe any tie between them. They seem conjoined, but never connected."[12] Hume then gives the example of someone watching a moving billiard ball collide with a stationary one, and he sees the second ball begin to move. But, according to Hume, the first time he had ever seen such a thing:

> He could not pronounce that the one event was connected but only that it was conjoined with the other. After he has observed several instances of this nature, he then pronounces them to be connected. What alteration has happened to give rise to this new idea of connection? Nothing, but that he now feels these events to be connected in his imagination, and can readily foretell the existence of one from the appearance of the other. *When we say, therefore, that one object is connected with another, we mean only that they have acquired a connection in our thought...*

I have italicized the last sentence to emphasize the fact that Hume explicitly denies the idea of necessary connection. He would thus undermine a great deal of modern science, since scientific laws involve precisely what Hume denies: cause-effect descriptions of the workings of a system. For example, Hume would admit that there are many cases of smoking being associated with lung cancer, but he would deny any causal relationship. If true, this would undermine the scientifically established relationship between smoking and lung cancer. And just think of what would be left of atomic physics, if we were not allowed to infer the existence of elementary particles from the tracks we observe in a bubble-chamber!

In a famous attack on Hume's theory of causation, the eminent mathematician and philosopher Sir Alfred North Whitehead pointed out that we all have many everyday experiences in which we are directly aware of cause and effect connections: for example, the reflex action in which a person in a dark room blinks when an electric light is turned on. Obviously, the person is aware that the light flash causes the blink. Research shows that the photon stream from the bulb impinges on the eye, stimulates activity in the optic nerve, and excites certain parts of the brain. This scientifically demonstrates that there is a complex causal chain.[13]

We conclude that there are two major reasons why Hume's view of miracles is deeply flawed:

1. Because he denies that the uniformity of nature can be established, he cannot turn round and use it to disprove miracle;

2. Because he denies necessary causation, he cannot regard nature as described by laws embodying necessary relationships that would preclude miracle.

Philosopher Anthony Flew, a world authority on Hume and one-time much feted atheist, radically revised his assessment of Hume, saying that his (Flew's) celebrated book needs to be re-written:

> ... in the light of my new-found awareness that Hume was utterly wrong to maintain that we have no experience, and hence no genuine ideas, of making things happen and preventing things from happening, of physical necessity and physical impossibility. Generations of Humeans have in consequence been misled into offering analyses of causation and of natural law that have been far too weak because they had no basis for accepting the existence of either cause and effect or natural laws... Hume's scepticism about cause and effect and his agnosticism about the external world are of course jettisoned the moment he leaves his study.[14]

Distinguished philosopher of science John Earman writes:

> It is not simply that Hume's essay does not achieve its goals, but that his goals are ambiguous and confused. Most of Hume's considerations are unoriginal, warmed over versions of arguments that are found in the writings of predecessors and contemporaries. And the parts of "Of Miracles" that set Hume apart do not stand up to scrutiny. Worse still, the essay reveals the weakness and the poverty of Hume's own account of induction and probabilistic reasoning. And to cap it all off, the essay represents the kind of overreaching that gives philosophy a bad name.[15]

In light of all this it is strange that authors like Christopher Hitchens think that Hume wrote "the last word on the subject".[16] He was not shy in pointing that out to me at our debate on his book in Birmingham, Alabama. Hitchens is not a scientist, but Dawkins and others do not have the same excuse.

To be fair, however, not all who regard miracles as violations of the laws of nature would argue along with Hume; and so we must further consider this issue from the perspective of contemporary science and its thinking about the laws of nature. Precisely because scientific laws embody cause-effect relationships, scientists nowadays do not regard them as capable merely of describing what has happened in the past. Provided we are not working at the quantum level, such laws can successfully predict what will happen in the future with such accuracy that, for example, the orbits of communication satellites can be precisely calculated, and moon and Mars landings are possible.

It is understandable, therefore, that many scientists resent the idea that some god could arbitrarily intervene, and alter, suspend, reverse, or otherwise "violate" these laws of nature. For that would seem to them to contradict the immutability of those laws, and thus overturn the very basis of the scientific understanding of the universe. As a corollary to this, many such scientists would advance two arguments:

Argument 1. Belief in miracles in general, and New Testament miracles in particular, arose in a primitive, pre-scientific culture where people were ignorant of the laws of nature, and readily accepted miracle stories.

Hume endorses this view, when he says that accounts of miracles "are observed chiefly to abound among ignorant and barbarous nations."[17] However plausible this explanation may seem at first sight, it is in fact nonsense when applied to the New Testament miracles. A moment's thought will show us that, in order to recognize some event as a miracle, there must be some perceived regularity to which that event is an apparent exception! You cannot recognize something that is abnormal, if you do not know what is normal.

This was recognized long ago. It is interesting that the historian Luke, who was a doctor trained in the medical science of his day, begins his biography of Christ by raising this very matter.[18] He tells the story of a man, Zechariah, and of his wife, Elizabeth, who for many years had prayed for a son because she was barren. When, in his old age, an angel appeared to him and told him that his former prayers were about to be answered and that his wife would conceive and bear a son, he very politely but firmly refused to believe it. The reason he gave was that he was now old and his wife's body decrepit. For him and his wife to have a child at this stage would run counter to all that he knew of the laws of nature. The interesting thing about him is this: he was no atheist; he was a priest who believed in God, in the existence of angels, and in the value of prayer. But if the promised fulfilment of his prayer was going to involve a reversal of the laws of nature, he was not prepared to believe it.

Luke here makes it obvious that the early Christians were not a credulous bunch, unaware of the laws of nature, and therefore prepared to believe any miraculous story, however absurd. They felt the difficulty in believing the story of such a miracle, just like anyone would today. If in the end they believed, it was because they were forced to by the sheer weight of the direct evidence presented to them, not through their ignorance of nature's laws.

Similarly, in his account of the rise of Christianity, Luke shows us that the first opposition to the Christian message of the resurrection of Jesus Christ came not from atheists, but from the Sadducean High Priests in Judaism.[19] They were highly religious men. They believed in God. They said their prayers and conducted the services in the temple. But that did not mean that the first time they heard the claim that Jesus had risen from the dead they believed it. They did not believe it; for they had embraced a worldview that denied the possibility of bodily resurrection of any one at all, let alone that of Jesus Christ.[20]

Indeed, they shared a widespread conviction. Historian Tom Wright says:

Ancient paganism contains all kinds of theories, but whenever resurrection is mentioned, the answer is a firm negative: we know that doesn't happen. (This is worth stressing in today's context. One sometimes hears it said or implied that prior to the rise of modern science people believed in all kinds of odd things like resurrection but that now, with two hundred years of scientific research on our side, we know that dead people stay dead. This is ridiculous. The evidence, and the conclusion, was massive and massively drawn in the ancient world as it is today.)[21]

To suppose, then, that Christianity was born in a pre-scientific, credulous, and ignorant world is simply false to the facts. The ancient world knew the law of nature as well as we do, that dead bodies do not get up out of graves. Christianity won its way by dint of the sheer weight of evidence that one man had actually risen from the dead.

Argument 2. Now that we know the laws of nature, belief in miracles is impossible.

The idea that miracles are "violations" of the laws of nature involves another fallacy, which C. S. Lewis illustrated by the following analogy:

> If this week I put a thousand pounds in the drawer of my desk, add two thousand next week and another thousand the week thereafter, the laws of arithmetic allow me to predict that the next time I come to my drawer, I shall find four thousand pounds. But suppose when I next open the drawer, I find only one thousand pounds, what shall I conclude? That the laws of arithmetic have been broken? Certainly not! I might more reasonably conclude that some thief has broken the laws of the State and stolen three thousand pounds out of my drawer. One thing it would be ludicrous to claim is that the laws of arithmetic make it impossible to believe in the existence of such a thief or the possibility of his intervention. On the contrary, it is the normal workings of those laws that have exposed the existence and activity of the thief.[22]

The analogy also helps point out that the scientific use of the word "law" is not the same as the legal use, where we often think of a law as constraining someone's actions.[23] There is no sense in which the laws of arithmetic constrain or pressurize the thief in our story! Newton's law of gravitation tells me that if I drop an apple it will fall towards the centre of the earth. But that law does not prevent someone intervening, and catching the apple as it descends. In other words, the law predicts what will happen, provided there is no change in the conditions under which the experiment is conducted.

Thus, from the theistic perspective, the laws of nature predict what is bound to happen if God does not intervene; though, of course, it is no act of theft, if the Creator intervenes in his own creation. It is plainly fallacious to argue that the laws of nature make it impossible for us to believe in the existence of God and the possibility of his intervention in the universe. It would be like claiming that an understanding of the laws of the internal combustion engine makes it impossible to believe that the designer of a motor car, or one of his mechanics, could or would intervene and remove the cylinder head. Of course they could intervene. Moreover, this intervention would not destroy those laws. The very same laws that explained why the engine worked with the cylinder head on would now explain why it does not work with the head removed.

It is, therefore, inaccurate and misleading to say with Hume that miracles "violate" the laws of nature. Once more C. S. Lewis is very helpful:

If God annihilates or creates or deflects a unit of matter, He has created a new situation at that point. Immediately all nature domiciles this new situation, makes it at home in her realm, adapts all other events to it. It finds itself conforming to all the laws. If God creates a miraculous spermatozoon in the body of a virgin, it does not proceed to break any laws. The laws at once take over. Nature is ready. Pregnancy follows, according to all the normal laws, and nine months later a child is born.[24]

In this vein we could say that it is a law of nature that human beings do not rise again from the dead *by some natural mechanism*. But Christians do not claim that Christ rose from the dead by such a mechanism. They claim that he rose from the dead by supernatural power. By themselves, the laws of nature cannot rule out that possibility. When a miracle takes place, it is the laws of nature that alert us to the fact that it is a miracle. It is important to grasp that Christians do not deny the laws of nature, as Hume implies they do. It is an essential part of the Christian position to believe in the laws of nature as descriptions of those regularities and cause-effect relationships built into the universe by its Creator and according to which it normally operates. If we did not know them, we should never recognize a miracle if we saw one.

THE ARGUMENT FROM THE UNIFORMITY OF EXPERIENCE

In anybody's book, miracles, by definition, are exceptions to what normally happens. If miracles were normal, they wouldn't be called miracles! What, then, does Hume mean by "uniform experience"? It is one thing to say "Experience shows that such and such normally happens, but there may be exceptions, although none has been observed, that is, the experience *we have had* has been uniform." It is an entirely different thing to say, "This is what we normally experience, and we must always experience it, for there can be and are no exceptions."

Hume appears to favour the second definition. For him, a miracle is something that has never been experienced before; for if it had been experienced before, you could no longer call it a miracle. But that is a very arbitrary statement. Why can there not have been a succession of miracles in the past, as well as the particular one we may be discussing at the moment? What Hume does is to assume what he wants to prove, namely that there have never been any miracles in the past, and so there is uniform experience against this present instance being a miracle. But here his argument runs into very serious trouble. How does he know? In order to know that experience against miracles is absolutely uniform, he would need to have total access to every event in the universe at all times and places, which is self-evidently impossible. It would seem that Hume has forgotten that humans have only ever observed a tiny fraction of the sum total of events that have occurred in the universe; and in any case, very few of the total of all human observations have been written down. Therefore, Hume cannot know that miracles have never occurred. He is simply assuming what he wants to prove – that nature is uniform, and no miracles have taken place!

The only real alternative to Hume's circular argument, of course, is to be open to the possibility that miracles have occurred. That is a historical question, and not a philosophical one, and depends on witness and evidence. But Hume does not appear willing to consider the question of whether there is any valid historical evidence that a miracle or miracles have taken place. He simply denies it, claiming that experience against miracles is "firm and unalterable". But, we repeat, his claim has no substance unless he has demonstrated that all reports of miracles are false. He singularly fails even to attempt to do this, so there is simply no way in which he can know the answer. The New Atheists follow him like sheep. But, on this issue, he is a blind guide.

HUME'S CRITERIA FOR EVIDENCE, AND THE CREDIBILITY OF WITNESSES

Not unreasonably, Hume thinks, "A wise man proportions his belief to the evidence."[25] It means that, when faced with, say, the report of a miracle, the wise person will weigh up all the evidence for the miracle on the one side, and all the evidence against it on the other, and then come to his decision. Hume adds a further criterion to aid this process:

> **No testimony is sufficient to establish a miracle, unless the testimony be of such a kind, that its falsehood be more miraculous, than the fact which it endeavours to establish... When anyone tells me that he saw a dead man restored to life, I immediately consider with myself, whether it be more probable that this person should either deceive or be deceived, or that the fact, which he relates, should really have happened. I weigh the one miracle against the other; and according to the superiority, which I discover, I pronounce my decision, and always reject the greater miracle. If the falsehood of his testimony would be more miraculous, than the event which he relates; then, and not until then, can he pretend to command my belief or opinion.[26]**

Let us examine what Hume is saying here. Suppose someone tells you that a miracle has happened. You have to decide whether it is true or false. If the character of the witness is dubious, you would be likely to dismiss his story out of hand. However, if the witness is of known moral integrity, you turn next to the actual thing that is claimed. Hume's view is that you must reject it as false, unless believing in its falsity would land you in such an impossible situation, and have such totally inexplicable implications in history, that you would need an even bigger miracle to explain them.

HUME'S CRITERIA APPLIED TO THE IDEA THAT THE DISCIPLES WERE FRAUDSTERS

This criterion of Hume's is precisely what Christians will use! Academician Professor Sir Norman Anderson, formerly Director of the Institute of Advanced Legal Studies in the University of London, writes in the opening words of his book *The Evidence for the Resurrection*:

> Easter is not primarily a comfort, but a challenge. Its message is either the supreme fact in history or else a gigantic hoax... If it is true, then it is the supreme fact of history; and to fail to adjust one's life to its implications means irreparable loss. But if it is not true, if Christ be not risen, then the whole of Christianity is a fraud, foisted on the world by a company of consummate liars, or, at best, deluded simpletons. St Paul himself realised this when he wrote: *If Christ be not risen, then our preaching is meaningless, and your faith worthless. More, we are found to be false witnesses.* [27]

Centuries before Hume, the Christian apostle Paul saw the issue clearly: either Christ is risen from the dead, or he and the other apostles are deliberate perpetrators of fraud.[28] But then the question cannot be avoided: is it possible to believe that Christ's apostles were the kind of men who would concoct a lie, foist it somehow upon their followers, and not only watch them go to their deaths for it, but themselves pay for their deliberate lie with prison, constant harassment and suffering, and eventually with their lives?

We must remember that, at the very beginning of Christianity, the apostles Peter and John were imprisoned twice by the authorities for preaching the resurrection.[29] Not long afterwards John's brother, James, was murdered by Herod. Can we imagine that John would have been prepared to keep silent while his brother suffered like that, if he knew the resurrection was a lie? By the time John died as an old man, exiled for his faith on the island of Patmos, many people had given their lives in the name of the risen Christ. John explicitly tells us that he would not be prepared to condone a lie even in a good cause. His reason was: *we know that no lie comes from the truth.*[30] Was John the kind of man then, who would watch his brother, and others as well, die for a lie that he himself had concocted? Hardly. And what about Peter? Historical tradition tells us that he was eventually martyred – as Jesus had indicated to him.[31] Was he likely to have allowed himself to be martyred for what he knew to be a lie?

In any case, is it reasonable to suppose that none of the disciples who perpetrated such a fraud would never have broken under torture, and confessed that it was a fraud? No – it is frankly impossible to believe that they were deliberate liars. Hence, according to Hume's criterion, if believing that the disciples were deliberate liars would involve a totally inexplicable historical and moral contradiction, then we must accept their testimony, as millions have done over the last twenty centuries.

HUME'S CRITERIA APPLIED TO THE CAUSE OF THE RISE OF CHRISTIANITY

The existence of the Christian church throughout the world is an indisputable fact. In the spirit of Hume's criterion we ask: what explanation is adequate to explain the transformation of the early disciples? From a frightened group of men and women – utterly depressed and disillusioned at what was to them the calamity that had befallen their movement when their leader was crucified – there suddenly exploded a powerful international movement which rapidly established itself all over the Roman empire, and ultimately all over the world. And the striking thing is that the early disciples were all Jews, a religion not noted for its enthusiasm in making converts from other nations. What could have been powerful enough to set all of this going?

If we ask the early church, they will answer at once that it was the resurrection of Jesus. Indeed, they maintained that the very reason and purpose for their existence was to be a witness to the resurrection of Christ. That is, they came into existence, not to promulgate some political programme or campaign for moral renovation; but primarily to bear witness to the fact that God had intervened in history, raised Christ from the dead, and that forgiveness of sins could be received in his name. This message would ultimately have major moral implications for society; but it was the message of the resurrection itself that was central.

If we reject the early Christians' own explanation for their existence, on the basis that it involves too big a miracle, what are we going to put in its place that will not involve an even greater strain on our capacity for belief? To deny the resurrection simply leaves the church without a *raison d'être*, which is historically and psychologically absurd.

Professor C. F. D. Moule of Cambridge wrote:

If the coming into existence of the Nazarenes, a phenomenon undeniably attested by the New Testament, rips a great hole in history, a hole the size and shape of the Resurrection, what does the secular historian propose to stop it up with?... the birth and rapid rise of the Christian Church... remain an unsolved enigma for any historian who refuses to take seriously the only explanation offered by the Church itself.[32]

HUME'S FURTHER OBJECTIONS TO MIRACLES

So far Hume's criterion makes good sense. But then he goes on to show that he is not content to proceed with an even-handed assessment of evidence in order to decide whether a miracle has happened or not. He has determined the verdict against miracles in advance, without allowing any trial to take place! In his very next paragraph he says that he has been far too liberal in imagining that the "testimony on which a miracle is founded may amount to an entire proof", since "there never was a miraculous event established on so full an evidence". But this is precisely what Christians will dispute. They will claim, for instance, that there is strong historical evidence for the resurrection of Christ, evidence that Hume never seems to have considered.

Hume's logic, then, looks something like this:

1. The laws of nature describe regularities.

2. Miracles are singularities, exceptions to the regular course of nature, and exceedingly rare.

3. Evidence for what is regular and repeatable must always be more than the evidence for what is singular and unrepeatable.

4. The wise man bases his belief on the weight of evidence.

5. Therefore no wise man can ever believe in miracles.

In other words, although at first Hume seems to be open to the theoretical possibility of a miracle having occurred provided the evidence is strong enough, he eventually reveals that from the beginning he is completely convinced that there can never be enough evidence to persuade a rational person that a miracle has happened, because rational people know that miracles cannot happen! Hume lays himself open to the charge of begging the question.

The idea in point 3 above, that evidence for what is regular and repeatable must always be more than the evidence for what is singular and unrepeatable, is heavily emphasized by Anthony Flew in his original defence of Hume's argument.[33] Flew argues that "the proposition reporting the (alleged) occurrence of the miracle will be singular, particular and in the past tense", and deduces that, since propositions of this sort cannot be tested directly in any case, the evidence for them will always be immeasurably weaker in logical strength, than the evidence for general and repeatable propositions.[34]

However, quite apart from the question of miracle, this argument is inimical to science, the classic example being the origin of the universe. The so-called "Big Bang" is a singularity in the past, an unrepeatable event. So, if Flew's argument is valid, no scientist should be prepared to believe in the Big Bang! Indeed, when scientists began to talk of the universe having a beginning in a singularity, they met strong objections from fellow scientists who held strong uniformitarian views, like those of Flew. However, it was studying the data supplied to them – not theoretical arguments on what was or what was not possible on the basis of an assumed uniformity – that convinced them that the Big Bang was a plausible explanation. It is very important, therefore, to realize that, even when scientists speak of the uniformity of nature, they do not mean absolute uniformity – especially if they believe in singularities like the Big Bang. Flew abandoned his earlier views and become a deist, on the basis of the evidence that the origin of life cannot be fitted into a naturalistic account of the uniformity of nature.

Turning to the question of the resurrection of Christ, what Hume and Flew have overlooked is that it is simply inadequate to judge the likelihood of the occurrence of the resurrection of Jesus on the basis of the observed, very high probability of dead people remaining dead. What they should have done (but did not do) was to weigh the probability of the resurrection of Jesus against the probability of the tomb of Jesus being empty *on any other hypothesis* than the resurrection.[35] We shall do this below.

Hume is aware of course that there are situations where people have understandable difficulty in accepting something because it is outside their experience, but which is nonetheless true. He relates a story of an Indian prince who refused to believe what he was told about the effects of frost.[36] Hume's point is that, although what he was told was not contrary to his experience, it was not conformable with it.

However, even here Hume is not on safe ground. In modern science, especially the theories of relativity and quantum mechanics, there are key ideas that do appear contrary to our experience. A strict application of Hume's principles might well have rejected such ideas, and thus impeded the progress of science! It is often the counterintuitive anomaly, the contrary fact, the exception to past repeated observation and experience, which turns out to be the key to the discovery of a new scientific paradigm. But the crucial thing here is that the exception is a *fact*, however improbable it may be on the basis of past repeated experience. Wise people, particularly if they are scientists, are concerned with facts, not simply with probabilities – even if those facts do not appear to fit into their uniformitarian schemes.

I agree that miracles are inherently improbable. We should certainly demand strong evidence for their happening in any particular case (see Hume's point 5). But this is not the real problem with miracles of the sort found in the New Testament. The real problem is that they threaten the foundations of naturalism, which is clearly Hume's worldview at this point. That is, Hume regards it as axiomatic that nature is all that there is, and there is nothing and no one outside nature that could from time to time intervene in nature. This is what he means when he claims that nature is uniform. His axiom, of course, is simply a belief that arises from his worldview. It is not a consequence of scientific investigation.

Ironically enough, Christians will argue that it is *only belief in a Creator that gives us a satisfactory ground for believing in the uniformity of nature in the first place*. In denying that there is a Creator the atheists are kicking away the basis of their own argument! As C. S. Lewis puts it:

If all that exists in Nature, the great mindless interlocking event, if our own deepest convictions are merely the by-products of an irrational process, then clearly there is not the slightest ground for supposing that our sense of fitness and our consequent faith in uniformity tell us anything about a reality external to ourselves. Our convictions are simply a fact about us – like the colour of our hair. If Naturalism is true we have no reason to trust our conviction that Nature is uniform. It can be trusted only if quite a different metaphysic is true. If the deepest thing in reality, the Fact which is the source of all other facthood, is a thing in some degree like ourselves – if it is a Rational Spirit and we derive our rational spirituality from It – then indeed our conviction can be trusted. Our repugnance to disorder is derived from Nature's Creator and ours.[37]

Thus, excluding the possibility of miracle, and making nature and its processes an absolute in the name of science, removes all grounds for trusting in the rationality of science in the first place. On the other hand, regarding nature as only part of a greater reality, which includes nature's intelligent Creator God, gives a rational justification for belief in the orderliness of nature, a conviction that led to the rise of modern science.

Secondly, however, if one admits the existence of a Creator in order to account for the uniformity of nature, the door is inevitably open for that same Creator to intervene in the course of nature. There is no such thing as a tame Creator, who cannot, or must not, or dare not get actively involved in the universe which he has created. So miracles may occur.

I stress once more that one can agree with Hume that "uniform experience" shows that resurrection *by means of a natural mechanism* is extremely improbable, and we may rule it out. But Christians do not claim that Jesus rose by some natural mechanism. They claim something totally different – that God raised him from the dead. And if there is a God, why should that be judged impossible?

This paves the way for a consideration of the resurrection from the perspective of history, as Wolfhart Pannenberg makes clear: "As long as historiography does not begin with a narrow concept of reality according to which 'dead men do not rise', it is not clear why historiography should not in principle be able to speak about Jesus' resurrection as the explanation that is best established of such events as the disciples' experiences of the appearances and the discovery of the empty tomb."[38]

In this chapter we have been considering essentially *a priori* reasons[39] for which Hume and others have rejected miracles. However, we have seen that it is not science that rules out miracles. Surely, then, the open-minded attitude demanded by reason is to proceed now to investigate the evidence, to establish the facts, and be prepared to follow where that process leads; even if it entails alterations to our preconceived ideas. So let us do precisely that – and challenge the New Atheists to leave Hume behind and follow us. We shall never know whether or not there is a mouse in the attic unless we actually go and look!

CHAPTER 8

DID JESUS RISE FROM THE DEAD?[1]

"We come down to the resurrection of Jesus Christ. It's so petty; it's so trivial; it's so local; it's so earthbound; it's so unworthy of the universe."

"Accounts of Jesus' resurrection and ascension are about as well documented as Jack in the Beanstalk."
Richard Dawkins

"The resurrection of Jesus does in fact provide a sufficient explanation for the empty tomb and the meetings with Jesus. Having examined all the other possible hypotheses I've read about anywhere in the literature, I think it's also a necessary explanation."
Tom Wright

The New Atheists never tire of citing Bertrand Russell's reply when he was asked what he would say if God were to ask him after his death why he had not believed: "Not enough evidence, God, not enough evidence." But then a curious thing happens. When evidence is offered to them, they refuse to examine it. I have already mentioned Richard Dawkins' contemptuous dismissal of the resurrection in our *God Delusion* debate; so his attitude is clear. Furthermore, I know of no serious attempt by any of the New Atheists to engage with the evidence for the resurrection of Jesus Christ. Indeed, it is even worse than that. Their whole attitude to history in general is characterized by sheer closed-mind prejudice: light-years removed from the open-minded scientific attitude that they pretend to hold in high esteem.

For instance, it is likely to be very difficult to get people to seriously consider historical evidence for the resurrection of Jesus, if they question his very existence. Christopher Hitchens speaks of "the highly questionable existence of Jesus".[2] Richard Dawkins concedes the probable existence of Jesus, although he says: "It is even possible to mount a serious, though not widely supported historical case that Jesus never lived at all, as has been done by, amongst others Professor G. A. Wells of London University."[3] A little further on in the same book Dawkins says: "Indeed, Jesus, if he existed (or whoever wrote his script if he didn't)..." What is interesting here is that neither Hitchens nor Dawkins appears to have bothered to consult a reputable ancient historian – Wells is an Emeritus Professor of German. If Wells' case is not "widely supported", why doesn't Dawkins, in the interests of accuracy, tell us why? Since I am interested in accuracy, and like Dawkins I am not a historian, I have therefore consulted the experts. Here are some examples of what I have found. Incidentally, some of these were pointed out in my presence to atheist physicist Victor Stenger by an ancient historian, who took exception to Stenger's insistence that there was no historical evidence for the existence of Jesus.[4]

First, a voice from the USA. Ed Sanders of Duke University, one of the leading figures in the historical study of Jesus over the last three decades, and a self-confessed agnostic, writes:

> There are no substantial doubts about the general course of Jesus' life: when and where he lived, approximately when and where he died, and the sort of thing that he did during his public activity... I shall first offer a list of statements about Jesus that meet two standards: they are almost beyond dispute; and they belong to the framework of his life, and especially of his public career: Jesus was born c. 4 BCE, near the time of the death of Herod the Great; he spent his childhood and early adult years in Nazareth, a Galilean village; he was baptized by John the Baptist; he called disciples; he taught in the towns, villages and countryside of Galilee (apparently not the cities); he preached 'the kingdom of God'; about the year 30 he went to Jerusalem for Passover; he created a disturbance in the Temple area; he had a final meal with the disciples; he was arrested and interrogated by Jewish authorities, specifically the High Priest; he was executed on the orders of the Roman prefect, Pontius Pilate. We may add here a short list of equally secure facts about the aftermath of Jesus' life: his disciples fled; they saw him (in what sense is not certain) after his death; as a consequence, they believed that he would return to found the kingdom; they formed a community to await his return and sought to win others to faith in him as God's Messiah.[5]

Next, a voice from England. Christopher Tuckett, University of Oxford, author of the Cambridge University textbook on the historical Jesus:

> All this does at least render highly implausible any far-fetched theories that even Jesus' very existence was a Christian invention. The fact that Jesus existed, that he was crucified under Pontius Pilate (for whatever reason) and that he had a band of followers who continued to support his cause, seems to be part of the bedrock of historical tradition. If nothing else, the non-Christian evidence can provide us with certainty on that score.[6]

Finally, a voice from Germany. Gerd Thiessen, a leading German New Testament historian at the liberal/sceptical end of the theological spectrum, says:

> The mentions of Jesus in ancient historians allay doubt about his historicity. The notices about Jesus in Jewish and pagan writers... – especially those in Josephus, the letter of Sarapion and Tacitus – indicate that in antiquity the historicity of Jesus was taken for granted, and rightly so, as two observations on the above-mentioned sources show:
> The notices about Jesus are independent of one another. Three authors from different backgrounds utilize information about Jesus independently: a Jewish aristocrat and historian, a Syrian philosopher, and a Roman statesman and historian.
> All three know of the execution of Jesus, but in different ways: Tacitus puts the responsibility on Pontius Pilate, Mara bar Sarapion on the Jewish people, and the Testimonium Flavianum (probably) on a co-operation between the Jewish aristocracy and the Roman governor. The execution was offensive for any worship of Jesus. As a "scandal" it cannot have been invented.[7]

All this shows that Bertrand Russell was talking in sheer ignorance of the facts, when he wrote in his book *Why I am not a Christian*, "Historically it is quite doubtful whether Christ ever existed at all, and if he did we know nothing about him."[8] I can well recall when I first read Russell's book as a student in Cambridge. It had been recommended to me as one of the most powerful and important intellectual rebuttals of Christianity ever written; and I took it up wondering what effect it would have on my thinking. I was totally unprepared for what I found. I had expected a careful, incisive examination of the evidence that was readily available, a lot of which I had already been exposed to; yet I came away with the impression that Russell simply had not engaged at any depth with the substantial body of evidence that supports Christianity. The net effect of the book was to leave me very disappointed with Russell (after all, he was a mathematician), and to confirm my Christian faith, not undermine it. Much more recently I have had many similar experiences reading the New Atheists.

It is very difficult to know how to proceed with people who, on the one hand, insist that we examine the evidence they claim in support for their views and who then, on the other hand, clamour loudly for our evidence, and peremptorily dismiss what we offer to them. I am aware that I cannot hope to persuade the minority, who have already decided their answer without looking at the evidence; so I must now write for those who, in the spirit of Socrates, are not content with remaining in the intellectual fog generated by the New Atheism, but are genuinely interested in following historical evidence where it leads.

I remind the reader that I use the term "evidence" and not the term "proof", since, as we pointed out in Chapter 2, proof in the rigorous mathematical sense is not available in any other discipline or area of experience, not even in the so-called "hard" sciences. In all other disciplines we speak of evidence; and it is up to each person to make up their mind whether the evidence is convincing for them or not. That is the approach I shall take here. I shall present the evidence as I understand it, and leave it to my readers to decide whether or not I have made my case.

The resurrection of Jesus Christ from the dead lies at the heart of Christianity. Indeed, it is to be noted that, whatever they may have in common at the level of ethical teaching (and it is considerable), the death and resurrection of Jesus are watershed issues that separate the three major monotheistic religions – Judaism, Islam, and Christianity – from each other. Judaism holds that Jesus died, but did not rise; Islam holds that Jesus never died; and Christianity holds that Jesus both died and rose again. It is clear that these three understandings of history are mutually exclusive – at most only one of them can be true.

For centuries Christians have greeted each other at Easter time with the confident, indeed triumphant, words "Christ is risen! He is risen indeed." It is, therefore, time to examine the basis for that confidence.

THE SOURCES OF THE EVIDENCE

That brings us at once to another difficulty. Most of our evidence comes from the New Testament, and there is a widespread notion that the New Testament is not historically reliable. The New Atheists have done their part in communicating this highly erroneous impression to the public. Richard Dawkins, for instance, writes: "Although Jesus probably existed, reputable biblical scholars do not in general regard the New Testament (and obviously not the Old Testament) as a reliable record of what actually happened in history, and I shall not consider the Bible further as evidence... The only difference between *The Da Vinci Code* and the gospels is that the gospels are ancient fiction while *The Da Vinci Code* is modern fiction."[9] Hitchens thinks that the New Testament is "a work of crude carpentry, hammered together long after its purported events, and full of improvised attempts to make things come out right".[10]

Once again this cavalier dismissal of the Gospels as ancient fiction tells us much more about Dawkins' and Hitchens' attitudes to history than it does about the authenticity of the Gospels. Like many others, they seem to be unaware of the evidence for the authenticity and reliability of the New Testament text. They do not appear to have consulted the literature – indeed Hitchens cites as his authority H. L. Mencken, an American journalist who apparently never even went to college. Here is just a little of what they might have found out, if they had done a bit of serious research.

THE NUMBER OF MANUSCRIPTS

No original manuscripts of the New Testament survive today. If what we possess, therefore, is the result of a centuries-long copying process, many people wonder how it bears any resemblance to the original text.

This difficulty is generally felt by people who are not aware of how overwhelmingly strong the evidence actually is for the original text of the New Testament. Firstly, there is the sheer number of the manuscripts that we now have. There are 5,664 partial or complete manuscripts of the New Testament in the original Greek language that have been catalogued; and over 9,000 in early translations into Latin, Syriac, Coptic, Arabic, and others. Added to this, there are 38,289 quotations from the New Testament by the early church fathers, who wrote between the second and the fourth centuries AD. If, then, we lost all the New Testament manuscripts, we could still reconstruct the entire New Testament from these quotations (except for eleven verses).

In order to get some idea of the weight of this manuscript support, it is helpful to compare it with the documentary evidence available for other ancient works of literature. For instance, the Roman historian Tacitus wrote *The Annals of Imperial Rome* around AD 116. The first six books of the *Annals* survive in only one manuscript, which was copied in about AD 850. Books 11 to 16 are in another single manuscript, dated to the eleventh century. The manuscript evidence is very sparse therefore; and the time gap between the original compilation and the earliest surviving manuscripts is over 700 years.

The documentary evidence for *The Jewish War*, written in Greek by the first-century historian Josephus, consists of nine manuscripts that were copied in the tenth to twelfth centuries AD; a Latin translation from the fourth century; and some Russian versions dating back to the eleventh and twelfth centuries. The ancient secular work with the most documentary support is Homer's *Iliad* (c. 800 BC), of which there are 643 manuscript copies, dating from the second and later centuries AD. Thus, in this case, the time gap between the original and the earliest surviving manuscripts is a thousand years.

The main point to be made here is that scholars treat these documents as authentic representations of the originals, in spite of the fewness of the manuscripts and their late dates. In comparison with these, the New Testament is by far the best-attested document from the ancient world.

THE AGE OF THE MANUSCRIPTS

The time-lapse between the date of certain ancient manuscripts, and the originals of which they are copies, is considerable. How does the New Testament fare in this respect? Here again, the evidence for the authenticity of the text is extremely impressive by comparison.

Some of the New Testament manuscripts are of a very great age. *The Bodmer Papyri* (in the Bodmer Collection, Culagny, Switzerland) contain about two-thirds of the Gospel of John in one papyrus, dated to around AD 200. Another third-century papyrus has parts of Luke and John. Perhaps the most important manuscripts are the *Chester Beatty Papyri*, which were discovered in 1930 and are now housed in the Chester Beatty Museum in Dublin, Ireland. Papyrus 1 comes from the third century, and contains parts of the four Gospels and Acts. Papyrus 2, dated to around AD 200, contains substantial portions of eight of Paul's letters, plus parts of the letter to the Hebrews. Papyrus 3 has a large part of the book of Revelation, and is dated to the third century.

Some fragments are even earlier. The famous *John Rylands Fragment* (in the John Rylands Library, Manchester, England), which consists of five verses from the Gospel of John, is dated by some to the time of the Emperor Hadrian, AD 117–138; and by others even to the reign of Trajan, AD 98–117. This refutes the influential view of sceptical nineteenth-century German scholars that John's Gospel could not have been written before AD 160.

The earliest surviving manuscripts containing all the books of the New Testament were written around AD 325–350. (Incidentally, it was in AD 325 that the Council of Nicea decreed that the Bible could be freely copied.) The most important of these manuscripts are the *Codex Vaticanus* and the *Codex Sinaiticus*, which are called uncial manuscripts because they are written in Greek capital letters. The *Codex Vaticanus* was catalogued by the Vatican Library (hence its name) in 1475; but, for 400 years after that, scholars were forbidden to study it – rather odd, in light of the original decision by the Council of Nicea!

The *Codex Sinaiticus* was found by Tischendorf (1815–44) in the Monastery of St Catherine, on Mount Sinai in Arabia, and is now in the British Museum in London. It is regarded as one of the most important witnesses to the text of the New Testament, because of its antiquity, accuracy, and lack of omissions.

MISTAKES IN THE COPYING PROCESS

We can now readily see that the objection – the New Testament cannot be reliable because it has been copied out so many times – is completely unfounded. Take, for example, a manuscript that was written around AD 200, and is therefore now some 1,800 years old.

How old was the manuscript from which it was originally copied? We do not know, of course; but it could very easily have been 140 years old at the time it was copied. If so, that manuscript was written out when many of the authors of the New Testament were still alive. Thus, we get from New Testament times to the modern day in just *two* steps!

Furthermore, whereas there are copying mistakes in most manuscripts (it is virtually impossible to copy out a lengthy document by hand without making some mistakes), no two manuscripts contain exactly the same mistakes. Therefore, by comparing all these manuscripts with each other, it is possible to reconstruct the original text to a point where expert opinion holds that less than 2 per cent of that text is uncertain, with a large part of that 2 per cent involving small linguistic features that make no difference to the general meaning. Moreover, since no New Testament doctrine depends solely on one verse or one passage, no New Testament doctrine is put in doubt by these minor uncertainties.

Summing up the situation, Sir Frederic Kenyon, who was Director of the British Museum and a leading authority on ancient manuscripts, wrote: "The number of manuscripts of the New Testament, of early translations from it, and of quotations from it in the oldest writers of the Church is so large that it is practically certain that the true reading of every doubtful passage is preserved in some one or other of these ancient authorities. This can be said of no other ancient book in the world."[11]

This verdict is approved by Bruce Metzger, Professor Emeritus of New Testament at Princeton Theological Seminary, one of the world's most eminent New Testament scholars, and author of *The Text of the New Testament, Its Transmission, Corruption and Restoration*.[12] He says: "We can have great confidence in the fidelity with which this material has come down to us, especially compared with any other ancient literary work."[13]

On this basis, then, we may have every confidence that, when we read the New Testament today, we have for all practical purposes what its original authors intended us to have. That leads us at once to a final important question: how authentic are the Gospels as history?

ARE THE GOSPELS ANCIENT FICTION?

We recall Dawkins' jibe mentioned earlier in this chapter, that the only difference between the Gospels and *The Da Vinci Code* is that the former were ancient fiction. Similarly, Hitchens thinks that Christians err in "assuming that the four Gospels were in any sense a historical record".[14] The error, however, is entirely theirs.

Take as an example the important case of the writings of Luke, whose contribution to the New Testament consists of his Gospel and his history of the beginnings of Christianity, the book of Acts. The first question to ask here (as of any document) is: how does the author expect to be understood? A reader of the New Testament will be struck almost immediately with its strong historical tones. For example, in his introduction to the third Gospel, Luke says:

Inasmuch as many have undertaken to compile a narrative of the things that have been accomplished among us, just as those who from the beginning were eyewitnesses and ministers of the word have delivered them to us, it seemed good to me also, having followed all things closely for some time past, to write an orderly account for you, most excellent Theophilus, that you may have certainty concerning the things you have been taught.[15]

So Luke claims to be writing about events that happened over a period of time, the report being traceable back to eyewitnesses. He also claims that he had conducted his own research, in order to prepare an orderly account for a Roman citizen of high standing called Theophilus, with the object of showing him the certainty of these events.

It belongs to his objectives to anchor his account of the life of Christ firmly in its setting in contemporary history, so he starts his account proper with the statement: "In the days of Herod, king of Judea." He then dates the events surrounding the birth of Christ in more detail: "In those days a decree went out from Caesar Augustus that all the world should be registered. This was the first registration when Quirinius was governor of Syria."[16] When he comes to the start of the public life of Christ, he gives even more dating information: "In the fifteenth year of the reign of Tiberius Caesar, Pontius Pilate being governor of Judea, and Herod being tetrarch of Galilee, and his brother Philip tetrarch of the region of Iturea and Traconitis, and

Lysanias tetrarch of Abilene, during the high priesthood of Annas and Caiaphas..."[17]

This kind of detail and method of dating is characteristic of serious ancient historians who wish to mark important events. Luke does not content himself with the "sometime, somewhere" of mythology or historical fiction. He pins down the events accurately to their historical context with checkable information. This demonstrates to his readers that he intends them to take what he writes as serious history. The question is, then: What is the evidence that Luke is credible?

Historical and archaeological research has repeatedly confirmed Luke's high status as a historian. For example, we quoted above his dating of the beginning of Christ's public life at a time when *Lysanias was tetrarch of Abilene*. For a long time this was cited as evidence that Luke could not be taken seriously as a historian; since it was said to be common knowledge that Lysanias was not a tetrarch, but the ruler of Chalcis half-a-century earlier. The critics fell silent when an inscription was found, dating to the time of Tiberius (AD 14–37), which named a certain Lysanias as tetrarch in Abila near Damascus – precisely as Luke had said!

Similarly, critics thought Luke was mistaken when he refers in his history of the early Christian church, the book of Acts, to city officials in Thessalonica as "politarchs,"[18] since there was no evidence from other contemporary Roman documents that such a term was used. Yet subsequently, archaeologists have found over thirty-five inscriptions referring to politarchs, some of them in Thessalonica, dating from the very same period to which Luke was referring.

An earlier generation of scholars felt that the mention of non-Jewish "God-fearers" in the book of Acts[19] showed that Luke could not be taken as a serious historian, since the existence of such a category of Gentiles was doubtful. However, the ancient historian Irina Levinskaya, of the Russian Academy of Sciences and St Petersburg University, demonstrates impressively that Luke's account has been vindicated by archaeological research.[20] Inscriptions have been found, indicating the existence of precisely such a class of Gentiles. They are, in fact, listed on one Greek inscription from Aphrodisias under a separate heading from the members of the Jewish community. Levinskaya writes: "The importance of this inscription for the historical controversy about Gentile sympathisers with Judaism lies in the fact that, once and for all, it has tipped the balance and shifted the onus of proof from those who believe in the existence of Luke's God-fearers to those who have either denied or had doubts about it."[21]

The eminent historian Sir William Ramsey, who spent over twenty years doing archaeological research in the areas about which Luke wrote, showed that, in his references to thirty-two countries, fifty-four cities and nine islands, Luke made no mistakes.[22]

In his definitive work Colin Hemer details many areas in which Luke displays very accurate knowledge.[23] We cite a few of Hemer's many examples, in order to give the flavour of what has been discovered:

1. **Acts 13:7 shows Cyprus correctly as a proconsular (senatorial) province at the time, with the proconsul resident at Paphos;**

2. **14:11 shows correctly that Lycaonian was (unusually) spoken in Lystra at the time;**

3. **14:12 reflects local interest in, and concepts of, the gods Zeus and Hermes;**

4. **16:12: Philippi is correctly identified as a Roman colony, and its seaport is correctly named Nea Polis;**

5. **16:14: Thyatira is identified as a centre of dyeing, confirmed by at least seven inscriptions in the city;**

6. **17:1 rightly shows Ampipholis and Apollonia as stations on the Egnatian Way from Philippi to Thessalonica;**

7. **17:16–18 shows accurate knowledge of Athens: its abundance of idols, its interest in philosophical debate, and its Stoic and Epicurean philosophers and their teachings;**

8. **Chapters 27–28 show detailed accurate knowledge of the geography and navigational details of the voyage to Rome.**

All this accurately recorded detail, and much more besides, supports the considered verdict of Roman historian Sherwin-White: "For Acts the confirmation of historicity is overwhelming... any attempt to reject its basic historicity even in matters of detail must now appear absurd."[24]

Thus Luke has proved to be a first-rate historian, and there is no reason to doubt his record. There is much more that could be said, but surely we can now proceed with some confidence in the historical reliability of our sources to examine what the New Testament offers us as evidence for the resurrection of Jesus.

THE EVIDENCE FOR THE RESURRECTION

Not only has there been a vast quantity of historical research on the documentary evidence for the New Testament text; there has also been an immense amount of scholarly effort put into studying the question of the resurrection of Jesus. Philosopher Gary Habermas, who has himself written prolifically on the subject, has compiled an extensive bibliography of over 3,000 scholarly articles and books written (in English, French, and German) in the past thirty-five years alone.[25] In a short work like this, we shall have to content ourselves with distilling the main lines of the argument.

I shall not necessarily expect the reader to share my convictions about the inspiration of the biblical documents; but rather to consider the argument on its own merits, in light of the evidence we can amass from various sources; as indeed we would do with any other texts from ancient history. Indeed, some of the evidence comes from sources other than the New Testament.

I mention this explicitly, since many sceptics seem to disregard the New Testament on the basis of their own *a priori* assumption that it is not inspired – an attitude that they would not adopt with regard to any other text from antiquity.

The evidence for the resurrection of Jesus is cumulative, and involves consideration of four different issues:

I. The death of Jesus

II. The burial of Jesus

III. The empty tomb

IV. The eyewitnesses

I. THE DEATH OF JESUS

It is self-evident that there could be no resurrection if Jesus did not really die on the cross. It is therefore important first of all to establish that he actually died. We note firstly that reports of his execution are to be found in a number of ancient non-Christian sources. Josephus (AD 37–100), a first-century Roman Jewish historian, wrote: "When

Pilate, upon hearing him accused by men of the highest standing amongst us, had condemned him to be crucified…"[26]

In the early second century Tacitus (AD 56–117), a senator and historian of the Roman empire, wrote: "Nero fastened the guilt [of the burning of Rome] and inflicted the most exquisite tortures on a class hated for their abominations, called Christians by the populace. Christus, from whom the name had its origin, suffered the extreme penalty [i.e. crucifixion] during the reign of Tiberius at the hands of one of our procurators, Pontius Pilatus."[27]

However, some point to Josephus' record of an instance where someone survived crucifixion, and in light of it they suggest that Jesus did not really die on the cross, but merely fainted; and then, when he was taken down from the cross, he revived in the cool air of the tomb. They claim that, although very weak, Jesus managed to get out of the tomb and was seen by some of his disciples, looking (not surprisingly) pale like a ghost. They imagined that a resurrection had occurred and spread the story around; but in fact Jesus probably simply wandered off and died of his wounds in some obscure, unknown place.

However, this theory does not stand up. Firstly, Josephus mentions that there were three men who were crucified – all of whom were friends of Josephus; and when he saw their plight he appealed at once to his friend Titus, the Roman Commander, who ordered them to be taken down. Only one of them survived, in spite of receiving the best medical attention of the day. In Jesus' case the evidence points overwhelmingly to the fact that he was dead before he was taken down from the cross. And even if he had still been alive his chances of survival would have been nil, considering the fact that not only was he pronounced dead, but he was also wrapped in lengthy bandage-type grave-cloths, covered in a great weight of spices, which would have had the effect of extinguishing any vestige of life.

In any case, the extent of Jesus' injuries guaranteed death. Before he was crucified, he was flogged and had a crown of thorns pressed on to his head.[28] Such flogging, as practised by the Romans, involved the use of a brutal instrument called a *flagrum*, which was like a whip with pieces of metal and bone attached to it. It bit deep into human flesh with the result that the victim sometimes died under its use. In Jesus' case, he was so weak as a result of the flogging that he was not able to carry the cross as far as the place of execution.[29]

Jesus was then crucified. This meant nailing him to a rough wooden structure in the shape of a cross, with an upright pole and a cross-piece: one large nail through both feet, fastening them to the upright, and other nails through the outstretched wrists, fastening them to the cross-piece. This arrangement was maximally cruel, because the nails through the feet meant that the legs could give support as the victim struggled to raise his body up so as to be able to breathe a bit easier; this prolonged the agony of death, sometimes for several days.

However, the Jewish Sabbath was approaching and, according to John's eyewitness account,[30] the Jewish authorities did not want the bodies, which they regarded as defiling, to remain on the crosses on the Sabbath. They therefore asked permission from Pilate to have death hastened by the expedient of administering the *crucifragium*; that is, breaking the legs of the three crucified men.[31] This would have the effect of removing support for the upper body, which would then hang with a dead weight and render the breathing action of the rib-cage very difficult, thereby hastening death if it had not already occurred. The permission was granted. However, when the soldiers came to Jesus they found he was dead already, so they did not break his legs. This means that they were absolutely sure he was dead – Roman soldiers knew a dead body when they saw one. However, presumably to make doubly sure that Jesus was dead, one of the soldiers pierced his side with a spear.

John tells us that the spear-thrust produced a flow of blood and water.[32] This supplies us with medical evidence of death. It indicates that massive blood clotting had taken place in the main arteries, which shows that Jesus had died even before the spear-thrust. Since John could not have known of the pathological significance of this, it is a powerful piece of circumstantial detail that establishes the Christian claim that Jesus really died.[33]

When the Sanhedrin Councillor, Joseph of Arimathea, subsequently came to Pilate to request the body for burial, Pilate was not willing to take any risks, not even for such a prominent person. In the very earliest of the Gospel accounts, Mark records that Pilate was surprised to hear that Jesus was already dead (recall the fact mentioned above, that crucified people often lived in agony for some days); so he took the precaution of checking with the duty centurion. Only when he had received this confirmation of death did Pilate release the corpse of Jesus for burial.[34]

The evidence for Jesus' death is so strong that John Dominic Crossan, the highly sceptical co-founder of the Jesus Seminar admitted: "That [Jesus] was crucified is as sure as anything historical can ever be."[35] And atheist scholar Gerd Lüdemann wrote: "Jesus' death as a consequence of crucifixion is indisputable."[36]

II. THE BURIAL OF JESUS

1. Who buried Jesus?

All four Gospels tell us that Joseph of Arimathea, a wealthy man, went to Pilate and requested the body of Jesus in order to bury it in a tomb that he owned.[37] Presumably Joseph was able to get access to Pilate because of his status as a member of the Jewish Sanhedrin Council.

His motivation was clear: he had become a follower of Jesus, and wanted to ensure that he had a decent burial. But in all probability, he had another motive. By his action he wanted to show that he had no part in the Sanhedrin's decision to execute Jesus, and was protesting against it. He had not joined the Sanhedrin in condemning him.[38] Indeed, it might well be that burying the body of Jesus as he did effectively amounted to handing in his resignation from the Sanhedrin. In light of his action, it is very unlikely that the Sanhedrin would have tolerated his membership any longer.

From John's account of the trial of Jesus, we have already deduced that Pilate had nothing but contempt for the Sanhedrin. He had seen that their case against Jesus was pathetically thin, and had acceded to their request to crucify Jesus only because they had blackmailed him. It may be, therefore, that in Joseph he was glad to see at least one member of the Sanhedrin who had disagreed with the general verdict; and in giving the body to Joseph he may well have felt a slight easing of his conscience.

This account of Pilate's acceding to Joseph's request for the body has all the hallmarks of authentic history. Bearing in mind the antagonism of the Sanhedrin to Christ and his followers, it is highly improbable that those same followers would have invented the story of a member of the Sanhedrin being prepared to stand with Jesus by ensuring he had an honourable burial, while many of the disciples themselves had run off in fear! In addition, if the story were false, it would have been fatal for the Christian version of events for the

Gospel writers to name someone with such a high public profile as Joseph. It would have been so easy for opponents to check the details afterwards, and prove the story untrue.

2. The place of the burial

According to the record, Joseph, together with another member of the Sanhedrin, Nicodemus,[39] buried the body of Jesus in a private tomb belonging to Joseph.[40] In addition, other witnesses saw where the tomb was: the women from Galilee saw it,[41] as did the two Marys.[42]

The fact of Jesus' burial in a tomb plays an important role in the evidence for the resurrection. If Jesus' corpse had simply been thrown into a common grave – as often happened to criminals – the determination of whether a specific body was no longer there would have been made very difficult, if not impossible. And not only was Jesus buried in a tomb; it was a new tomb in which no one had ever been laid before, so there was no question of his body being accidentally confused with that of someone else.[43] Moreover, since, as we have just noticed, some of the women-believers followed Joseph, and saw the tomb in which Christ's body was laid,[44] it makes it extremely unlikely that, when the women came early on the first day of the week while it was still dark, they mistook the tomb, as some scholars have suggested.

What is likely is that one of those women was Joanna, the wife of Chuza, the steward or manager of Herod's household. Luke tells us that she was a follower of Jesus from Galilee,[45] and that these women from Galilee not only witnessed the crucifixion, but also the burial.[46] As a member of the upper-crust of society, and as a follower of Jesus, she would have been well known to Joseph of Arimathea and Nicodemus. With such prominent people involved, it is inconceivable that a mistake could have been made regarding the location of the tomb, especially in light of the additional information that John gives us, to the effect that the tomb was in Joseph's private garden, near to the place where Jesus was crucified.[47]

3. The manner of the burial

Together with Nicodemus, Joseph wrapped the body in linen cloths interlaced with spices.[48] They were following a time-honoured custom for the burial of an important person; and in the process they would have used a mixture of myrrh and aloes – about 25 kg in all. As wealthy people, in all probability they would have had a store of such spices readily available at home. It is possible that they were helped in this by the wealthier women from Galilee.[49] In any case, between them they had enough spices for the preliminary embalming. The rest could wait until the Sabbath was over.

The other women, who were not so prosperous, had no such spices available; they would have to wait until the shops reopened after the Sabbath in order to buy them.[50]

Implications
One thing is very clear from all of this: they were not expecting a resurrection. If you expect a body to rise from the dead, you do not embalm it in this way! Indeed, when the women arrived the next morning (Sunday), they were only concerned with the problem of gaining access to the tomb in order to continue the embalming[51] – clear evidence once more that they were not expecting a resurrection.

It is also to be noted that the weight of the spices, and the way in which the grave-cloths would have been tightly bound around the body, render incredible the theory mentioned earlier – that Christ swooned on the cross, revived in the tomb, and then managed to escape.

Security at the tomb
The body was placed in a tomb that had been hewn out of the rock, not in a grave dug in the earth. The tomb must have been of considerable size, since Peter and John were later able to go right into it.[52] In such tombs the body was usually placed in an alcove on a rock-ledge, the ledge having an elevated part at one end where the head could rest slightly higher than the body. The tomb was then secured by Joseph with a large disc-shaped stone that fitted into a slanting groove at the entrance to the tomb: though easily rolled into place, it would have required several men to move it away.[53] In addition, acting on the authority of Pilate, the next day the Jewish leaders had the stone officially sealed, so that no one could break that seal without incurring the wrath of officialdom.[54]

Moreover, at the request of the Pharisees and with Pilate's permission, guards were placed around the tomb. Matthew tells us that this was to prevent the disciples coming, removing the body of Jesus, and fraudulently announcing a "resurrection". Here are the details of his account:

> The next day, that is, after the day of Preparation, the chief priests and the Pharisees gathered before Pilate and said, "Sir, we remember how that impostor said, while he was still alive, 'After three days I will rise.' Therefore order the tomb to be made secure until the third day, lest his disciples go and steal him away and tell the people, 'He has risen from the dead,' and the last fraud will be worse than the first." Pilate said to them, "You have a guard of soldiers. Go, make it as secure as you can." So they went and made the tomb secure by sealing the stone and setting a guard.[55]

Although some have questioned the authenticity of the story about the guards, there is strong evidence of its truth. First of all, it is not hard to imagine the unease and nervousness of the priests as they recalled Christ's prediction of his resurrection. They could not afford to run any risk of a deception here, so it was in their interests to get the tomb guarded. In addition to this, the story is confirmed by its sequel, as we shall see in a moment. Here, however, we should notice in passing that it was not until the day after the burial that the priests posted the guard. The women, who had gone home immediately after the burial, would have known nothing about the guard. This accounts for the fact that, as they were going to the tomb the next (Sunday) morning, they questioned among themselves: "Who will roll away the stone for us?" According to Mark, the stone had in fact been rolled away by angelic intervention.[56]

III. THE EMPTY TOMB

It is the constant and unvarying testimony of the Gospels that the tomb was found to be empty when the Christian women came early in the morning of the first day of the week, to complete the task of encasing the body of Jesus in spices. And when the apostles went to investigate the women's report, they likewise found the tomb empty.

It is impossible to exaggerate the significance of this fact, for it shows us what the early Christians mean when they testify to the resurrection of Jesus. They mean that the body of Jesus which they had buried in the tomb, knowing it to be dead – that same body was raised from the dead and had vacated the tomb. However much that body was changed (and the descriptions of what that body was like, when they eventually saw and handled it alive, will indicate some of these changes), they insist that it was the same body that had been laid in the tomb. It was not another, new, body, unconnected with the original body of Jesus. It was a genuine resurrection of the original body, not the substitution of a new body in place of the original.

This fact is very important, because, in the last century and a half, some theologians have argued that the testimony of the early Christians to the bodily resurrection of Christ was never more than a mythical way of expressing their faith that Christ's spirit had survived death; and therefore it would not have made any difference to their claim that Christ had risen from the dead, if it could have been demonstrated to them that his body was still in the tomb.

But this is a comparatively modern, and indeed a modernist, theory based on the *a priori* assumption of naturalism. It cannot be made to square with the insistent emphasis that the early witnesses placed on the fact that the tomb was empty. When they explain that fact by saying that Christ had risen from the dead, they mean by that the literal resurrection of his body.

1. The Jewish authorities: the first witnesses to the fact of the empty tomb

According to the Gospel of Matthew, the first people to tell the world that the tomb of Jesus was empty were the Jewish authorities, and not the Christians at all! They started a story circulating in Jerusalem to the effect that the disciples had stolen the body while the guards slept:

> Some of the guard went into the city and told the chief priests all that had taken place. And when they had assembled with the elders and taken counsel, they gave a sufficient sum of money to the soldiers and said, "Tell people, 'His disciples came by night and stole him away while we were asleep.' And if this comes to the governor's ears, we will satisfy him and keep you out of trouble." So they took the money and did as they were directed. And this story has been spread among the Jews to this day.[57]

The question arises: is Matthew's story authentic? Some have suggested that it is a late myth, invented long after the event. But that explanation is unlikely. Matthew's Gospel, in which the story is related, is by common consent the most characteristically Jewish Gospel in the New Testament. It bears every mark of having been written for circulation among Jews. It was probably published in the late AD 60s. By that time the facts about the crucifixion and burial of Christ would have been widely circulated in Jewish synagogues in that part of the Middle East. If the story were a late invention concocted by Matthew, it would immediately have been seen as a recent fiction. Matthew certainly would not have risked telling such a story to Jewish communities.

There is, therefore, no reason to suppose that this story is not true. The question now arises: why would the Jewish authorities have put their money into circulating such a story? The only reason could have been to achieve a pre-emptive strike. They knew from the guards that the tomb was empty. They could see immediately that the Christians would publish this, and as an explanation they would say that Jesus was risen from the dead. So the authorities decided to strike first, tell the story that the tomb was empty, and then give their explanation of it to counter the force of the inevitable Christian explanation. However, the very fact that they circulated such a story is proof that the tomb was empty.

It must have been much to their embarrassment, therefore, when (contrary to their logical expectation) the Christians did not say anything publicly for another seven weeks.[58] During those seven weeks of Christian silence, however, the rumour of the empty tomb would have been filling Jerusalem.

It is not hard to imagine that many in Jerusalem perceived how thin the guards' story was. It was scarcely conceivable that the Jewish authorities would entrust such a highly sensitive mission to the kind of men who would fall asleep. In any case, if they were asleep, how did they know what had happened, let alone identify the disciples as the culprits? The story was evidently a product of bewilderment and desperation. As propaganda coming from the enemies of Christ, the circulation of this story is historical evidence of the highest quality that *the empty tomb of Jesus was a fact.*

Furthermore, if the tomb had not been empty, the authorities would have had no difficulty in producing the body of Jesus, demonstrating conclusively that no resurrection had happened. When the apostles subsequently proclaimed that he had risen, they would have met with nothing but derision, and Christianity could never have got started.

Alternatively, if they had had the slightest evidence that the tomb was empty because the disciples had removed the body, then they had the authority and the forces to hunt down the disciples, arrest them, and charge them with tomb-robbing, which at the time was a very serious offence.

An interesting side light is thrown on all of this by an inscription, found in the nineteenth century, dating to AD 30–40. It contains the so-called Edict of Nazareth, and warns that robbery from, or desecration of tombs was an offence carrying the death penalty. Historians think that something very unusual must have happened around that time to cause such a severe edict to be issued – the most likely thing being the circumstances surrounding Joseph's empty tomb.[59]

2. The Christian disciples: their explanation of the empty tomb

We are now at the point in our investigation where we have an empty tomb to be explained. The disciples claimed that Jesus had risen, but could they have been deceived about that? What if somebody had stolen the body away without the disciples' knowing, and now had deceived them into thinking that there had been a resurrection? But who would have been interested in doing that? In our discussion of the moral character of the disciples, we have seen why it could not have been any one of the friends of Christ; and the last thing the enemies of Christ wanted was for anything to happen that could lead people to believe in a resurrection. After all, it was for this very reason they had ensured that the tomb was guarded. The idea, then, that the disciples were deceived, has no explanatory power whatsoever; especially when it comes to the evidence that they advanced for positively believing that Jesus had risen; and this we must now consider.

3. The people involved

It is clear from the Gospel records that the events at the cross and tomb of Jesus involved several groups of women.

Matthew says: "There were also many women there, looking on from a distance, who had followed Jesus from Galilee, ministering to him, among whom were Mary Magdalene and Mary the mother of James and Joseph and the mother of the sons of Zebedee."[60]

Mark says: "There were also women looking on from a distance, among whom were Mary Magdalene, and Mary the mother of James the younger and of Joses, and Salome. When he was in Galilee, they followed him and ministered to him, and there were also many other women who came up with him to Jerusalem."[61]

John specifically records that the mother of Jesus and three other women were standing by the cross – Jesus' mother's sister, Mary the wife of Clopas, and Mary Magdalene.[62]

It is natural to presume that the three women specially distinguished in the descriptions were the same in each case, having come to support Mary the mother of Jesus in her hour of acute distress. John Wenham, in his detailed study of the events surrounding the resurrection,[63] points out that this would mean that Jesus' mother's sister was called Salome, and was the wife of Zebedee and mother of James and John (the author of the fourth Gospel). Mary the wife of Clopas was the mother of James the Younger and of Joses (or Joseph).[64]

From this we see that between these women there are family relationships, which become important for our purposes when we remember that it was Passover-time at Jerusalem. The city would be crowded with pilgrims, who would naturally lodge with relatives wherever possible. One very important detail here is the fact that, from the cross, Jesus explicitly instructed John to look after his mother, Mary; and we read that he took her at once to his own home.[65] In all probability this was in Jerusalem, possibly not far from the house of the High Priest, Caiaphas. Presumably John's mother, Salome, and her husband, Zebedee, were staying there also, along with Peter, who, as John records, accompanied John to the tomb on Easter morning.[66]

But clearly other women were involved as well; and in all probability one of them was Joanna,[67] the wife of Chuza, Herod's steward.[68] She was a wealthy woman who, as the wife of a very senior civil servant in Herod's Court, would have been living in the Hasmonean Palace in Jerusalem, where Herod and his retinue stayed on their visits to the city. Joanna's name is linked with that of Susanna;[69] and it is possible that she, too, was one of the unnamed women in the crucifixion narrative.

What about the other apostles? Where were they? Just before the Feast of Passover they had been staying in Bethany.[70] This was a village just over the Mount of Olives, about 3 km from Jerusalem and therefore within walking distance. The arrest of Christ took place in a garden at the foot of the Mount of Olives: a garden that may well have belonged to the family of John Mark, the author of the second Gospel. We read that, after the arrest of Christ, all the disciples forsook Him and fled.[71] The most likely place for them to flee to was back over the Mount of Olives to the comparative safety of Bethany. As far as we know, John and Peter were the only two to remain in the city.

We see, therefore, that there were different groups of people staying in a variety of locations: some in Jerusalem, and some outside the city. These facts assume great importance when we come to study the events of Easter morning, as detailed in the Gospel narratives. The narratives are often compressed; and one might be tempted to think that they contain contradictory elements, if unaware of the complexities of the situation, and the fact that there were different groups of people going to and coming from the tomb of Christ, not only from different directions and by different routes, but also at different times. Matthew's brief account has telescoped these features, as we shall later see.

4. Physical evidence found at the tomb: the grave-cloths of Christ

The Gospel accounts tell us that a number of women disciples of Christ came early to the tomb, to embalm his body more thoroughly than Joseph and Nicodemus had done.[72] Incidentally, their intention shows again that resurrection was the last thing they were expecting.[73]

According to Mark, Mary Magdalene, the mother of James the Younger and Joseph (the "other Mary", see Matthew 27:61, 28:1), and Salome, had bought spices the previous evening at sundown (*after the Sabbath was past*).[74] Wenham makes the very plausible suggestion[75] that Mark's account is told from the perspective of these three women; whereas Luke's account, which records how certain women returned from the burial and prepared spices and ointments and then rested on the Sabbath, is most likely to have been written from the perspective of Joanna, the wife of Herod's Steward. As a wealthy Jewess she would have had her own store of spices and ointments, and so would not have had to wait, as the other groups of women did, until the Sabbath ended, for the shops to open to enable her to buy them.

As Wenham says, it is likely that these two groups of women arrived at the tomb separately. The first group – Mary Magdalene, the "other Mary", and Salome – arrived at the tomb first. To their astonishment, they found the stone rolled away from the tomb, and the tomb empty! One of them, Mary (perhaps without entering the tomb), ran at once to tell the apostles Peter and John. Mary did not speak of a resurrection, but simply presumed that the body of Jesus had been removed.[76] Archaeologists point out that tomb-robbing was a very common activity in the ancient world – in ancient Egypt, for example. Thieves would show particular interest in the tombs of the wealthy, as the cloths in which the corpse was wrapped and the spices used for embalming were valuable, re-sellable items; to say nothing of the jewellery and other possessions that might accompany the corpse. Now Jesus was not wealthy, but Joseph was; so Mary may have thought that tomb-robbers had been active.

Peter and John ran to the tomb. John got there first, stooped, and looked inside. Immediately he noticed something strange: the linen grave-cloths that had been wrapped around the body of Jesus were still there. Stranger still, they were lying just as they had been when his body was in them, but the body had gone. Peter caught up with John, who must therefore have been the faster runner (one of those little details that give the narrative the ring of eyewitness writing). Both of them went into the tomb and saw what was possibly the strangest sight of all: the cloths which had been wrapped around Jesus' head were lying on the slightly elevated part of the ledge within the tomb; and, though his head was no longer in them, they were still wrapped round as if it had been, except that they had probably collapsed flat. The effect on John was powerful: *he saw and believed.*[77] This does not merely mean that he now believed what Mary had said: from his first glimpse into the tomb it was obvious that the body was missing. Now he believed that something very mysterious indeed must have happened. It looked as if in some way the body of Jesus had come right through the grave-cloths and left them exactly where they were when the body was inside. John had no doubt that he was seeing the evidence of a miracle!

What was it about the grave-cloths that carried such convincing power? The obvious question for him, or for anyone else, to ask is, how did they get to be like that? Tomb-robbers would not have taken the corpse, and left the valuable linen and spices. And even if, for some unfathomable reason, they had wanted only the corpse, they would have had no reason whatever for wrapping all the cloths round again as if they were still round a body, except, perhaps, to give the impression that the tomb had not been disturbed. But if they wanted to give that impression they would surely have done better to roll the stone back into its place! But here we meet another matter:

how could any tomb-robber have removed the stone when the guard was there? The noise would have been considerable. The rolled-away stone was a complete give away that the tomb had been disturbed. It was an open invitation to come and have a look inside.

If it wasn't tomb-robbers, then, who could it have been? Perhaps misguided followers of Jesus, trying to get the body away from under the noses of the authorities to a safer place? But if they had done that, they would not have kept it secret from the other apostles. They would have reburied him reverently (as Mary was intending to do)[78], and eventually all the Christians would have come to know where his tomb was. In any case, we are still left with the noisy problem of rolling away the stone within earshot of the guard.

The way in which the grave-cloths were lying convinced John that something supernatural had happened. We can imagine him thinking it through. So, could someone have taken the body and rewound the cloths deliberately to give the impression that a miracle had happened? But who could this have been? It was morally impossible for the followers of Christ to have done it. It was also psychologically impossible, since they were not expecting a resurrection. And it was practically impossible, because of the guards.

Finally, it would be absurd to think of the authorities doing anything remotely suggestive of a resurrection. After all, it was they who had ensured that the tomb was guarded, to avoid anything like that!

For John and Peter, it was an electrifying discovery. They had ruled out impossible explanations, so they were left with only one alternative: that the body had come through the grave-cloths. But what did that mean? And where was Jesus now?

Well-known historian Michael Grant of Edinburgh University writes: "True, the discovery of the empty tomb is differently described by the various Gospels, but if we apply the same sort of criteria that we would apply to any other ancient literary sources, then the evidence is firm and plausible enough to necessitate the conclusion that the tomb was, indeed, found empty."[79]

So Peter and John left the empty tomb. They thought there was nothing more to be gained by remaining there. However, as events proved, they were wrong.

IV. THE EYEWITNESSES

The empty tomb is important: if it were not empty, you could not speak of resurrection. But we need to be clear that the early Christians did not simply assert that the tomb was empty. Far more important for them was the fact that subsequently they had met the risen Christ, intermittently over a period of forty days culminating in his ascension.[80] They had actually seen him, talked with him, touched him and even eaten with him. It was nothing less than this that galvanized them into action, and gave them the courage to confront the world with the message of the Christian gospel. And what is more, when the apostles began to preach the gospel publicly, the fact that they had personally witnessed these appearances of the risen Christ formed an integral part of that gospel. The evidence for this is so strong that even atheist scholar Gerd Lüdemann writes: "It may be taken as historically certain that Peter and the disciples had experiences after Jesus' death in which Jesus appeared to them as the risen Christ."[81] Not surprisingly, Lüdemann's atheism forbids a resurrection as the cause. He holds that the appearances were visions – a view that turns out to be highly improbable as we shall see below.

First, let us look at the documentary record:

Peter in Jerusalem (1): On the day of Pentecost, at the first public announcement of the resurrection of Jesus in Jerusalem, Peter says: "This Jesus God raised up, and of that we all are witnesses."[82]

Peter in Jerusalem (2): Shortly after Pentecost, in the second major speech recorded by Luke, Peter says: "You killed the Author of life, whom God raised from the dead. To this we are witnesses."[83]

Peter in Caesarea: In the first major announcement of the Christian message to non-Jews, Peter says to Cornelius, the Roman centurion, that he and others "ate and drank with him after he rose from the dead".[84]

Paul at Pisidian Antioch: In a major speech in a synagogue, Paul says of Christ: "They took him down from the tree and laid him in a tomb. But God raised him from the dead, and for many days he appeared to those who had come up with him from Galilee to Jerusalem, who are now his witnesses to the people."[85]

When Paul eventually came to write down a brief, but definitive, statement of the gospel, he included a selection of Christ's appearances to various witnesses as an essential part of that statement:

Now I would remind you, brothers, of the gospel... that Christ died for our sins in accordance with the Scriptures, that he was buried, that he was raised on the third day in accordance with the Scriptures, and that he appeared to Cephas, then to the twelve. Then... to more than five hundred brothers at one time, most of whom are still alive, though some have fallen asleep. Then... to James, then to all the apostles. Last of all... he appeared also to me.[86]

Hume's criteria for witnesses

As we saw in the last chapter, Hume lists several criteria that he regards as important for assessing the strength of evidence for an alleged event, particularly the number and character of the witnesses, and the way in which they deliver their testimony. In that chapter, in response to Hume, we thought about the character and integrity of the apostles as witnesses; now we shall look at other aspects.

Criterion 1. The number and variety of witnesses
According to Paul's list in 1 Corinthians 15 there were originally well over 500 people who at different times saw the risen Christ during the forty days between his resurrection and ascension. Twenty years later, in the mid-fifties AD when Paul was writing 1 Corinthians, more than half of them were still alive, and presumably, if need be, available for questioning. There was no shortage then of eyewitnesses to the resurrection during the early phase of the growth of the Christian church.

But it is not only the number of eyewitnesses who actually saw the risen Christ that is significant. It is also the widely divergent character of those eyewitnesses, and the different places and situations in which Christ appeared to them. For instance, some were in a group of eleven in a room, one was by herself in a garden, a group of fishermen were by the sea, two were travelling along a road, others on a mountain. It is this variety of character and place that refutes the so-called hallucination theories.

The inadequacy of hallucination theories
Lüdemann and others suggest that the so-called resurrection "appearances" were actually psychological occurrences, like visions or hallucinations: the disciples "saw" something, but it was not objectively real, rather something going on inside their minds.

However, psychological medicine itself witnesses against this explanation.

1. Hallucinations usually occur to people of a certain temperament, with a vivid imagination. The disciples were of very different temperaments: Matthew was a hard-headed, shrewd tax-collector; Peter and some of the others, tough fishermen; Thomas, a born sceptic; and so on. They were not the sort of people one normally associates with susceptibility to hallucinations.

2. Hallucinations tend to be of expected events. Philosopher William Lane Craig points out: "Since a hallucination is just a projection of the mind, it cannot contain anything that is not already in the mind."[87] But none of the disciples was expecting to meet Jesus again. The expectation of Jesus' resurrection was not in their minds at all. Instead, there was fear, doubt, and uncertainty – exactly the wrong psychological preconditions for a hallucination.

3. Hallucinations usually recur over a relatively long period, either increasing or decreasing. But the appearances of Christ occurred frequently, over a period of forty days, and then abruptly ceased. None of those first disciples ever claimed a similar experience again. The only exceptions were Stephen and Paul. Stephen, the first Christian martyr, in the moments before he was stoned to death, exclaimed: "Behold, I see the heavens opened, and the Son of Man standing at the right hand of God."[88] Paul records having met the risen Christ once, and that he was the last to do so.[89] This pattern is not consistent, therefore, with hallucinatory experiences.

4. It is difficult to imagine that the 500 people who saw him at once[90] were suffering from collective hallucination. Indeed, Gary Sibcy, a clinical psychologist, comments:

I have surveyed the professional literature... written by psychologists, psychiatrists and other relevant health care professionals over the past two decades and have yet to find a single documented case of a group hallucination, that is, an event in which more than one person purportedly shared in a visual or other sensory perception where there was clearly no external referent.[91]

5. Hallucinations would not have led to belief in the resurrection. Hallucination theories are severely limited in their explanatory scope: they only attempt to explain the appearances. They clearly do not account for the empty tomb – no matter how many hallucinations the disciples had, they could never have preached the resurrection in Jerusalem, if the nearby tomb had not been empty!

C. S. Lewis makes a characteristically perceptive remark on the topic: "Any theory of hallucination breaks down on the fact (and if it is an invention it is the oddest invention that ever entered the mind of man) that on three separate occasions this hallucination was not immediately recognized as Jesus (Luke 24:13–31; John 20:15; 21:4)."[92]

Criterion 2. The consistency of the testimony
If several witnesses to an event make statements in court that agree in every detail, word-for-word, any judge would be likely to deduce that the testimonies were not independent; and, worse still, that there had possibly been collusion to mislead the court. On the other hand, testimonies of independent witnesses, which were hopelessly in disagreement on all the main points, would be of no use to a court either. What is looked for in independent testimonies is agreement on all the main facts, with just that amount of difference which can be accounted for by different perspectives, etc. There may even be what appear to be minor discrepancies or inconsistencies in the secondary details, which can either be harmonized with one another in a natural way, when more background information is available, or else must be left hanging for the time being, in the hope that further information will clear them up; but which are of such a nature that none of the primary details is affected.

Historians proceed in a similar way to lawyers. No historian would dismiss multiple versions of an event, just because there were discrepancies in the secondary details. Indeed, that is true even if some of the details are irreconcilable; as is the case, for example, with the two versions of Hannibal's journey across the Alps to attack Rome. Although they differ in many details, no scholar doubts the truth of the core-story – that Hannibal did indeed cross the Alps in his campaign against Rome.

When we apply these criteria to the records of the resurrection, we find that the Gospel narratives have the same primary details.

There is a clear core-story: Joseph of Arimathea puts the body of Jesus in his tomb; a small group, or groups, of women-disciples visit the tomb early on the first day of the week, and find the tomb to be empty. They, and the apostles, subsequently meet Jesus on a number of occasions.

In the secondary details there are some apparent discrepancies. For example, Matthew says that Mary Magdalene came to the tomb at dawn;[93] whereas John says, "while it was still dark" Mary went to the tomb.[94] Such statements are easily harmonized: Mary may well have set out while it was still dark, and got to the tomb as dawn broke.

In addition, in any attempt at a detailed reconstruction of events, it is important to be aware, as we pointed out above, that there were different groups of women associated with the death and resurrection of Christ. The group consisting of Mary Magdalene, the "other Mary", and Salome arrived at the tomb first. On approaching the tomb they saw the tomb opened, and Mary ran back into the city to tell Peter and John. While she was gone, Joanna (and possibly Susanna), who had set out from the Hasmonean Palace, arrived by a different route. They would have come through a different gate of the city, and so they did not meet Mary Magdalene. The four women now went into the tomb, where they are told to go back into the city and tell the disciples. As there are many routes through the narrow streets of Jerusalem, they did not meet Peter and John running towards the tomb, followed by Mary Magdalene. On arriving at the tomb John and Peter saw the evidence of the grave-clothes that indicated to them that Jesus had risen. They left the tomb. Mary Magdalene lingered, and it was at this point that she saw Jesus.[95] She then returned to the others at the house in Jerusalem.

Now the women had been told to tell the disciples. So far, only two of them knew – John and Peter. The other nine, who had presumably spent the night in Bethany, had to be told. At this point, Wenham argues, a group of women (probably including "the other" Mary and Salome) set out for Bethany, and on the way they too met Jesus.[96]

Another apparent discrepancy lies in the fact that Luke describes Jesus as appearing to "the eleven";[97] whereas John's description of what appears to be the same event says that Thomas was not present on that occasion.[98] Thus, in fact, only ten disciples were there. However, there is no necessary contradiction here, since the term "the eleven" can mean "the disciples as a group", rather than implying that all of them were there without exception on every occasion. For instance, there are eleven players in an English cricket team. If a sports reporter said that he had gone to Lord's Cricket Ground in London to interview the English Eleven, his statement would not necessarily be taken to imply that he had seen all eleven players, but perhaps only a representative group of them.

For further discussion of the detailed historical questions involved in the events surrounding the burial and resurrection of Christ, see Wenham's *Easter Enigma*.[99]

Criterion 3. The possible bias of witnesses
It is often said that, because the evidence for the resurrection of Jesus Christ comes predominantly from Christian sources, there is a danger of it being partisan, and therefore not carrying the weight of independent testimony. This objection sounds plausible at first, but it looks very different in the light of the following considerations. Those who were convinced by the evidence for the resurrection of Jesus became Christians. *But they were not necessarily Christians when they first heard of the resurrection.* The prime example is Saul of Tarsus. Far from being a Christian, he was a leading academic Pharisee who was fanatically opposed to the Christians – so much so that he was persecuting the Christians, and having them imprisoned and tortured. He wanted to destroy the resurrection story, and stamp out Christianity at its roots. When he heard that Christianity was beginning to spread beyond Jerusalem, he got permission from the High Priest's Office to go to Damascus in Syria and arrest all Christians. But by the time he got to Damascus something utterly unexpected had happened – he had become a Christian![100]

Paul's conversion and subsequent writing have marked the history of Europe and of the world. In his lifetime he founded many churches, and even to the present day his writings (more than half of the New Testament) have influenced millions of people from every nation under the sun. The conversion of Saul has proved a turning point in history, and demands once more an explanation big enough to explain that effect. His own explanation was: "Last of all... he appeared also to me."[101]

Paul's witness is significant, then, for the reason that he was not a believer when he met the risen Christ. It was that meeting which was the cause of his conversion.

But there is another question that should be asked in this connection. Where is the evidence, on the part of those who did not believe the resurrection of Jesus, to prove that he did not rise? The religious authorities, having condemned and executed Jesus, could not afford to ignore, or dismiss, the Christian claim. They desperately wanted to stop a mass movement based on the resurrection. They had at their disposal all their own official resources, and the help of the Roman military machine if they wanted it. Yet strangely they seem to have produced no evidence, except for the patently silly story (for which they had to pay a great deal!) about the disciples stealing the body while the guards slept. So they resorted to crude scare tactics. They put the apostles in prison, and tried to intimidate them by threatening them with serious consequences if they continued preaching the resurrection.[102] The complete absence of contemporary evidence against the resurrection, from the authorities or anyone else, tells its own eloquent story. There does not seem to have been any to publish!

Criterion 4. The attitude of the witnesses
Hume would have us consider here the manner in which the Christians put forward their views. Were they over-hesitant; or, just the opposite, too violent? Certainly they were not hesitant. In Acts, Luke gives us many examples of the courageous way in which the disciples gave their witness to the resurrection, often to very hostile audiences. But they were never violent. Indeed, one of the striking things about the early Christians is their non-violence, which they had learned from Christ himself. He had taught them not to use the sword to protect either him or his message.[103] His kingdom is not the kind of kingdom where people fight.[104] Think of the effect that his conversion had upon Paul. Before he was converted, he was a religious bigot and fanatic, who persecuted his own fellow Jews when they had become Christians. After his conversion, he did not persecute anyone, of any religion, ever again. On the contrary, for his belief in the resurrection of Christ he himself suffered grievous persecution, and eventually gave his life.

It would seem therefore that, in the case of the early disciples, Hume's criteria for credible witnesses are well satisfied.

Women as witnesses

To anyone who knows anything about the ancient laws regarding legal testimony, it is very striking that the first reports mentioned in the Gospels of appearances of the risen Christ were made by women. In first-century Jewish culture, women were not normally considered to be competent witnesses. At that time, therefore, anyone who wanted to invent a resurrection story would never have thought of commencing it in this way. The only value of including such a story would be if it were both true and easy to verify, whatever people thought of the fact that it figured women as witnesses. Its very inclusion, therefore, is a clear mark of historical authenticity.

The psychological evidence

There is no mention in John's account[105] that John and Peter attempted to discuss with Mary the logical implications of the grave-cloths. Psychologically, it is most unlikely that they did; for she was weeping, evidently distraught at the thought of having irreparably lost the body of the one who had brought forgiveness, peace of heart, and honour back into her life. And if "resurrection" meant that she had permanently lost all contact with him, it would have been no comfort to her. After all, she had come to the tomb with the other women in order to complete the embalming of the body, and it is easy to see what was ultimately in their minds. Had the resurrection not happened, they would very quickly have made the tomb into a shrine, to which they could come, and pray, and show devotion to their dead spiritual hero. Yet the extraordinary thing is that there is no record of their ever doing any such thing. Nowhere in the New Testament do we find the apostles encouraging the faithful to make pilgrimages to the tomb of Christ for special blessing, or for healing. On the contrary, in the earliest Christian era there is no evidence of any real interest in the tomb of Christ.

So what was powerful enough to break the strong, natural desire, particularly on the part of those early Christian women, to venerate the tomb? Mary is perhaps the best person to tell us, for she felt very strongly that desire to remain close to the tomb on the day she found it empty. Since she had come to complete the task of embalming the body, she needed to find that body. As she stood there weeping, through her tears she was conscious of someone else nearby, whom she thought was the gardener. Perhaps he had taken the body? So she spoke to him: "Tell me where you have laid him, and I will take him away." Together with the other women, she would have taken him away and reburied him with honour, in a place to be venerated forever.[106]

But she didn't. Something so powerful happened in the garden that day, that Mary and the others never showed any interest in the tomb again. John tells us that the one whom she had taken to be the gardener was actually the risen Christ. "Mary," he said, and as she instantly recognized his voice, she knew that her quest was over. If Jesus was risen, what interest could there possibly be in holding on to his tomb? None whatsoever! No one makes a shrine to a person who is alive.

But there is another issue. Granted that the tomb was abandoned because the disciples were convinced that Jesus had risen from the dead, there then arises the important question of what was to be the relationship between the disciples and the risen Christ. Having found that he was alive, Mary wanted, very naturally, to cling on to him. But Christ had something to say to her – indeed a message for all his followers: "Do not cling to me [that is, in Greek, do not keep holding on to me, or stop holding on to me], for I have not yet ascended to the Father; but go to my brothers and say to them, 'I am ascending to my Father and your Father, to my God and your God.'"[107]

Mary knew he was real and that he was really there: she had heard his voice and touched him; but he was telling her that he was not going to remain with her in that way. She would keep him, but not in the same sense as before. Now, from the other side of death, he was assuring her, and through her all of his followers, that he had created a new and permanent relationship between them and him and his Father, that death itself could not destroy. It was this living relationship with the living Christ that satisfied her heart, and the hearts of millions since. The bare fact of knowing that he had risen from the dead would not have been enough to do that.

SOME FINAL CONSIDERATIONS

The nature of the resurrection body

That evening, Christ appeared to the main group of disciples.[108] They were meeting somewhere in Jerusalem in a room with the doors locked, because they were frightened of the Jewish authorities. He showed them his hands and side with the marks of the nails and spear. Now at last John knew what resurrection meant! The body that had come through the grave-cloths, had come through closed doors – but it was real, tangible, and, above all, alive.

Now some readers will wish at once to raise the question: in this advanced scientific age, how can one possibly believe that a physical body came through grave-cloths, and through locked doors into a room? But perhaps this advanced scientific age has made such a thing more conceivable, rather than less so. We know what the disciples did not know: matter consists largely of empty space; elementary particles can penetrate matter; some – like neutrinos – to immense depth.

In addition to that, there is the question of dimensionality. We are familiar with the four dimensions of space-time; but God is not limited to those four dimensions. Maybe nature itself involves more dimensions than we thought – string theory would suggest there may be more. An analogy can help us here. In 1880 a delightful book called *Flatland* was written by a mathematician, Edwin Abbott, as a satire on class structure.[109] Abbott asks us to imagine a two-dimensional world called Flatland, whose inhabitants are two dimensional figures, straight lines, triangles, squares, pentagons, etc., all the way up to circles. We are introduced to a Sphere from Spaceland (three-dimensions), who tries to explain to one of the creatures in Flatland what it means to be a sphere. The sphere passes through the plane of Flatland, appearing first as a point, then a circle that gets larger, then smaller until it disappears. This, of course, seems impossible to the Flatlanders, simply because they cannot conceive any dimension higher than two. The sphere mystifies them even further by saying that, by moving around above the plane of Flatland, it can see into their houses and can appear in them at will, without the doors having to be open. The sphere even takes one incredulous Flatlander out into space to give him a view of his world from outside. However, on his return, he cannot get his new knowledge accepted by the Flatlanders, who know nothing other than their two-dimensional world. Is it possible that our world is something like Flatland – but with four dimensions rather than two? If so, a reality of higher dimensionality could interact with our world, as the sphere does in the Flatland world.

The physics of matter, and such analogies as that of Flatland, can help us at least to see that it might be very short-sighted and premature to dismiss out of hand the New Testament account of the properties of Christ's resurrection body. If there is a God who transcends space and time, it is not surprising if the resurrection of his Son reveals aspects of reality that also transcend space and time.

Some will take issue, however, with the idea that the resurrection body of Christ is physical, by pointing out that the New Testament itself speaks of the resurrection body as a "spiritual body".[110] The objection, then, asserts that "spiritual" means "non-physical". But a moment's reflection shows that there are other possibilities. When we speak of a "petrol engine", we do not mean an "engine made of petrol". No, we mean an engine powered by petrol. Thus the term "spiritual body" could well be referring to the power behind that body's life, rather than a description of what it is *made* of.

To decide between these possibilities we need only to refer to the text of the New Testament; for there we find that Christ says to his disciples: "See my hands and my feet, that it is I myself! Touch me, and see. For a spirit does not have flesh and bones as you see that I have."[111] That is, he was explicitly pointing out that his resurrection body was not "made of spirit". It had flesh and bone: it was tangible. And to prove the point even further, Christ asked them if they had anything to eat. He was offered a fish, and he ate it in front of them.[112] The eating of that fish proved beyond all doubt that his resurrection body was a physical reality. They must have spent a long time staring at the empty plate on the table after he had gone. Whatever the nature of the world to which he now belonged, he had taken a fish into it. It certainly therefore had a physical dimension.

Doubt and the resurrection

The New Testament writers tell us honestly that there were several occasions on which the first reaction of some of the disciples was to entertain doubts about the resurrection. For example, when the apostles first heard the report of the women, they simply did not believe them, and regarded what they said as nonsense.[113] They were not in the end convinced, until they had seen Jesus for themselves.

Thomas was not with the other disciples in Jerusalem on the evening when the risen Christ appeared in the locked room; and he simply refused to believe their claim that they had seen him. He issued a challenge: "Unless I see in his hands the mark of the nails and place my finger into the mark of the nails, and place my hand into his side, I will never believe."[114] Thomas was not prepared to give in to group pressure – he wanted the evidence for himself. A week later, they all found themselves once more in the locked room in Jerusalem. Jesus appeared, spoke to Thomas, and invited him to put his finger in the nail marks, and his hand in the spear wound. Christ offered him the evidence that he demanded (which proves, incidentally, that the risen Christ had heard him ask for it), gently reproaching him for not believing what the others had said. We are not told whether Thomas did touch Christ on this occasion. But we are told what his response was. He said: "My Lord and my God!"[115] He recognized the risen Jesus as God.

What about those who have not seen Christ?

In this lengthy section on the appearances of Christ we have been thinking of those early Christians who saw him. We also have made the point that after about forty days the appearances stopped – apart from those to Stephen and Paul. It is a simple historical fact, therefore, that the vast majority of Christians throughout history have become Christians without literally seeing Jesus. Christ said something very important about this to Thomas and the others: "Have you believed because you have seen? Blessed are those who have not seen and yet have believed."[116]

They saw and believed – but most have not seen. This, as we saw in Chapter 1, does not mean that Christ is asking all the rest of us to believe without any evidence. In the first place, the evidence that is offered to us is the eyewitness evidence of those who did see. But Christ is also alerting us to the fact that there are different kinds of evidence. One of them is the way in which the communication of God's message penetrates the heart and conscience of the listener.

Christ's death and resurrection predicted by the Old Testament

Among the disciples there was a deeper sort of incredulity than that of Thomas, which was not overcome simply by seeing. Luke tells us of two of Jesus' followers who were taking a journey from Jerusalem to the nearby village of Emmaus on that event-packed first day of the week.[117] They were utterly dispirited at the events that had just taken place in Jerusalem. A stranger joined them. It was Jesus, but they did not recognize him. Luke explains that their eyes were "held", presumably supernaturally, and for the following reason. They had thought that Jesus was going to be their political liberator; but, to their dismay, he had allowed himself to be crucified. To their way of thinking, a liberator who allowed himself to be crucified by his opponents was useless as a liberator. Rumours spread by women about his resurrection were therefore irrelevant.

To solve their problem, Jesus did not immediately open their eyes to see who he was. What he did was to take them through a concise summary of the Old Testament, arguing that it was the consistent testimony of the Old Testament prophets that the messiah, whoever he was, would be rejected by his nation, put to death, and then eventually be raised and glorified. This was news to the two travellers. Hitherto they had read from the Old Testament what they had wanted to see. They had studied the prophecies about the triumphant coming of messiah, but had overlooked the fact that messiah also had to fulfil the role of the suffering servant; and in order to do that he must suffer, and only then enter into his glory.

Perhaps the most remarkable of those predictions is contained in Isaiah. Over 500 years before it occurred, the rejection, suffering, and death of the messiah for human sins is graphically portrayed: "He was wounded for our transgressions; he was crushed for our iniquities; upon him was the chastisement that brought us peace, and with his stripes we are healed."[118] Isaiah then speaks of him being "cut off out of the land of the living", and being put in a grave; after which we read the remarkable words: "Out of the anguish of his soul he shall see and be satisfied."[119] According to Isaiah, then, the messiah was going to die. Therefore, far from the death of Jesus proving that he was not the messiah, it proved that he was. When the two travellers had grasped that, it made the story of Jesus' resurrection that they had heard from the women credible. It removed the grounds of their despair, and filled them with new hope.

But still they didn't recognize that the stranger was Jesus. So far it was enough that they had been brought to see the objective fact that the Old Testament proclaimed the death of messiah. How did they come to recognize him? The answer is that they recognized him by something he did when they invited him into their home. He performed an act that would be intensely revealing to those who belonged to the inner core of the early disciples. As they were partaking of a simple meal, Jesus broke the bread for them – and suddenly they recognized him! This detail has a powerful ring of genuineness and truth. They had seen Jesus break bread before –

when he fed the multitudes, for instance – and there was something indefinable, but characteristic about the way he did it that was instantly recognizable.

We all know this kind of thing from our experience of family and friends: characteristic ways of doing things that are special to them and which we would recognize anywhere. To the disciples it was evidence, conclusive evidence, that this really was Jesus. No impostor would ever have thought of imitating such a tiny detail.

This has been a lengthy and detailed account – necessarily so, because of the importance of the topic. We give the last word on the evidence for the resurrection to legal expert Professor Sir Norman Anderson: "The empty tomb, then, forms a veritable rock on which all rationalistic theories of the resurrection dash themselves in vain."[120]

The reader will note that there have been relatively few references to the New Atheists in this section on the resurrection. There is a simple reason for that. For all their vaunted interest in evidence, there is nothing in their writings to show that they have seriously interacted with the arguments, many of them very well known, that we have presented here. The silence of the New Atheism on this matter tells its own story.

CHAPTER 9

FINAL REFLECTIONS

There is another kind of evidence that we have not yet discussed in this book. It is the evidence of God that is available through direct perception. Suppose I say to you: "The roses have started to bloom in our garden." You would not dream of thinking that I had come to this conclusion as the result of a long chain of philosophical and scientific reasoning. No, you would correctly infer that I had perceived it directly. There are many things in our daily experience just like that. They are directly perceived, rather than established by a long chain of inference and reasoning. It is so with God. Logical arguments are important of course; but, if there is a God worthy of the name, they cannot possibly be the whole story. Otherwise access to God would be the provenance of a few intellectuals. There must be something more. And there is. The Bible speaks clearly of at least three distinct ways in which God reveals himself to human beings: (1) through creation, (2) moral conscience, and (3) through the written revelation of Scripture.

In his famous letter to the Romans, the apostle Paul discusses this important matter of revelation. In the first chapter we find the following passage that deals with our point (1). Speaking of human beings Paul says: "For what can be known about God is plain to them [*lit*: 'in them'],[1] because God has shown it to them.[2] For his invisible attributes, namely, his eternal power and divine nature, have been clearly perceived, ever since the creation of the world, in the things that have been made. So they are without excuse. For although they knew God, they did not honour him as God or give thanks…"[3]

This passage makes several assertions:

1. God has taken the initiative in making himself known to us by first creating us and placing us in a universe designed and

created to express not merely his existence, but something of what he is like.

2. The visible creation objectively shows us two of God's attributes: his eternal power and divinity.

3. We perceive these attributes directly, intuitively; not by a long process of discursive, logical reasoning.

4. So that we could perceive the significance of what we see as we contemplate God's creation, he created within us not only our cognitive faculties in general, but an instinctive faculty of awareness of God.

This faculty of perception is at work in everyone, including Richard Dawkins. We can see this in his famous definition of biology as: "the study of complicated things which give the impression of having been designed for a purpose".[4] Indeed, he writes elsewhere that it is "terribly tempting" to say that the universe has been designed. The spectacular success of science in elucidating the unbelievably sophisticated mechanisms of the workings of the universe has done nothing but enhance that initial impression. The New Atheists, however, spend their lives in denial, hiding behind the idea that, because they have found what they think is the only mechanism involved in life's origin and variation, they have somehow explained life. They seem unaware of their elementary category mistake, in thinking that the existence of a mechanism somehow obviates the need for an agent who designed the mechanism. Their concept of "explanation" is inadequate – in several different ways, in fact.

The distinguished German philosopher Robert Spaemann of Munich University says:

> Science does not try to find out, as Aristotle did, why the stone falls downwards. It rather tries to discover the laws according to which it falls. And that constitutes scientific "explanation". But Wittgenstein writes: "The great delusion of modernity is that the laws of nature explain the universe for us. The laws of nature describe the universe, they describe the regularities. But they explain nothing."[5]

Dawkins needs to pay attention to Wittgenstein. The "great delusion" has Dawkins so thoroughly in its grip, that he thinks science has given the ultimate explanation, making God redundant and enabling him to deny the evidence of God that he experiences every day of his life. Spaemann[6] gives an interesting analogy to illuminate this flaw in atheist thinking. He refers to the work of musicologist Helga Thoene, who discovered a remarkable double coding in the D-minor *Partita* by J. S. Bach. If you apply to the music a formal scheme of numbers corresponding to letters of the alphabet[7] the following ancient proverb appears: *Ex Deo nascimur, in Christo morimur, per Spiritum Sanctum revivisicimur.*[8] Clearly one does not have to know about this hidden text in order to enjoy the Sonata – it has been enjoyed for hundreds of years without people having any idea that the message was there.

Spaemann addresses the New Atheists: "You can describe the evolutionary process, if you so decide, in purely naturalistic terms. But the text that then appears when you see a person, when you see a beautiful act or a beautiful picture, can only be read if you use a completely different code." Spaemann goes on to imagine that our musicologist then said that the music of Bach had explained itself completely; that it was simply chance that the message pops out, and so it was enough to interpret the music purely as music without thinking about any text. Would that not strain our credulity? Of course it would. We would not accept for a moment that the text just happened to be there by chance, without someone having encoded it and put it there. So it is with science. You can, if you wish, restrict yourself to a purely naturalistic science. But then you cannot hope to explain the text that appears. The musicologist, as a musicologist, can explain how the music was composed; but only if they ignore the text. The New Atheists would appear to be in exactly that position. They openly confess that they are not prepared even to listen to arguments that go outside the bounds of their naturalism. Of course it is honest of them to say that they have decided to imprison themselves inside the small world of their naturalistic castle. But whether that attitude is reasonable, or whether there is a world outside that they have put beyond their own reach, is of course quite a different matter.

The second source of evidence for God that we perceive directly has to do with our innate sense of morality – our point (2). We perceive ourselves to be moral beings. The apostle Paul points out that our daily experience of people accusing and excusing each other and themselves is evidence of the fact that we intuitively believe that there is a standard of morality outside of ourselves. If you accuse me of something, your accusation is based on the fact that you expect me to share your moral standard. If I then begin to make excuses, it proves that I do accept that standard. In other words, this everyday human behaviour shows that people believe there is a universal standard outside of themselves; and each of us expects others to conform to it. This universally observed phenomenon constitutes strong evidence for the existence of God. As the Oxford philosopher J. L. Mackie, an atheist, admitted: "If there are objective values, they make the existence of a god more probable than it would have been without them. Thus we have a defensible argument from morality to the existence of a god."[9]

Immanuel Kant, though he argued that God's existence could not be proved by pure reason, nevertheless confessed his belief in God on the basis of practical reason. As evidence he listed the two sources we have just discussed: "Two things fill the mind with ever new and increasing admiration and reverence, the more often and more steadily one reflects on them: the starry heavens above me and the moral law within me."[10] Those words are engraved on the headstone of his grave in Kaliningrad.

As this book comes to its conclusion I should like to point out that Dawkins gives the game away in the Dedication at very beginning of his book *The God Delusion*. He cites Douglas Adams (of *The Hitchhiker's Guide to the Galaxy* fame): "Isn't it enough to see that a garden is beautiful without having to believe that there are fairies at the bottom of it too?" Some may think that Dawkins does a great job of getting rid of the fairies; although it must be said that most of us have never believed in them anyway – and if we did we soon grew out of it. But when he sees the beauty of a garden, does Dawkins really believe that there is no gardener? Will he hold that its sublime beauty has come about from raw nature by pure chance? Of course not – for gardens are distinguished from raw nature precisely by the operation of intelligence. And that is just the point. Dawkins has a deserved reputation for describing, in enviable prose, the breathtaking beauty of the garden that is this universe. I find it incomprehensible and rather sad that he presents us with such an obviously false set of alternatives: the garden on its own, or the garden plus fairies. Real gardens do not produce themselves: they have gardeners and owners. Similarly with the universe: it did not generate itself. It has a creator – and an owner.

Twenty centuries ago, in the dawn of an oriental day, a woman, distraught at finding an empty tomb in a garden near the place of crucifixion, saw a man standing in the shadows. Thinking that he was the gardener, she asked him if he had removed the body of Jesus. He spoke her name, "Mary"; and, in a moment of overwhelming understanding, she realized that this was not the gardener but the owner, the Lord of Creation, the one who was ultimately responsible not only for all the beauty of flowers and trees, but for the whole universe in all of its prodigious glory. Jesus had risen from the dead. Death itself had been overcome.

Atheism has no answer to death, no ultimate hope to give. It is an empty and sterile worldview, which leaves us in a closed universe that will ultimately incinerate any last trace that we ever existed. It is, quite literally, a hope-less philosophy. Its story ends in the grave. But the resurrection of Jesus opens the door on a bigger story. It is for each one of us to decide whether it is the true one or not.

NOTES

Introduction

1. Richard Dawkins, *The God Delusion* (hereafter *GD*), London, Bantam Press, 2006.

2. Stephen Hawking, *A Brief History of Time*, London, Bantam Press, 1988, p.175.

3. Stephen Hawking and Leonard Mlodinow, *The Grand Design*, London, Bantam Press, 2010.

4. Christopher Hitchens, *God is not Great* (hereafter *GNG*), London, Atlantic Books, 2008.

5. Daniel C. Dennett, *Breaking the Spell*, London, Penguin, 2007.

6. *Ibid*, p.21.

7. Sam Harris, *The End of Faith*, London, Free Press, 2006.

8. Sam Harris, *Letter to a Christian Nation*, New York, Alfred A. Knopf, 2006.

9. Sam Harris, *The Moral Landscape*, New York, Free Press, 2010.

10. Michel Onfray, *In Defence of Atheism* (hereafter *IDA*), London, Profile Books, 2007.

11. *Perché non possiamo essere cristiani (e meno che mai cattolici)*, Longanesi, 2007.

12. *GD*, p.27.

13. Reproduced by permission of Fixed-Point Foundation.

14. Ruth Gledhill, *The Times*, 21 November 2009, p.14.

15. *The God Delusion Debate*, a Fixed-Point DVD, www.fixed-point.org. See also www.dawkinslennoxdebate.com.

16. John C. Lennox, *God's Undertaker: Has Science Buried God?* 2nd ed, Oxford, Lion Hudson, 2009.

17. *Has Science Buried God?* A Fixed-Point DVD, www.fixed-point.org.

18. *Can Atheism Save Europe?* A Fixed-Point DVD, www.fixed-point.org.

19. *Is God Great?* A Fixed-Point DVD, www.fixed-point.org.

20. Intelligence Quotient Squared is a series of public debates sponsored by the Sydney Morning Herald.

21. *Duelling Professors*, http://www.youtube.com/watch?v=Yx0CXmagQu0.

22. www.veritas.org/Media.aspx#!/v/925.

23. John C. Lennox, *God and Stephen Hawking*, Oxford, Lion Hudson, 2011.

24. Alister & Joanna McGrath, *The Dawkins Delusion?* London, SPCK, 2007.

25. Keith Ward, *Why There Almost Certainly Is a God*, Oxford, Lion Hudson, 2008.

26. David Bentley Hart, *The Dawkins Letters*, Fearn, Christian Focus Publications, 2007.

27. David Bentley Hart, *Atheist Delusions*, New Haven and London, Yale University Press, 2009.

28. *GD*, p.141.

29. *GNG*, p.5.

30. Dennett, *Breaking the Spell*, p.21.

31. Alasdair MacIntyre, *After Virtue*, London, Duckworth, 2003.

32. See Ward, *Why There Almost Certainly Is a God*, Chapter 8.

33. Christopher Hitchens, *Letters to a Young Contrarian*, New York, Basic Books, 2001.

34. *GNG*, p.13.

35. *A Bitter Rift Divides Atheists*, Barbara Bradley Hagerty, NPR, 19 October 2009.

36. Harris, *Letter to a Christian Nation*, p.ix.

37. *Der Spiegel*, 26 May 2007, pp.56–69.

38. *Der Spiegel*, 10 September 2007.

39. Richard Dawkins, *A Devil's Chaplain*, London, Phoenix, 2004, p.185.

40. *GD*, pp.23–24.

41. And yet the New Atheists are prepared to accuse God of totalitarianism.

42. *GD*, p.28.

43. http://www.timesonline.co.uk/tol/comment/faith/article2368534.ece.

44. http://news.bbc.co.uk/1/hi/programmes/wtwtgod/3518375.stm.

45. www.gc.cuny.edu/faculty/research_briefs/aris/key_findings.htm.

46. Richard Dawkins, *River Out of Eden*, New York, Basic Books, 1995, see also his, *A Devil's Chaplain, op cit.* pp.17–22.

47. *New Scientist*, 18 November 2006, pp.8–11.

48. See David C. Lindberg and Ronald L. Numbers (eds.), *Where Science and Christianity Meet*, Chicago, University of Chicago Press, 2003, pp.198–200.

49. *GD*, p.33.

50. *A Bitter Rift Divides Atheists*, Barbara Bradley Hagerty, NPR, 19 October 2009.

51. McGraths, *The Dawkins Delusion?*

52. John Humphrys, *In God We Doubt*, London, Hodder and Stoughton, 2007.

53. I have interwoven Humphrys' comments with his statements for sake of clarity.

54. This role played by evolution in the debate is discussed in more detail in my *God's Undertaker*.

55. 2 January 2011.

Chapter 1: Are God and Faith Enemies of Reason and Science?

1. *IDA*, pp.12, 13.

2. Please note the significance of this step in Genesis where hitherto it is God who has provided the names (see Genesis 1 "And God called...").

3. Peter Harrison, *The Bible, Protestantism and the Rise of Science*, Cambridge, Cambridge University Press, 1998.

4. That is, reasons that have to do with the convictions, beliefs, and principles that we already have, *before* we bring them to bear on a situation.

5. Sir Arthur Eddington, *The End of the World: From the Standpoint of Mathematical Physics*, Nature, 127, 1931, p.450.

6. Sir John Maddox, *Nature*, 340, 1989, p.425.

7. See my *God's Undertaker* for more on the use of science by the New Atheists.

8. Hawking and Mlodinow, *The Grand Design*, p.180.

9. Hawking and Mlodinow, *The Grand Design*, p.5.

10. Hawking, *A Brief History of Time*, p.174.

11. I am well aware that chaotic considerations (sensitivity to initial conditions) make this prediction

practically impossible for all but the first few ricochets of the ball.

12. See Clive Cookson, "Scientists Who Glimpsed God", *Financial Times*, 29 April 1995, p.20.

13. C. S. Lewis, *Miracles*, London, Fontana, 1974, p.63.

14. Richard Feynman, *The Meaning of it all*, London, Penguin, 2007, p.23.

15. Allan Sandage, *New York Times*, 12 March 1991, p.B9. Or see http://www.nytimes.com/1991/03/12/science/sizing-up-the-cosmos-an-astronomer-s-quest.html.

16. Hawking and Mlodinow, *The Grand Design*, p.164.

17. For more on this concept, see my *God's Undertaker*, pp.69–77.

18. Sir John Polkinghorne, *One World*, London, SPCK, 1986, p.80.

19. Hannah Devlin, "Hawking: God Did Not Create the Universe" *The Times Eureka*, 12 September 2010.

20. *Eureka*, 12 September 2010, p.23.

21. Hannah Devlin, "Hawking: God Did Not Create the Universe" 12 September 2010.

22. For more on this issue see my *God and Stephen Hawking*, Oxford, Lion Hudson, 2011.

23. *GD*, p.74.

24. Richard Dawkins, "Is science a religion?" *The Humanist*, Jan/Feb 1997, pp.26–39.

25. Richard Dawkins, *Daily Telegraph* Science Extra, 11 September 1989.

26. *IDA*, p.28.

27. We note in passing that this statement is a rather blatant instance of begging the question.

28. Julian Baggini, *Atheism – A Very Short Introduction*, Oxford, Oxford University Press, 2003, pp.32, 33.

29. http://atheistempire.com/atheism/faith.php.

30. Baggini, *Atheism*, p.31.

31. *GD*, p.348.

32. It is perhaps worth pointing out that revelation (in the biblical sense) is not a feeling but involves the claim that God can and has shown us things that would otherwise be inaccessible to the unaided human intellect. Nor does revelation preclude reason since reason has to be used on it to see whether it makes sense and to consider evidence for its truth-claims.

33. Dawkins, *A Devil's Chaplain*, pp.288–89.

34. Baggini, *Atheism*, p.33.

35. *GNG*, p.5.

36. Immanuel Kant, *Critique of Pure Reason*, p. 29 Bxxix-xxx.

37. We should note here a further common use of "faith" to describe a body of doctrine.

38. I am writing as a Christian. It is only fair and right that the representatives of other religions should respond to any New Atheist charge against them.

39. John 20:25.

40. John 20:26–29. The New Atheists might notice the use of the term "believe" in the translation rather than the term "faith" even though they are equivalent.

41. Baggini, *Atheism*, p.33.

42. Baggini is not alone. Philosopher A. C. Grayling is equally confused about the definition of faith – see p.49.

43. John 20:30–31.

44. For example, John 2:11, 3:2, 4:41, 4:53, 6:14.

45. *Times Higher Education Supplement* review of *GD*, 1 September 2006. Or see http://www.lrb.co.uk/v28/n20/terry-eagleton/lunging-flailing-mispunching.

46. *GD*, p.347.

47. *GD*, p.28.

48. Acts 26:24.

49. Alister McGrath, *Dawkins' God: Genes, Memes, and the Meaning of Life*, Oxford, Blackwell, 2005, p.87.

50. Sigmund Freud, *The Future of an Illusion (Die Zukunft einer Illusion, 1927)* English translation by James Strachey, New York, London, W. W. Norton & Company, 1975.

51. *IDA*, p.23.

52. *IDA*, p.27.

53. Manfred Lütz, *Gott: Eine kleine Geschichte des Grössten*, München, Pattloch, 2007.

54. See the New York Review of Books http://www.nybooks.com/articles/archives/1998/nov/19/discreet-charm-of-nihilism/.

55. Lütz, *Gott: Eine kleine Geschichte des Grössten* – Lütz also argues in detail that the same holds for Jung and Frankl.

56. *GD*, p. 51.

57. *Daily Telegraph* Science Extra, 11 September 1989.

58. Templeton Prize Address, 1995, http://www.origins.org/articles/davies_templetonaddress.html.

59. See Max Jammer, *Einstein and Religion*, Princeton, University Press, 1999, p.94.

60. *GD*, p.34.

61. See particularly Jammer, *Einstein and Religion*, p.50.

62. Jammer, *Einstein and Religion*, p.48.

63. *Letter from Einstein to Phyllis Wright*, 24 January 1936, Albert Einstein Archive 52-337. Cited by Walter Isaacson, *Einstein*, London, Simon and Schuster, 2007, p.388.

64. *New Scientist*, 8 November 2007.

65. I am of course aware that Einstein is an advance on Newton; but we should not forget that Newton's laws are still accurate enough to do the necessary calculations to put a man on the moon.

66. At a deeper level there are uncertainties within mathematics as shown by the work of Kurt Gödel, but we cannot digress to discuss them here.

67. As is the case in my own field of algebra with the Classification of Finite Simple Groups.

68. *IDA*, p.1.

69. *GD*, p.125.

70. Eugene Wigner *Communications in Pure and Applied Mathematics*, Vol.13, No.1 (February 1960), New York, John Wiley & Sons, Inc.

71. Which argument, if valid, would of course, by the same token, dismiss atheism also.

72. See John Haught, *God and the New Atheism*, Louisville, Westminster John Knox Press, 2008, p.57.

73. Hawking and Mlodinow, *The Grand Design*, p.181.

74. John Gray, *Straw Dogs*, London, Granta Books, 2002, p.26.

75. For the detail of this argument see http://plato.stanford.edu/entries/religion-science/.

76. Materialism is the view that nothing exists apart from matter (or "mass-energy" in more technical terms) so that ultimate reality is the material universe.

77. *GD*, p.351.

Chapter 2: Is Religion Poisonous?

1. Richard Brooks, *Sunday Times*, 2 September 2007.

2. http://news.bbc.co.uk/1/hi/programmes/wtwtgod/3518375.stm.

3. Humphrys, *In God We Doubt*, p.117.

4. *GNG*, Chapter 13.

5. *GD*, p.49.

6. *GD*, p.342.

7. Keith Ward, *Is Religion Dangerous?*, Oxford, Lion Hudson, 2006, p.55.

8. In an edited transcript of a talk given at the Atheist Alliance conference in Washington D.C. on 28 September 2007.

9. http://www.positiveatheism.org/hist/russell2.htm.

10. Although Onfray entitles his book more broadly: *In Defence of Atheism: The Case against Christianity, Judaism and Islam.*

11. E.g. Dawkins: "Unless otherwise stated, I shall have Christianity mostly in mind…", *GD*, p.58.

12. *GNG*, p.11.

13. Sam Harris, *Letter to a Christian Nation* New York, Alfred A. Knopf, 2006.

14. It is not hard to see how such ideas could fan the flames of persecution against Christians.

15. Matthew 26:52.

16. For a discussion of miracles see Chapter 7.

17. Luke 22:51.

18. It is therefore clear that, when Christ said he had "not come to bring peace but a sword" (Matthew 10:34), he did not mean a physical sword; but rather that attitudes to him would lead to spiritual division within society and family. Some would accept him, and others reject him.

19. John 19:12.

20. John 18:28 – 19:16.

21. Zechariah 9:9; John 12:12–19.

22. John 18:36. In Greek the tenses in this hypothetical conditional sentence can refer either to the present, i.e. "my servants would now be fighting", or to a past process, "my disciples would have been fighting". According to Greek scholar Professor David Gooding, this second translation is to be preferred. Christ is referring to what happened in Gethsemane, when he forbade his disciples to fight in order to prevent his arrest by the Jews.

23. John 18:37.

24. It is important to note, however, that not all of that community supported these charges. By far the majority of Jesus' early followers were Jews. In addition, two prominent members of the Sanhedrin, Nicodemus and Joseph of Arimathea, disassociated themselves from the verdict against Christ by requesting his body to give it a proper burial.

25. Matthew 23:23–28.

26. Klaus Müller, *Streit um Gott*, Regensburg, 2006, p.33 (translation mine).

27. Arnold Angenendt, *Toleranz und Gewalt*, Münster, Verlag Aschendorff, 2009.

28. *Die Tageszeitung*, 5th January 2008.

29. Maarten t'Hart, *Mozart und Ich*, Munich, Piper, 2006.

30. Angenendt, *Toleranz und Gewalt*, p.15.

31. *GD*, p.354.

32. *GD*, p.52.

33. *GD*, p.298.

34. *Times Higher Education Supplement* review of *GD*, 1 September 2006. Or see http://www.lrb.co.uk/v28/n20/terry-eagleton/lunging-flailing-mispunching.35. Jürgen Habermas, *Glaube und Wissen*, Friedenspreis des Deutschen Buchhandels 2001, Frankfurt am Main, 2001, p.25.

36. Jürgen Habermas, *Time of Transitions*, New York, Polity Press, 2006.

37. http://www.ttf.org/index/journal/detail/atheism-and-moral-clarity/.

38. David Sloan Wilson "Beyond Demonic Memes: Why Richard Dawkins is Wrong about Religion", Internet magazine *eSceptic*, 4 July 2007.

39. See Helen Phillips, *New Scientist*, 1 September 2007, pp.32–36.

40. *Ibid.*

41. Nicholas Beale and Sir John Polkinghorne, *Questions of Truth*, Westminster, John Knox Press, 2009.

42. Professor Andrew Sims, *Is Faith Delusion?: Why Religion is Good For Your Health*, London, Continuum, 2009.

43. *Ibid.*, p.100.

44. *Ibid.*, from the Preface.

45. Matthew Parris, *The Times*, 27 December 2008.

46. Ward, *Is Religion Dangerous?*, p.40.

47. David Berlinski, *The Devil's Delusion – Atheism and its Scientific Pretensions*, New York, Crown Forum, 2008, p.21.

48. Noam Chomsky, *New Scientist*, 26 July 2008, p.46.

Chapter 3: Is Atheism Poisonous?

1. Marilynne Robinson, "Review of *The God Delusion*", *Harper's Magazine*, 2006. See http://solutions.synearth.net/2006/10/20/.

2. *GNG*, p.230.

3. Peter Berkowitz, *The Wall Street Journal*, 16 July 2007, p.A13.

4. Chris Hedges, *I Don't Believe in Atheists*, New York, Free Press, 2008, p.54.

5. *GNG*, p.57.

6. John Gray, *Black Mass: Apocalyptic Religion and the Death of Utopia*, London, Penguin, 2007, pp.36, 39.

7. *GD*, p.34.

8. *GD*, p.309.

9. *GD*, pp.315–16.

10. Peter Berkowitz, "The New New Atheism", *The Wall Street Journal*, 16 July 2007, p.A13.

11. *GNG*, p.12.

12. *The Difference between the Natural Philosophy of Democritus and the Natural Philosophy of Epicurus*, translated in K. Marx and F. Engels, *On Religion*, Moscow, Foreign Languages Publishing House, 1955, p.15.

13. *Ibid.* p.5.

14. *Black Book of Communism*, ed. Stephane Courtois, Cambridge Mass., Harvard University Press, 1999.

15. Michael Rissmann, *Hitlers Gott: Vorsehungsglaube und Sendungsbewusstsein des deutschen Diktators*, Zürich, Pendo, 2001.

16. The main ideas of his book are also to be found in Rissmann's essay, "Hitlers Vorsehungsglaube und seine Wirkung" (Communio 4/2002, S.358-367).

17. *Hitler's Table Talk*, stenographic notes of Hitler's private conversations, London, Weidenfeld and Nicolson, 1953.

18. *GD*, p.309.

19. Berlinski, *The Devil's Delusion*, pp.26–27.

20. Richard Schröder, *Abschaffung der Religion*, Freiburg im Breisgau, Herder, 2008, p.18, translation mine.

21. Richard Dawkins, *The Greatest Show on Earth*, London, Bantam Press, 2009.

22. In *50 Voices of Disbelief*, eds. Russell Blackford and Udo Schüklenk, Oxford, Wiley-Blackwell, 2009, p.290.

23. Cited by Ruth Gledhill, *The Times*, 2 April 2010.

24. *GD*, p.342.

25. Gray, *Black Mass*, p.198.

26. Romans 5:12.

27. Gray, *Black Mass*, p.36.

28. Revelation 6.

29. Harris, *The End of Faith*, pp.52–53.

30. Aleksandr Solzhenitsyn, Templeton Prize Address, 1983.

Chapter 4: Can We be Good Without God?

1. *GNG*, p.97.

2. *GNG*, p.109.

3. *GD*, pp.51, 59.

4. Michael Ruse, *Defining Darwin: Essays on the History and Philosophy of Evolution*, Amherst New York, Prometheus Books, 2009, Chapter 10, p.237.

5. Peter Singer, "Sanctity of Life or Quality of Life?", *Pediatrics*, Vol. 72, No.1, July 1983, pp.128–129.

6. In *50 Voices of Disbelief*, Blackford and Schűklenk, p.171.

7. Marc Hauser, *Moral Minds*, New York, HarperCollins, 2006.

8. M. Hauser and P. Singer, "Morality Without Religion", *Free Inquiry* Vol. 26, No. 1, 2006, pp.18–19.

9. C. S. Lewis, *The Abolition of Man*, London, Geoffrey Bles, 1940.

10. For this and Einstein's stance on religion and science see the definitive work of Max Jammer, *Einstein and Religion*, Princeton, Princeton University Press, 1999. The citation here is from p.69.

11. Richard P. Feynman, *The Meaning of it All*, London, Penguin, 2007, p.32.

12. *Ibid.* p.43.

13. Dawkins, *A Devil's Chaplain*, p.39.

14. Harris, *The Moral Landscape*.

15. Holmes Rolston III, *Genes, Genesis and God*, Cambridge, Cambridge University Press, 1999, pp.214–15.

16. Alasdair MacIntyre raises the question as to which "ought" Hume is talking about, and also whether the transition from is to ought needs great care and is usually fallacious, or whether any such transition is logically impossible. MacIntyre warns about Hume's well-known inconsistency in other areas (*A Short History of Ethics*, London, Macmillan, 1967, p.174).

17. We note, however, that this use of the word "naturalism" is, as Raphael has indicated, rather broader than that used by contemporary thinkers, where, in ethics, the term refers to "theories which *define* value terms as equivalent to expressions describing a natural fact, e.g. theories which say that 'good' means the same as 'pleasant' or 'desired'" (*Moral Philosophy*, Oxford, Oxford University Press, 1994, footnote p.18).

18. Lewis, *The Abolition of Man*.

19. Julian Baggini, "The Moral Formula", *The Independent*, 11 April 2011.

20. Harris, *The Moral Landscape*, p.39.

21. Perhaps Harris is vaguely aware of this himself since, towards the end of his book, he attenuates the claim of his cover sub-title to the lesser and very different "claim that science could have something important to say about values" (*The Moral Landscape*, p.189).

22. Kwame Anthony Appiah, "Science knows best", *The New York Times*, 1 October 2010.

23. http://scienceblogs.com/pharyngula/2010/05/sam_harris_v_sean_carroll.php?.

24. http://www.huffingtonpost.com/sam-harris/a-science-of-morality_b_567185.html.

25. A term coined around the turn of the twentieth century and popularized by the American historian Richard Hofstadter.

26. Herbert Spencer, *Social Statics*, New York, D. Appleton, 1851.

27. Michael Ruse, *Can a Darwinian be a Christian?* Cambridge, Cambridge University Press, 2001, p.170.

28. Ruse points out that G. E. Moore called Spencer's "is to ought" logic a prime example of the naturalistic fallacy (Ruse, *Can a Darwinian be a Christian?*).

29. Ruse, *Can a Darwinian be a Christian?*, p.182.

30. See Jonathan Hodge and Gregory Radick, *The Cambridge Companion to Darwin*, Cambridge, Cambridge University Press, 2003, pp.214ff.

31. Charles Darwin, *The Descent of Man*, 2nd ed, New York, A. L. Burt Co., 1874, p.178.

32. Charles Darwin, *Life and Letters I*, Letter to W. Graham, 3 July 1881, p.316.

33. See Richard Hofstadter, *Social Darwinism in American Thought*, Boston, Beacon Press, 1955, p.204.

34. Horgan's first objection is that he disagrees with Harris about Hume: "Hume was right: The realm of ought is qualitatively different from the realm of is." For the reference, see below.

35. http://www.theglobeandmail.com/news/arts/books/book-review-the-moral-landscape-how-science-can-determine-human-values-by-sam-harris/article1749446/page2/.

36. There are now various schools of sociobiology, but their primary thesis remains essentially the same.

37. Jacques Monod and A. Wainhouse, *Chance and Necessity*, London, Collins, 1971, pp.110, 167.

38. Gaia is the Greek earth-goddess whose name is attached to James Lovelock's theory of earth as a self-regulating mechanism (*Gaia: The Practical Science of Planetary Medicine*, London, Gaia Books, 1991).

39. Gray, *Straw Dogs*, p.33.

40. Peter Singer, *Practical Ethics*, 2nd ed, Cambridge, Cambridge University Press, 1993, reprint of 1999, p.331.

41. William B. Province, "Scientists, Face It! Science and Religion are Incompatible", *The Scientist*, 5 September 1988.

42. Alasdair Palmer, "Must Knowledge Gained Mean Paradise Lost?" *The Sunday Telegraph*, 6 April 1977.

43. Monod and Wainhouse, *Chance and Necessity*.

44. Materialistic reductionism holds that everything can, in the end, be reduced to nothing but physics and chemistry – that is, to matter and its behaviour.

45. Michael Ruse and Edward O. Wilson, "Evolution and Ethics", *New Scientist*, Vol. 108, 17 October 1985, pp.50–52.

46. Gray, *Straw Dogs*, p.31.

47. Gray, *Black Mass*, p.26.

48. *Ibid.* p.37.

49. *Ibid.* pp.107, 109.

50. There is an interesting discussion of the difficulties of explaining altruism within the framework of evolutionary theory in Rolston, *Genes, Genesis and God*, Chapter 5.

51. Edward O. Wilson, *Sociobiology*, Cambridge USA, Harvard University Press, 1975, p.3.

52. Holmes Rolston III, *Biology, Ethics and the Origins of Life*, Boston, Jones and Bartlett, 1995, p.96.

53. Rolston, *Biology, Ethics and the Origins of Life*, p.127.

54. Rolston, *Biology, Ethics and the Origins of Life*, pp.128, 129. A further investigation of the arguments would take us beyond our present remit and the reader is referred to biologist Denis Alexander, *Rebuilding the Matrix: Science and Faith in the 21st Century*, Oxford, Lion, 2001, ch.11, for an analysis of the empirical and philosophical inadequacies of these arguments from the perspective of a theist who holds to Darwinian theory.

55. For a critique of sociobiology from an evolutionary perspective, see Langdon Gilkey's article in Rolston, *Biology, Ethics and the Origins of Life*, p.163ff.

56. For a critical analysis of an earlier, equally desperate attempt by C. H. Waddington, see Lewis, *The Abolition of Man*, p.29.

57. Richard Dawkins, *The Selfish Gene*, Oxford, Oxford University Press, 1976, p.215.

58. Dawkins, *The Selfish Gene*, p.ix.

59. *Ibid.* p.205.

60. See Lewis, *The Abolition of Man*, p.28.

61. Richard Dawkins, *River Out of Eden*, New York, Basic Books, 1992, p.133.

62. Steven Rose, who has no quarrel with Dawkins over evolution itself as a biological theory, argues strongly against the reductionism that lies at the heart of Dawkins' genetic determinism. He thinks that it is simply wrong: "I am distressed with the arrogance with which some biologists claim for their – our – discipline explanatory and interventionist powers which

it certainly does not possess, and so cavalierly dismiss the counter-evidence" (*Lifelines*, London, Penguin, 1997, p.276). He goes on to say: "The phenomena of life are always and inexorably simultaneously about nature *and* nurture, and the phenomena of human existence and experience are always simultaneously biological and social. Adequate explanations must involve both" (*Lifelines*, p.279).

63. Jean-Paul Sartre, *Existentialism*, New York, Bernard Frechtman, 1947.

64. Berlinski, *The Devil's Delusion*, p.26.

Chapter 5: Is the God of the Bible a Despot?

1. *GD*, p.287.

2. *GD*, p.287.

3. Leviticus 19:33–34.

4. *GD*, p.292.

5. "Der freiheitliche säkularisierte Staat lebt von Voraussetzungen, die er selbst nicht garantieren kann."

6. "Vorpolitische Grundlagen des demokratischen Rechtsstaates?" in Jürgen Habermas, *Zwischen Naturalismus und Religion*, Frankfurt, Suhrkampf Verlag, 2005, p.106–18.

7. Arnold Angenendt, *Toleranz und Gewalt*, Münster, Aschendorff Verlag, 2009 p.581.

8. *GD*, p.298.

9. See the comments on Marc Hauser's work earlier p.98f.

10. A very important observation, to the significance of which we must return later.

11. Dawkins also suggests four new commandments of his own in *GD*, p.300.

12. Proverbs 17:22.

13. Luke 2:10 [NKJV]

14. Libby Purves, "God rest you merry atheist", *The Times*, 18 December 2007.

15. *GNG*, p.12.

16. 1 Thessalonians 5:21.

17. Matthew 15:14.

18. *GD*, p.283.

19. Deuteronomy 7:2.

20. Joshua 11:5–11.

21. Deuteronomy 10:18.

22. See also Christopher J. H. Wright, *The God I Don't Understand*, Grand Rapids, Zondervan, 2008, p.92ff.

23. Deuteronomy 9:4.

24. Chief Rabbi Lord Jonathan Sacks, "Credo", *The Times*, 12 August 2006, http://www.timesonline.co.uk/tol/comment/faith/article1084389.ece.

25. Deuteronomy 10:18.

26. Deuteronomy 12:31; 18:10.

27. Genesis 15:16.

28. Deuteronomy 9:4.

29. Deuteronomy 8:19–20.

30. Deuteronomy 1:1. See also 27:9; 29:2; 31:1.

31. Deuteronomy 31:11.

32. 1 Samuel 25:1.

33. 1 Kings 8:62.

34. "Reading Joshua", Conference *My Ways Are Not Your Ways*, University of Notre Dame, 10–12 September 2009.

35. Isaiah 2:4.

36. John 5:22.

37. Usually translated as something like: "On the nature of the physical universe".

38. "Cues Of Being Watched Enhance Cooperation In a Real-World Setting", Melissa Bateson, Daniel Nettle, and Gilbert Roberts, *Biol Lett*, 22 September 2006; 2(3): pp.412–414.

39. H. Butterfield, *Christianity and History*, London, G. Bell & Sons, 1949, Chapter 2, pp. 29, 30, 31, 35.

40. *Ibid.* p.33.

41. Cited in "The Nation: Looking For a Reason", *Time Magazine*, 25 July 1977.

42. See Richard Alleyne, Science Correspondent, *Daily Telegraph*, 7 September 2009.

43. Psalm 96:11–13.

44. Dawkins, *River Out of Eden*, p.133.

45. Cited in "Believe it or not", New York, *First Things*, May 2010.

46. Acts 17:31

47. For they hold that science has long since put miracles in their rightful place – in the pigeon-hole marked "Fantasy" along with Santa Claus, tooth-fairies and flying spaghetti monsters. However, science has done no such thing. See my *God's Undertaker,* Chapter 12.

48. C. S. Lewis, *The Problem of Pain*, London, Geoffrey Bles, 1940, p.133.

49. Romans 8:18, 38–39.

50. C. S. Lewis, *Mere Christianity*, New York, Macmillan, 1952, Book 2, Chapter 3, p.53.

51. I used the Hebrew word for Jesus.

Chapter 6: Is the Atonement Morally Repellent?

1. *GD*, p.287.

2. *GD*, p.285.

3. Romans 6:23.

4. Nicholas Lash, *Theology for Pilgrims*, London, Darton, Longman and Todd, 2008, p.10.

5. *GD*, pp.286–87.

6. Richard Dawkins, "Forgive me, spirit of science", *New Statesman*, 20 December 2010, p.80.

7. 1 Corinthians 1:23.

8. James Boswell, *The Life of Samuel Johnson*, London, John Sharpe, 1830, p.513.

9. Luke 11:13.

10. In light of the caricatures of "original sin" by Dawkins, Hitchens, and others, it is important to notice that the last clause in this quotation does not say (as is sometimes suggested) that "all men sinned *in him* (i.e. in Adam)". The last clause is introduced by the Greek conjunction *eph' hō* which cannot mean "in whom", or "in him", for that would have required *en hō*. *Eph' hō* means "because".

11. Romans 5:12.

12. *GD*, p.304.

13. Genesis 3:5. The Bible here indicates that an alien evil intelligence was involved to which many people react with instant dismissal. I find it interesting (and rather ironical) that many of the very same people will argue for the existence of (as yet undiscovered) alien intelligences in the universe – and they expect one day to find them. For more on the Genesis narrative see my *Seven Days that Divide the World*, Grand Rapids, Zondervan, 2011.

14. Genesis 3:7–10.

15. *GNG*, p.209.

16. Romans 3:23.

17. Romans 5:19.

18. Romans 3:24, 28; 4:5.

19. This mistake seems to be made by Christopher Hitchens when he accuses God of totalitarianism and says that: "The essential principle of totalitarianism is to make laws that are *impossible to obey*." See *GNG*, p.212.

20. Ephesians 2:8–9.

21. Though Hitchens appears to think it is, *GNG*, p.209.

22. The Greek word *metanoia* used in the New Testament for "repentance" means "change of mind".

23. *GD*, p.287.

24. *Ibid.*

25. In the context of his question, "Why can't God just forgive?" Dawkins tellingly says: "Progressive ethicists today find it hard to defend any kind of retributive theory of punishment…" If that is the case, may we be protected from "progressive ethicists". For the danger of the "progressive ethics" that involves replacing "punishment" with "treatment", see C. S. Lewis's essay "On the Humanitarian Theory of Punishment" in *Undeceptions*, London, Geoffrey Bles, 1971, p.250ff.

26. In Simon Wiesenthal, *The Sunflower*, New York, Schocken Books Inc., 1997, p.123.

27. Luke 23:34.

28. D. W Gooding, *According to Luke*, Leicester, IVP, 1987, p.342. Christ's attitude to those who did know what they were doing was very different. See Matthew 11:20ff.

29. *GNG*, p.211.

30. For instance, Matthew 21:12–13, Mark 11:15–17, Luke 19:45–46, and John 2:13–17.

31. 1 Timothy 2:5–6a [NKJV]

32. It is worth recording Carton's words: "It is a far, far better thing that I do, than I have ever done; it is a far, far better rest that I go to than I have ever known."

33. Matthew 9:2.

34. Wiesenthal, *The Sunflower*.

35. Matthew 1:20–21.

36. John 1:29.

37. See Hebrews 10:4.

38. Mark 10:45.

39. Luke 22:19–20.

40. 1 Corinthians 15:3–4.

41. Isaiah 53:5.

42. 2 Corinthians 5:19–21.

43. For further explanation of this terminology at a popular level the interested reader might consult *Key Bible Concepts* by David Gooding and John Lennox, Grand Rapids, Gospel Folio Press, 1997. The book is available for download at www.keybibleconcepts.org.

44. Luke 23:11, 35–37.

45. The Greek word used denotes a spectrum including robber, brigand, bandit, or outlaw.

46. In Charles Williams, *Taliessin through Logres*, Grand Rapids, Eerdmans, 1974, p.307.

47. Luke 23:40–41 (Jerusalem Bible translation).

48. David Gooding, *According to Luke*, Leicester, Inter-Varsity Press, 1987, pp.344–45.

Chapter 7: Are Miracles Pure Fantasy?

1. An earlier version of this chapter appears as Chapter 12 in my book *God's Undertaker*. It is included here since it forms an essential bridge to the next chapter on the evidence for the resurrection.

2. *GD*, p.83.

3. http://daily.stanford.edu/article/2008/1/28/hitchensKnocksIntelligentDesign.

4. Francis Collins, *The Language of God*, London, Simon & Schuster Ltd, 2006, pp.51–52.

5. Acts 1:22.

6. Lewis, *Miracles*, p.148.

7. 1 Corinthians 15:14.

8. See David Hume, *An Enquiry Concerning Human Understanding*: *A Letter from a Gentleman to His Friend in Edinburgh*, Indiana, Hackett Publishing Co., 1993, 10.1, pp.76–77.

9. This is the meaning of the Greek word for "resurrection" (*anastasis*).

10. David Hume, *An Enquiry Concerning Human Understanding*, 4.1, p.15.

11. *GD*, p.187.

12. David Hume, *An Enquiry Concerning Human Understanding*, p.49.

13. Alfred North Whitehead, *Process and Reality*, Macmillan, London, 1929.

14. Anthony Flew, *There is a God*, New York, HarperOne, 2007, pp.57–58.

15. John Earman, *Hume's Abject Failure*, Oxford, Oxford University Press, 2000, p3.

16. *GNG*, p.141.

17. *GNG*, p.79.

18. Luke 1:5–25.

19. Acts 4:1–21.

20. Acts 23:8.

21. Tom Wright, James Gregory Lecture, University of Durham, 2007.

22. Lewis, *Miracles*, p.62.

23. In this connection one thinks of the words of Wittgenstein: "The great delusion of modernity is that the laws of nature explain the universe for us. The laws of nature describe the universe, they describe the regularities. But they explain nothing."

24. Lewis, *Miracles*, p.63.

25. David Hume, *An Enquiry Concerning Human Understanding*, p.73.

26. *Ibid.* p.77.

27. Norman Anderson, *The Evidence for the Resurrection*, Inter-Varsity Press, Leicester, 1990, p.1.

28. Corinthians 15:15.

29. Acts 4:3; 5:18.

30. John 2:21.

31. John 21:18.

32. C. F. D. Moule, *The Phenomenon of the New Testament*, London, SCM, 1967, pp.3, 13.

33. See his article "Miracles" in *The Encyclopedia of Philosophy*, ed. Paul Edwards, Macmillan, New York, 1967, vol.5, pp.346–53; see also the essay, "Neo-Humean Arguments about the Miraculous", in *In Defence of Miracles*, eds. R. D. Geivett and G. R. Habermas, Leicester, Apollos, 1997, pp.45–57.

34. Edwards, *Encyclopedia of Philosophy*, p.252.

35. Another defect in the Hume-Flew view is that it does not appear to be falsifiable (in the sense that they do not appear to be able to conceive of an observation that would prove their view false).

36. David Hume, *An Enquiry Concerning Human Understanding*, p.76.

37. Lewis, *Miracles*, p.109.

38. Wolfhart Pannenberg, *Jesus – God and Man*, translated by L. L. Wilkins and D. A. Priebe, Philadelphia, Westminster, 1974, p.109.

39. That is, reasons that have to do with the convictions, beliefs, and principles that we already have, *before* we bring them to bear on a situation.

Chapter 8: Did Jesus Rise from the Dead?

1. This chapter is based on material that appeared in D. W. Gooding and J. C.

Lennox, "Worldview", Yaroslavl, Nord, 2004.

2. *GNG*, p.114.

3. *GD*, p.122.

4. This incident occurred just after a debate organized by the *Sydney Morning Herald* in which both Stenger and I took part. The debate may be seen at http://www.iq2oz.com/events/event-details/2008-series/08-08-19.php.

5. E. P. Sanders, *The Historical Figure of Jesus*, Penguin Books, 1993, p.11.

6. Christopher Tuckett, "Sources and Methods", in *The Cambridge Companion to Jesus*, ed. Markus Bockmuehl, Cambridge, Cambridge University Press, 2001, p.124.

7. Gerd Theissen and Annette Merz, *The Historical Jesus: a comprehensive guide*, Minneapolis, Fortress Press, 1998, pp.93–94.

8. Bertrand Russell, *Why I Am Not a Christian*, London, George Allen and Unwin, 1957, p.16.

9. *GD*, p.122.

10. *GNG*, p.110.

11. Frederic G. Kenyon, *Our Bible and the Ancient Manuscripts*, 4th ed, Harper, New York, 1958, p.55.

12. Bruce M. Metzger and Bart D. Ehrman, *The Text of the New Testament, Its Transmission, Corruption and Restoration*, Oxford, Oxford University Press, 3rd enlarged ed, 1992.

13. Interview recorded by Lee Strobel, *The Case for Christ*, Zondervan, Grand Rapids, Michigan, 1998, p.63.

14. *GNG*, p.111.

15. Luke 1:1–4.

16. Luke 2:1

17. The times and dates are to be found in Luke 1:5, 2:1, and 3:1–2, respectively.

18. Acts 17:6, original Greek.

19. See, e.g., Acts 17:17, original Greek.

20. Irina Levinskaya, *The Book of Acts in its First Century Setting, Volume 5 Diaspora Setting*, Michigan, Eerdmans, Grand Rapids, 1996, p.51ff.

21. *Ibid.* p.80

22. William Ramsey, *St. Paul The Traveller and The Roman Citizen*, New York, G. P. Putnam's Sons, 1896.

23. Colin J. Hemer and Conrad H. Gempf, *The Book of Acts in the Setting of Hellenistic History*, London, Coronet Books Inc, 1989, p.107ff.

24. Sherwin White, *Roman Society and Roman Law in the New Testament*, Oxford, Oxford University Press, 1963, p.189.

25. For an informative introduction written by a philosopher and a historian see Gary R. Habermas and Michael R. Licona, *The Case for the Resurrection of Jesus*, Grand Rapids, Kregel, 2004.

26. Josephus, *Antiquities of the Jews*, 18.64.

27. Tacitus, *Annals*, 15.44.

28. Matthew 27:26–31.

29. See Matthew 27:32.

30. John 19:31ff.

31. See, again, John 19:31ff.

32. John 19:34.

33. For further comments on the medical aspects of the crucifixion, see Raymond Brown, *The Death of the Messiah*, New York, Doubleday, 1994, 2:1088, and see also Charles Foster QC, *The Jesus Inquest*, Oxford, Monarch, 2006, Appendix 1.

34. Mark 15:44–45.

35. John Dominic Crossan, *Jesus, A Revolutionary Biography*, San Francisco, HarperCollins, 1991, p.145.

36. Gerd Lüdemann, *The Resurrection of Christ*, Amherst, Prometheus Books, 2004, p.50.

37. Matthew 27:57–60; Mark 15:42–46; Luke 23:50–53; John 19:38–42.

38. Luke 23:50–51.

39. See John 7:50–52; 19:39–42.

40. Matthew 27:50.

41. Luke 23:55.

42. Matthew 27:62; Mark 15:47.

43. Luke 23:53.

44. Mark 15:47; Luke 23:55.

45. Luke 8:3.

46. Luke 23:49–55.

47. John 19:42.

48. John 19:39.

49. Luke 23:55–56.

50. Mark 16:1.

51. Mark 16:1–3.

52. John 20:3–9.

53. Mark 15:46; Matthew 27:60.

54. Matthew 27:62, 65–66.

55. Matthew 27:62–66

56. Mark 16:3–4.

57. Matthew 28:11–15.

58. The reasons for this are clear. Firstly, the disciples were initially afraid of the Jewish authorities, as is evidenced by the fact that for some time afterwards they met behind closed doors (John 20:19, 26). Secondly, Jesus met with them on various occasions soon after his resurrection, and told them to wait until the day of Pentecost before telling the nation that he had risen from the dead (Acts 1:4–5).

59. See Ethelbert Stauber, *Jesus – Gestalt und Geschichte*, Bern, Francke Verlag, 1957, p.163f.

60. Matthew 27:55–56.

61. Mark 15:40–41.

62. John 19:25.

63. John Wenham, *Easter Enigma – Do the Resurrection Stories Contradict One Another?* Exeter, Paternoster Press, 1984, p.34.

64. There is no further information about Joses, but in the lists of the Apostles (see, e.g., Matthew 10:3ff, Mark 3:13ff) there are two men with the same name, James: James the son of Zebedee, and James the son of Alphaeus. Alphaeus and Clopas could well be versions of the same Aramaic name, which is usually transliterated *Chalphai*. The reason for this is that the first letter of the name in Aramaic is a guttural, which can either be transliterated as a "k", thus yielding Clopas (or *Cleopas*, in its nearest Greek equivalent, according to Wenham, *Easter Enigma,* p.37); or as an "h". The latter is represented in Greek by a small sign called a rough breathing, and it was commonly dropped both in speaking or writing, so yielding the Greek *Alphaios*, which is Latinized as Alphaeus. It is also of interest that the historian Eusebius, in his *Ecclesiastical History*, written towards the beginning of the fourth century, mentions that Clopas was the brother of Joseph (that is, Joseph, the husband of Mary, Jesus' mother).

65. John 19:27.

66. John 20:3.

67. See Luke 24:10.

68. Luke 8:3.

69. Luke 8:3.

70. John 12:1.

71. Matthew 26:56; Mark 14:50. It is thought by many that the young man who was in the garden at the time of Jesus' arrest, and who just managed to escape the arrest party, may well have been Mark himself (Mark 14:51–52).

72. Mark 16:1; Luke 23:56 – 24:1.

73. It is interesting to note that, although Jesus had told his disciples he would die and rise again (for example, Matthew 16:21), it had clearly not sunk in. The psychological reason for this is clear: it ran counter to all they hoped that Jesus, being the messiah, would do (see Luke 24, which is discussed later, for an instance of this). The Jewish authorities, however, had noticed Jesus' predictions, which was their reason for guarding the tomb (Matthew 27:62–65).

74. Mark 16:1.

75. Wenham, *Easter Enigma – Do the Resurrection Stories Contradict One Another?* p.69.

76. John 20:2.

77. John 20:3–8.

78. See John 20:15.

79. Michael Grant, *Jesus: An Historian's Review of the Gospels*, New York, Charles Schribner & Sons, 1977, p.176.

80. Acts 1:3.

81. Gerd Lüdemann, *What Really Happened to Jesus? A Historical Approach to the Resurrection*, translated by John Bowden, Louisville, Westminster John Knox, 1995, p.80.

82. Acts 2:32.

83. Acts 3:15.

84. Acts 10:41.

85. Acts 13:29–31.

86. 1 Corinthians 15:1–8. A full list of references to the post-resurrection appearances of Christ is: Matthew 28:1–10, 16–20; Mark 16:9ff; Luke 24:13–31, 34, 36–49; John 20:11–18, 19–23, 24–29; 21:1–23; Acts 1:1–3, 6–11; 9:1–9; 22:3–11; 26:12–18; 1 Corinthians 15:5–9.

87. William Lane Craig, *Reasonable Faith*, Wheaton, Illinois, Crossway, 1994, p.288.

88. Acts 7:56.

89. 1 Corinthians 15:8.

90. 1 Corinthians 15:6.

91. See Michael Licona, *The Evidence for God*, Ada, Baker Academic, 2010, p.178.

92. Lewis, *Miracles*, p.151.

93. Matthew 28:1.

94. John 20:1.

95. John 20:11–18.

96. Matthew 28:9.

97. Luke 24:33ff.

98. John 20:19–25.

99. Wenham, *Easter Enigma – Do the Resurrection Stories Contradict One Another?*

100. Acts 9:1–19.

101. 1 Corinthians 15:8.

102. Acts 4:17–22.

103. Matthew 26:52.

104. John 19:36.

105. John 20:1–10

106. See John 20:10–18.

107. John 20:17.

108. John 20:19–23; Luke 24:36–49.

109. Edwin Abbott, *Flatland*, Oxford, Blackwell, 1884.

110. 1 Corinthians 15:44.

111. Luke 24:39.

112. Luke 24:41–43.

113. Luke 24:11.

114. John 20:25.

115. John 20:28.

116. John 20:29.

117. Luke 24:3–35.

118. Isaiah 53:5.

119. Isaiah 53:11.

120. Anderson, *The Evidence for the Resurrection*, p.11. For a more recent evaluation of the evidence both for and against the resurrection by a legal expert, see *The Jesus Inquest*, by Charles Foster QC, Oxford, Monarch, 2006.

Chapter 9: Final reflections

1. Greek: *en autois*.

2. Greek: *autois*.

3. Romans 1:19–21.

4. Richard Dawkins, *The Blind Watchmaker*, London, Longman, 1986, p.1.

5. Interview with *Wirtschaftswoche*, August 2007. Translation mine.

6. Robert Spaemann, *Das unsterbliche Gerücht: Die Frage nach Gott und die Täuschung der Moderne*, Stuttgart, Klett-Cotta, 2007, p.63.

7. Similar to the gematria of the classical world where a boy, using a simple letter / number code might inscribe on a wall: "I love the girl whose number is 467". A famous biblical example is the number 666.

8. In God we are born, in Christ we die, through the Holy Spirit we are made alive.

9. J. L. Mackie, *The Miracle of Theism*, Oxford, Clarendon, 1982, pp. 115–116.

10. Kant, *Critique of Practical Reason*, Conclusion, p.113.